Alberta Mammals

An Atlas and Guide

Hugh C. Smith

Curator of Mammalogy
Provincial Museum of Alberta

with contributions from
Ross I. Hastings and James A. Burns

Prepared and Published by:

The Provincial Museum of Alberta

Edmonton, Alberta

1993

ALBERTA MAMMALS: AN ATLAS AND GUIDE

Published by: The Provincial Museum of Alberta
12845-102 Avenue, Edmonton, Alberta, T5N OM6

Editorial Staff: Bruce McGillivray, James Burns, Ross Hastings, Mark Steinhilber
Layout: Mark Steinhilber
Cover Design: Carolyn Lilgert

Canadian Cataloguing-in-Publication Data
Smith, Hugh C.
  Alberta Mammals: An Atlas and Guide / Hugh C. Smith — Edmonton; Provincial Museum of Alberta, 1993. 250 p.: ill.; 29 cm.
  Maps included
  Includes index and bibliography
  ISBN 0-7732-1073-3
  1. Mammals — Alberta. 2. Mammals — Geographical Locations — Alberta. I. Title

QL721.5.A3564 1993   599.09 7123

Printed in Canada

Foreword

The study of mammals in Alberta likely began the day humans first stepped into the Province. To this day, mammals continue to serve as a source of food, and also to instill fear and wonder. The mammal fauna of Alberta has undergone many changes in the 12,000 years of human occupancy. Our stewardship of the environment includes a responsibility to ensure that habitats continue to exist that will support the diversity of mammals found today in Alberta. The first step in this stewardship is to know what is there. The second is to educate the public about mammals and their requirements for survival. Hugh Smith has created a vehicle in this publication to begin both tasks.

The publication of *Alberta Mammals: An Atlas and Guide* marks the culmination of a career and the beginning of an ongoing database. Hugh Smith began his career at the Provincial Museum of Alberta in 1968, four years after the publication of Soper's (1964) *The Mammals of Alberta*. He retired in 1991 as the first and only Curator of Mammalogy in the first 25 years of the Provincial Museum. Hugh built the Mammalogy collection in a systematic fashion. Rather than use his research interests as the focus, he collected throughout the Province using mapsheets as sampling units. Over time the collection grew to be a valuable resource for distributional information, studies of geographic variation, and species' status.

Range maps for mammals are difficult to generate. Unlike birds, many mammals are rarely seen. Most rodents, shrews, bats, and carnivores are traditionally documented by specimens or other physical evidence, e.g., scats, tracks, or mounds. The range maps in this book provide two levels of distribution information. Townships in which physical evidence of the occurrence of a species has been collected and stored in a museum are marked with a dot. Lightly shaded areas on the maps indicate expected distributions based on other types of evidence. The benefit to this dual approach is the encouragement it provides readers to add records to our provincial database. The book has been designed deliberately to allow readers to judge the significance of an observation they might make and when physical evidence would be a valuable addition to their observation.

One goal in producing this book was to provide an identification guide for students and interested naturalists. To that end, much of the text is directed at the key features that can be used to distinguish species.

A chapter by Ross Hastings on the historical and ecological biogeography of Alberta mammals gives insight into the patterns of immigration shown by groups of species as they recolonized the province following the retreat of the glaciers. Dr. Jim Burns has added a section on methods of distinguishing domestic mammals from native mammals based primarily on skull characters. This is particularly valuable for separating skulls of domestic cattle from bison or those of domestic dogs from wolves.

The Provincial Museum is pleased to publish this book both as a record of the achievements of a distinguished mammalogist and as a guide to help train the next generation of researchers.

W. Bruce McGillivray, Ph.D.
Assistant Director, Curatorial
Provincial Museum of Alberta

Acknowledgments

I wish to thank all those who supplied me with information on Alberta's mammals: those people who allowed us access to their property while we did our field collecting and numerous people with the Alberta Fish and Wildlife Division for assisting us with collecting and making specimens available to the Provincial Museum that would have been difficult to collect.

There are individuals who need to be singled out because of their special assistance. Colleen Steinhilber and Mark Steinhilber both were instrumental in seeing this book come to fruition. Colleen typed numerous drafts of the manuscript. Her diligent efforts in putting together a bunch of handwritten notes into a comprehensive whole is truly remarkable. Mark took the edited manuscript and through his skill at desktop publishing made the final camera-ready copy. Thank you both.

The raw data for the distribution maps was provided by curators and collections managers in many North American museums. To each of these I extend my thanks. Special thanks to Dr. C. G. (Stan) van Zyll de Jong at the Canadian Museum of Nature, Ottawa; Dr. Judith Eger, Royal Ontario Museum, Toronto; and Mr. Wayne Roberts at the Zoology Museum, University of Alberta, Edmonton. Not only did these people provide me with information on their holdings of Alberta specimens, they also allowed me access to their collections.

I prepared the initial maps and from these a series of working maps was prepared by Lori Convey. Harold Bryant, current curator of Mammalogy at the Provincial Museum of Alberta, added range limits to the distribution maps. The final distribution maps were prepared by Wendy Johnson of Johnson Cartographic Services. Marvin Weiss, Assistant Director, Provincial Mapping, Alberta Forestry, Lands and Wildlife, Land Information Services Division, kindly provided the 1993 provincial base map.

The illustrations of the skulls (with the exception of those of domestic animals which were drawn by Dr. James Burns) and microtine teeth were drawn by Diane Hollingdale. They add greatly to the usefulness of a book such as this. In many cases the identification of an individual mammal is based on skull or teeth characteristics. Without excellent illustrations, identifications are extremely difficult.

Photographs, unless otherwise indicated, are from the E. T. Jones collection at the Provincial Museum of Alberta.

Dr. David Boag and Mr. William Wishart read an early draft of the manuscript. Their comments and suggestions were gratefully received. Dr. James Burns, Dr. Bruce McGillivray, and Mr. Ross Hastings reviewed the final draft and contributed many editorial suggestions which have enhanced the final product.

I am pleased to include a chapter on Zoogeography of Alberta Mammals prepared by Ross Hastings and a section on Domestic Animals commonly encountered written by Dr. James Burns.

Several museum technicians, with whom I had the pleasure of working, also made a contribution to this book. These people are Michael Hampson, Jasper Keizer, Rodney Burns, Anne Allen, Michael Luchanski, and William Weimann. Without the skills each of these people brought to their jobs, the work of compiling these records would have been greatly increased. Each of these people worked at collecting and preparing mammal specimens over the course of their employment at the Provincial Museum and each made a major contribution to the success of the mammal program at the institution.

To the people for whom I worked as Curator of Mammalogy I wish to express my thanks. First, David Spalding gave me the opportunity of becoming a curator at a very young and developing museum. Under his leadership, I was able to learn much of what a museum is and how to be a curator. Second, Dr. Philip Stepney provided the insight into the importance of building collections. Also, through Phil's leadership, I was given the opportunity and time to compile the data and records necessary for this book. Finally, Dr. Bruce McGillivray was instrumental in pursuing various ways of obtaining funds so that the book could be published. His persistent efforts eventually were successful when an agreement to purchase 2000 copies was reached with the Alberta Recreation, Parks and Wildlife Foundation. As a colleague and supervisor, Bruce supported the project and encouraged me to finish it.

Following my retirement in September 1991, a committee consisting of Bruce McGillivray, Jim Burns, Ross Hastings, and Mark Steinhilber took over the responsibility of editing and proofing text and designing the book. Their efforts over the past year, particularly those of Mark Steinhilber in overcoming technical problems and computer intractability, improved the manuscript considerably. I'm grateful for their desire to make this an outstanding contribution to Alberta mammalogy.

Finally, I wish to thank my wife, Joyce. Without her constant support, through many years of education, extended field trips, and other work-related demands, I would never have been in a position to start, let alone finish, a task such as writing about the distribution of mammals in Alberta.

Contents

Introduction

Staff at the Provincial Museum of Alberta have been collecting mammals actively since its inception in 1964. This collection, along with those mammals housed in the Museum of Zoology collection at the University of Alberta, provide important resources for examining the distributions of mammals in the province. Up to now, the basis for our knowledge about the distribution of Alberta's mammals has been *The Mammals of Alberta* (Soper 1964). Unfortunately, this book has been out of print for several years and its wealth of information has been unavailable to both the public and interested specialists. It is evident that a new book is necessary to reflect what is currently known about the distribution of Alberta's mammals.

The collections at the Provincial Museum of Alberta and the University of Alberta have a good representation of Alberta mammals. I used the data associated with the specimens in these collections and consulted other major museums in North America with respect to their holdings of specimens of Alberta mammals. In the present volume, I have developed a fresh look at the distribution of the mammals found in Alberta.

A number of natural history picture books provide the interested reader with illustrations and general information about mammals. The scope of these books is generally fairly broad and covers those mammals that are large and spectacular. However, most mammals are small, nondescript, nocturnal creatures that are infrequently encountered; they are not usually photogenic or spectacular. In addition, these books are so general and cover such a large geographic area that they are not very useful as regional references. The first purpose of this current book is to provide a specific reference to those mammals that occur in Alberta and to provide a means whereby they may be identified.

Much of our knowledge of the distribution and biology of the birds of Alberta has been contributed by amateur naturalists, people who describe themselves as 'bird watchers.' By contrast, there is not a comparably large group of 'mammal watchers.' Mammals are not watched in the same way that birds are watched. This does not mean that amateur naturalists cannot contribute to the knowledge of mammals in the province. For example, a brief study of the maps that accompany the species accounts in this volume will indicate where information on distribution is lacking. Surprisingly, this information is often missing even for those species that are relatively common, are reasonably well known, and are readily identified. The second purpose of this book is to encourage the amateur naturalist and the professional biologist to fill the gaps in our knowledge of mammalian distribution, by depositing specimens in public natural history museums such as the Provincial Museum of Alberta.

To have the confidence to identify a mammal, it is important to know if that animal occurs in the area. One way to become familiar with the mammals of an area is to consult a checklist. Thus, the final purpose of this work is to provide a checklist of the mammals that have been found in Alberta, and to provide their currently accepted English common names and their scientific names. Unfortunately, checklists often become dated because species not previously recorded are found and because taxonomic studies may result in name changes. Nevertheless, this checklist will be useful in learning about the mammals of Alberta.

Taxonomy

While systematics deals with the diversity of organisms, taxonomy is the assignment of scientific names to organisms. This book is not intended to be a taxonomic treatise. I have not examined any species group to determine if there are any subspecific differences evident between populations. Recently there has been a number of taxonomic studies that have involved species found in Alberta. For example, van Zyll de Jong (1980) examined the Masked Shrew complex and concluded that two species were lumped together. On the basis of morphological and ecological considerations he indicated that a subspecies of the Masked Shrew *(Sorex cinereus haydeni)* was in fact a separate species now named the Prairie Shrew *(Sorex haydeni)*. Similarly, a subspecies of the Wandering Shrew (*Sorex vagrans obscurus*) has been raised to species status—Dusky Shrew (*Sorex monticolus*) (Hennings and Hoffmann 1977). Until more species complexes are examined and species relationships resolved, the use of subspecies as previously understood is not useful in a publication such as this. For anyone interested in the number of subspecies in the province, reference to Soper (1964) and Hall (1981) will be useful.

The names that I have selected to use in this paper, both the scientific and the English common names, are those used by Jones et al. (1986). When a more recent publication is available or a study of a species group has used a different name I have selected the name that is most current or is most commonly used. For example, I consulted van Zyll de Jong (1985) for the names of the bats found in Alberta.

Maps

A provincial base map of townships and ranges was used in preparing the distribution maps in this book. For those not familiar with this system of mapping the following brief description may prove useful.

Prior to the settlement of the province, the Government of Canada surveyed this area. Meridians were established along lines of longitude. For Alberta, the first of these meridian lines is 110° West longitude, constituting the border between Alberta and Saskatchewan. It is also known as the fourth meridian. The fifth meridian lies along 114° West longitude and the sixth meridian along 118° West longitude. Commencing at the United States border (49° North latitude) and proceeding north to the Northwest Territories border (60° North latitude) a series of townships was surveyed.

A "township" is a plot of land 6 miles square or 36 square miles. In order to provide a means of locating a point of land within a township, a grid system was established. For every six miles north an east-west line was established, known as a township line. For every six miles west of a meridian a north-south line was established, known as a range line. In Alberta there are 126

township lines and a variable number of range lines. To find a particular area in this type of grid system it is necessary to know the township line, the range line, and the meridian line. Hence, the first township in Alberta in the extreme southeast of the province is Township 1, Range 1, West of the 4th Meridian. This is shortened to 1-1-W4. Similarly, the township in the farthest northwest corner of the province is Township 126, Range 12, West of the 6th Meridian (126-12-W6).

In the maps that follow, a dot within a township indicates that at least one specimen of that species has been collected in that township and that the specimen is housed in a public museum. Generally, a dot implies that the species can be expected to occur in the township where suitable habitat is available. As many records are quite old, suitable habitat may no longer be found in the township.

The shaded area in each map represents the best estimate of the distribution of a species in the province. Data from collected specimens are supplemented by published reports to delineate estimated ranges. The reader should be cautious in interpreting these ranges though, as they represent extrapolations from existing data. Many mammals have very specific habitat requirements and connecting the dots, as is done to produce range maps, will likely include many areas of unsuitable habitat within a species range. Specimen evidence documenting the occurrence of species outside their estimated range would be welcome by the Provincial Museum of Alberta.

Keys

In order to assist a person in identifying an unknown specimen, a set of keys has been developed. The keys consist of a series of couplets. By using characters that are reasonably easily observed, a person using the keys should be able to arrive at the correct species name. By consulting the description in the species accounts, the identification should be confirmed. The key is based on the assumption that the unknown specimen is an adult animal. In some species immature individuals may not key out. In cases of uncertainty, the specimen can be sent or brought to the Provincial Museum of Alberta for confirmation.

Species Accounts

In preparing the species accounts, the following format was used:

Species Name: Jones et al. (1986) was selected as the most current authority for the scientific names. The English common name was taken from several sources, principally Jones et al. (1986) but van Zyll de Jong (1983, 1985) and Hall (1981) were also consulted. Common names have been capitalized to eliminate ambiguities and to set them apart from the surrounding text.

Identifying Characters: Those characters that I believe best separate one species from another were used. A description of the pelage and skull are provided as well as a reference to size, teeth, and dental formula.

Measurements: The measurements used are of those specimens housed in the Provincial Museum of Alberta. Where specimens were not available in the institution, other sources were used. The measurements include weight [in either grams (g) or kilograms (kg)], total length, tail length, hindfoot length, and ear length [in millimetres (mm)]. Where possible a mean, range, number of specimens, and sex of specimens are indicated.

Distribution: The distribution includes a description of the entire range of a species in Alberta as it is believed to be at this time.

Habitat: This includes a general statement regarding the preferred habitat.

Status: The assessment of abundance (i.e., common, rare) is subjective and open to argument. Under this heading the assessment is based on my interpretation of the available information.

Similar Species: This heading is used to point out key characters that distinguish superficially similar species.

Zoogeography of Alberta Mammals

Zoogeography is the scientific study of the patterns of animal distribution. One pattern of interest concerns the distribution of animals as a function of current ecological conditions. In studying these patterns, zoologists correlate the distributions of groups of animals with underlying environmental conditions, such as vegetation and climate, and attempt to discover how current habitat structures influence the distribution of animals. This field of study is known as ecological biogeography. A second pattern of interest is related to the history of the biota. In studying these patterns, zoologists attempt to correlate the distribution of groups of animals with past geological events, such as continental drift or glaciation. This field is known as historical biogeography. Questions in this field of endeavour are usually framed in broad terms; for example, where is the centre of origin of a taxon and what is its evolutionary history? However, historical biogeography can also be approached from determining the centres of radiation of unrelated taxa which have shared a common refugium from some major, but geologically recent, environmental perturbation.

In this outline of the distributional patterns of Alberta mammals I shall classify animal distributions both from historical and ecological biogeographical approaches. History and ecology combine to give us a picture of the modern distribution patterns of Alberta's mammalian fauna.

Methods of Zoogeographic Analysis

This book does not deal with taxa below the species level, and because mammals have repopulated Alberta only recently in geological time, I approach historical biogeography by determining relatively recent centres of radiation of unrelated taxa. I grouped animals together on the basis of shared patterns of distribution. Hultén (1937) pioneered this method of analysis in a study of the Quaternary flora of the Holarctic region. By mapping the modern distributions of a large number of plant species he found recurring patterns of distributional limits in unrelated taxa. He called these patterns "equiformal progressive areas." Groupings of animals which share a common

distributional pattern have been termed "faunal elements" *sensu* Armstrong (1972). I have classified the mammals of Alberta into eight faunal elements, plus one group which is widespread (Figs. 1-8). The elements are named for the locality of the focal point of their distribution.

The centre of distribution of a faunal element is where all or most of the species occur and it is from this area that they are presumed to have dispersed. This area will contain: "the ecosystem which provides the prime habitat of these species and which at present occupies the area central to the distribution" (Udvardy 1969). Hultén's analysis of the arctic and boreal biota found that most of these centres were in areas which were not glaciated during the Pleistocene. These centres were taken to be refugial areas, from which the organisms dispersed during deglaciation.

It must be realized that centres of dispersal as defined by current, not historical, distributions will have shifted over time as species have migrated in response to postglacial conditions. Therefore, the location of the so-called centres of dispersal, as indicated by the modern biota, must be tempered with the geological evidence. For example, the centre of dispersal of the boreal element is currently in central Saskatchewan and Manitoba. However, as this area was covered by ice during the Wisconsinan glaciation, it obviously cannot have been the centre from which animals of this element dispersed. Delcourt and Delcourt (1984) have shown that during the Wisconsinan glaciation the boreal forest existed in a broad belt south of the continental ice sheet in the Great Plains and eastern mountains of the United States. This latter area is taken to be the real centre of dispersal for the boreal element.

By grouping species on the basis of shared habitats we can develop hypotheses to explain the ecological limits on the ranges of animals as they emigrate from their centres of dispersal. Although animals may have survived together in a single refugium, it is not necessary that they share identical environmental tolerances or dispersal abilities. The occurrence of a species from one faunal element in a geographic area dominated

4

by members of a second faunal element is evidence that the former species has successfully "escaped" from the environment of its dispersal centre and that it shares some ecological adaptations with organisms of the second element. It is this meeting of the historical and ecological which provides the explanation for the mosaic of distributions found in an area.

From an environmental perspective, many biologists have argued that both plants and animals follow similar rules of ecological distribution. Perhaps the most persuasive arguments were those of Clements (1916, 1936) and Shelford (1963). Clements believed that soil formation in a given climatic zone allows for the development of a unique climax association with a well defined pattern of successional sequences. Given both soil and climate data, the climax plant community of any given area could be predicted and the vegetation of large areas could be mapped. Clements and Shelford postulated that animal members associated with the plant communities followed similar rules of ecological succession and could therefore be classified as belonging to a particular climax plant community. The animals, like the plants, could be grouped into life-forms and the life-forms of the plant and animal communities would be correlated. This correlated plant-animal complex defined the highest unit of classification in their system, the biome.

This method of ecobiogeographic analysis, incorporating both plant and animal groups, probably reached its zenith with the works of Dice (1943, 1952). Dice defined biotic provinces as "characterized by the occurrence of one or more important ecological associations that differ, at least in proportional area covered, from the associations of the adjacent provinces." As the communities occupying the provinces are able to modify their environment, and their constituent species are able to spread, each province can be considered as a centre for ecological dispersal for the dominant community types.

Dice's was a complete system in the sense of Clements and Shelford; his provinces were defined from the ground up. The provinces were organized such that each had a unique combination of climate, topography, soil, and vegetation. The animal communities were superimposed upon this environmental complex. This concept of biotic provinces, based on a correlation between animals and their phytological (plant) and physical environments has seldom again been applied. Provinces are now defined typically on the basis of their animal distributions, and are, therefore, zoological provinces. The underlying biotic and physical bases of the provinces are either just assumed to match the zoological pattern, or are commonly supported by anecdotal correlations.

This form of ecogeographic classification of mammalian provinces was well exemplified in the works of Hagmeier and Stults (1964) and Hagmeier (1966) who analyzed all of North America and by Armstrong (1972) who applied Hagmeier's method to a detailed analysis of the mammals of Colorado. In these studies, the faunal provinces (Armstrong's "faunal areas") are defined on the basis of a shared, relatively homogeneous mammalian fauna and are separated from other areas by zones of heterogeneity. These latter zones are "boundaries" of rapid faunal change.

The boundaries of faunal provinces may follow readily observable topographic barriers such as the Rocky Mountains but in other areas the zoological boundaries may correspond with no discernible physiographic feature (e.g., the Boreal vs. Plains faunal provinces in Alberta). In these latter cases the "boundaries" may be due to some other factor, such as a shift in dominant air mass which correlates with a change in vegetation. In these cases the boundaries of the faunal provinces are quite arbitrary and could be shifted many kilometres in either direction. The basic underlying pattern and controls for each province, however, are presumed to remain intact.

The realization that, in many cases, the boundaries of communities cannot be well defined is one point that has led to a weakening of the biotic province concept. The idea that biotic provinces exist as definable biological entities has been severely undermined by Gleason (1926, 1939) and Whittaker (e.g., 1952, 1960, 1967). They argued that the range limits of floral and faunal species are clinal, changing gradually from area to area. From this perspective, biotic provinces based on ecological rules cannot be delimited by lines. Armstrong himself (1972) points out that in the field all boundaries are "dynamic fronts" with individual species of a faunal province taking advantage of, or being limited by, ecological perturbations.

While I agree with this latter viewpoint, I still recognize that the system of biotic provinces provides a useful tool for initial conceptualization of an ecological relationship between animals and an underlying phytological-physical base. It may be best to think of this system as forming a baseline hypothesis about environmental controls on animal distributions, rather than as comprising a strict system of laws which govern their distribution.

I use the faunal provinces of North America, as defined by Hagmeier and Stults (1964) and modified by Hagmeier (1966), as a basis for the ecogeographic classification of Albertan mammals into faunistic provinces. These provinces correspond in a general way with the ecoregions of Alberta (cf. Strong and Leggat 1981) that are defined by soil, climate, and vegetation.

Of the 91 mammals discussed in the species accounts, six species are not considered in this biogeographic discussion: Gray Squirrel, Black Rat, Norway Rat, House Mouse, Gray Fox, and Black-footed Ferret. The first four of these species occur in Alberta through introductions by man. Of the latter two species, the Gray Fox is so far outside its current known range that its occurrence in Alberta is accidental. The occurrence of the Black-footed Ferret in Alberta is questionable as the only known specimen may have been acquired elsewhere and transported here (Anderson et al. 1986).

Historical Biogeography

The mammals that occur in Alberta today have not always been here. Starting about 2 million years ago a dramatic change in climate occurred throughout the world, causing massive ice sheets to cover much of the northern hemisphere several times. This time of widespread glaciation is known as the Quaternary Period. The Quaternary is further sub-divided into two epochs: the Pleistocene and the Holocene, or Recent. During the Pleistocene, there were periods of cold-and-wet, alternating with warm-and-dry, which corresponded to cycles of glaciation and deglaciation.

There were about 12 glacial periods during the last half-million years. The Holocene, or Recent, is the interval since the retreat of the last continental ice sheets in the Northern Hemisphere.

During periods of deglaciation, mammals and other animals, as well as plants, occupied the area we now know as Alberta. Harington (1978) has summarized the findings of several workers with respect to the Pleistocene mammals in Alberta. Such mammals as mammoths, lions, various forms of bison and horses, and muskoxen have all been part of the fauna at some time in the past. During the last major glaciation, the late Wisconsinan, continental and mountain glaciers covered most of Alberta for a period of about 10 thousand years. At the glacial maxima, no mammals were in the province. Plants and animals retreated to refugia, both south of the ice sheets in the contiguous United States, and north in Beringia which extended from the western Yukon into eastern Siberia. Some species now occurring in Alberta may also have survived in small refugia in the Canadian Arctic Islands.

During the Wisconsinan, there were a number of interstadials in which the climate ameliorated and the ice retreated from its maximal position. During part of at least one significant interstadial, at about 22-33,000 years before present, a number of mammals were able to emigrate into Alberta. For example, Burns (1980) reports Brown Lemming and Collared Lemming from a fossil locality at January Cave on Plateau Mountain. During subsequent reglaciations, however, these interstadial resident species were again forced into their refugial areas. Their occupation of the province during the interstadials had no affect on their Holocene repopulation of the province.

About 12 thousand years ago the ice began its final retreat and habitats became available to the mammals we are familiar with today. These animals migrated into the province from their various centres of distribution, presumably corresponding to major refugia. From the analysis of the continental distributions of Alberta's mammals, I have classified them into eight faunal elements plus one general category termed "widespread." These faunal elements correspond to those used by Armstrong (1972) and Jones et al. (1983).

Widespread Species

The 26 species assigned to the widespread category (Table 1) have ranges that are so extensive that a common centre cannot be identified. Species in this category include five bats, four rodents, 13 carnivores, and four ungulates. Many of these species have wide ecological tolerances as well as being geographically widespread. It is likely that these animals survived in a number of different refugia during the Wisconsinan glaciation.

It is also significant that 18 of these species, the 13 carnivores and five bats, are carnivorous. These species do not rely directly on plants for food and roam more freely in search of prey. Therefore, it is not surprising that their distributions cannot be correlated closely with vegetation elements. Further, the bats depend more on the structure of their environment for shelter elements than they do on particular plant species associated with glacial refugia. For example, the Silver-haired and Hoary Bats use a wide range of tree species for roosting and these trees are distributed across a range of forest types. The Little Brown and Big Brown Bats have found structures made by European settlers especially useful for their needs and have expanded their ranges in response to the availability of these artificial roosts. The Western Small-footed Bat uses rock outcrops for roosting; such habitats would have been available in a wide range of refugia and are currently widely distributed but localized in a number of ecosystems.

The Beaver, Muskrat, Mink, and River Otter are adapted to specialized aquatic habitats that cross virtually all terrestrial ecosystems and which existed in all refugia. These species are of localized occurrence in aquatic ecosystems but are widely distributed in Alberta.

The four ungulates are large and mobile species. They have the ability to cross the boundaries that define a number of faunal elements and occupied a wide range of refugia in the contiguous United States and Beringia during the Wisconsinan glaciation.

Occupation of the province by Europeans has definitely affected the distributions of several of these species in addition to the bats. In the past, the Gray Wolf, Grizzly Bear, Wapiti, and Bison were all more widely distributed in Alberta than at present. Due to a combination of agricultural practices, overhunting, and extermination programs, these species have been pushed into remote areas not representative of the limits of their ecological tolerances. By contrast, some species such as the Coyote, Red Fox, Raccoon, and White-tailed Deer, have been able to expand their ranges even in the face of human persecution.

Arctic Faunal Element

The Arctic Faunal Element has contributed three species to the mammalian fauna of the province. Currently, the centre of distribution for the Brown Lemming, Arctic Fox, and Caribou is in an area north of the treeline in central Canada (Fig. 1). This suggests that these species survived in and dispersed from a centre in an arctic refugium. However, such refugia are known to have occurred south of the continental ice sheet, as well as in Beringia and perhaps the Canadian Arctic Islands. The fossil evidence suggests that these three species survived in the Beringian refugium and that the Brown Lemming and Caribou also survived south of the ice sheet. Harington (1978) reported fossils of all three species from Wisconsinan age deposits in Alaska. Kurtén and Anderson (1980) reported finds of Arctic Fox from the Old Crow Basin in the Yukon and those of the Brown Lemming from Fairbanks in Alaska. Caribou fossils have also been recovered from south of the Wisconsinan ice sheet in a number of sites from Idaho, eastwards to New York, and as far south as Tennessee (Kurtén and Anderson 1980) and Alabama (Churcher et al. 1989).

Boreal Faunal Element

Four species in Alberta have distributions which centre in the forests of central Canada and so belong to the Boreal Faunal Element (Fig. 2). Paleontological evidence suggests that members of this element survived the Wisconsinan glaciation in boreal forest refugia immediately south of the ice sheet, and subsequently immigrated north and westwards with the retreat of the ice (Macpherson 1965; Kelsall and Telfer 1973; Kurtén and Anderson 1980; Junge et al. 1983). The Woodchuck has a distribution which extends far to the south and east of most members of the Boreal Element and could be placed in the Eastern Faunal Element. Its distribution indicates that

Table 1. Distribution of Alberta mammals according to faunal elements.

Widespread
Little Brown Bat
Western Small-footed Bat
Silver-haired Bat
Big Brown Bat
Hoary Bat
Beaver
Deer Mouse
Muskrat
Porcupine
Coyote
Gray Wolf
Red Fox
Black Bear
Grizzly Bear
Raccoon
Long-tailed Weasel
Mink
Striped Skunk
Badger
River Otter
Cougar
Bobcat
Wapiti
Mule Deer
White-tailed Deer
Bison

Arctic
Brown Lemming
Arctic Fox
Caribou

Boreal
Arctic Shrew
Woodchuck
Taiga Vole
Meadow Jumping Mouse

Cordilleran
Dusky Shrew
Wandering Shrew
Pika
Yellow-pine Chipmunk
Red-tailed Chipmunk
Yellow-bellied Marmot
Hoary Marmot
Columbian Ground Squirrel
Golden-mantled Ground Squirrel
Bushy-tailed Woodrat
Long-tailed Vole

Water Vole
Western Jumping Mouse
Mountain Goat
Bighorn Sheep

Boreal-Cordilleran
Masked Shrew
Water Shrew
Pygmy Shrew
Snowshoe Hare
Least Chipmunk
Red Squirrel
Northern Flying Squirrel
Southern Red-backed Vole
Heather Vole
Meadow Vole
Northern Bog Lemming
Marten
Fisher
Ermine
Least Weasel
Wolverine
Canada Lynx
Moose

Eastern Forest
Northern Long-eared Bat
Red Bat

Campestrian
Prairie Shrew
White-tailed Jack Rabbit
Richardson's Ground Squirrel
Thirteen-lined Ground Squirrel
Franklin's Ground Squirrel
Olive-backed Pocket Mouse
Northern Grasshopper Mouse
Prairie Vole
Swift Fox
Pronghorn

Great Basin
Long-eared Bat
Long-legged Bat
Nuttall's Cottontail
Northern Pocket Gopher
Sagebrush Vole

Chihuahuan
Ord's Kangaroo Rat
Western Harvest Mouse

8

it too survived south of the continental ice sheet, perhaps farther south than other members of this element. Woodchuck from 25 Pleistocene localities have been found in east-central United States from Georgia to Maryland and westwards to Missouri (Kurtén and Anderson 1980). It has successfully dispersed across much of eastern North America up to, but not including, the western mountains. Along with the Woodchuck, the Arctic Shrew and Meadow Jumping Mouse are essentially confined to the northern forest areas in Alberta. None of these species has yet been found in the mountains.

Cordilleran Faunal Element

Fifteen species have extensive distributions with no well defined centre but cover an area from the southern Rocky Mountains and Sierra Nevadas to the northern Rockies in the Yukon Territory (Fig. 3). Some species (Dusky Shrew, Yellow-bellied Marmot, Columbian Ground Squirrel, Bushy-tailed Woodrat, Long-tailed Vole, and Western Jumping Mouse) may extend eastwards beyond the mountains but these are all typically mountain animals. While the habitats of these mountain-dwelling species are not conducive to fossil formation, existing evidence suggests that these species survived the Wisconsinan glaciation principally in unglaciated sites in the central Rocky Mountains. For example, Pika, Columbian Ground Squirrel, Golden-mantled Ground Squirrel, Bushy-tailed Woodrat, Long-tailed Vole and Mountain Goat fossils have all been recovered in sites from Idaho, southern Wyoming, and northern Colorado (Kurtén and Anderson 1980). Hoary Marmot fossils have been found in the Big Horn Mountains of Wyoming (Walker 1987). A few species (Yellow-bellied Marmot, Golden-mantled Ground Squirrel, Bushy-tailed Woodrat, Western Jumping Mouse and the Wandering Shrew) have been recovered in northern California, eastern Nevada, or in the mountains of southern Texas. Environmental indicators suggest that these latter sites were occupied by animals typical of cooler, more humid, more northerly environments and may have been southern outliers of the Cordilleran Faunal Element. No fossils of any mammals of the Cordilleran Element have been found in the arid southwest mountains or in Beringian sites and, except for the Vagrant Shrew, few Cordilleran species are

known as fossils from outside mountainous areas.

It appears that species of the Cordilleran Element survived in a number of unglaciated, relatively high-elevation, forested-to-subalpine mountain sites. They probably migrated northwards into Alberta along the Rocky Mountain chain following the retreat of both the continental and Cordilleran ice sheets.

Boreal-Cordilleran Faunal Element

The 18 Albertan species comprising this faunal element occupy a broad range across the boreal forest from Alaska to Newfoundland with southward extensions along both the western and eastern North American mountain chains (Fig. 4). The distinctions between the Cordilleran and Boreal-Cordilleran have been well described by Armstrong (1972). Both the northern and southern limits of the Boreal-Cordilleran Element are farther north than those of the Cordilleran Element. Further, the Boreal-Cordilleran Element extends across northern North America and down the Appalachians, a pattern of distribution not achieved by the Cordilleran Element. Seven Albertan species from the Boreal-Cordilleran element occur both in the Rockies of the American Southwest and in the central Appalachians (Masked Shrew, Water Shrew, Pygmy Shrew, Snowshoe Hare, Red Squirrel, Southern Red-backed Vole, and Meadow Vole). As is to be expected of such a widely distributed element, the fossil record indicates its members survived in a number of refugia, but all fossil sites have indicators of more northern or higher-altitude environments.

Most species in this element have fossil records that reflect a southward extension of their current ranges; that is, the fossils are found in mountain sites in the northwestern United States, along the Appalachians in the east, and at higher-elevation sites in the central Great Plains of the United States. These latter sites probably supported southward extensions of the boreal forest during the Wisconsinan glaciation. Four species — Masked Shrew, Ermine, Least Weasel, and Wolverine — are believed to have Old World ancestors. However, all these species were in North America prior to the Wisconsinan glacial period. Pleistocene fossils of Masked Shrew

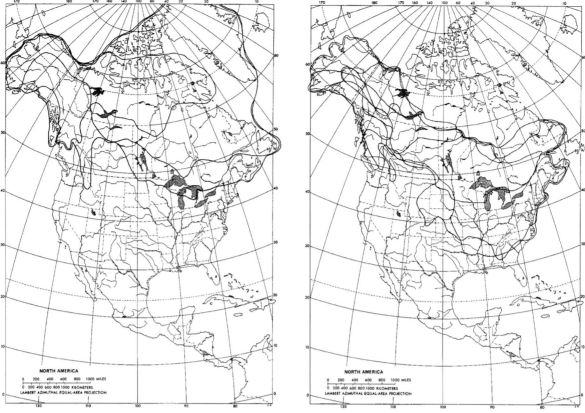

Figure 1. Arctic Faunal Element

Figure 2. Boreal Faunal Element

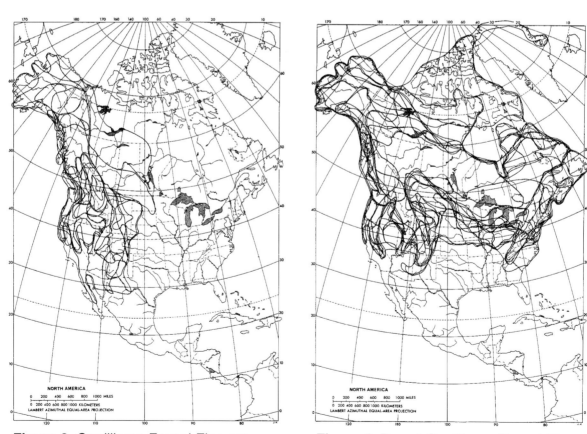

Figure 3. Cordilleran Faunal Element

Figure 4. Boreal-Cordilleran Faunal Element

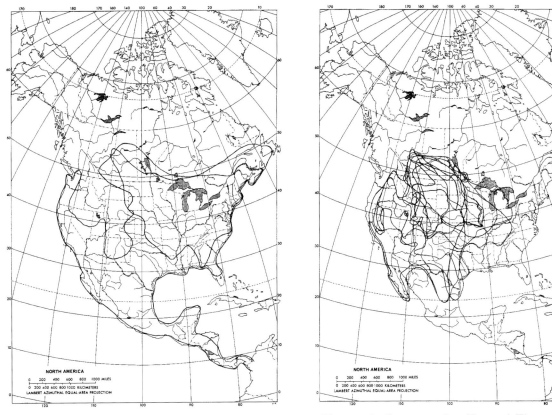

Figure 5. Eastern Forest Faunal Element

Figure 6. Campestrian Faunal Element

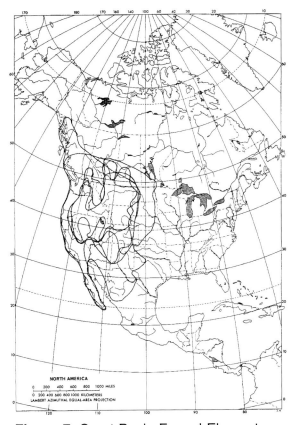

Figure 7. Great Basin Faunal Element

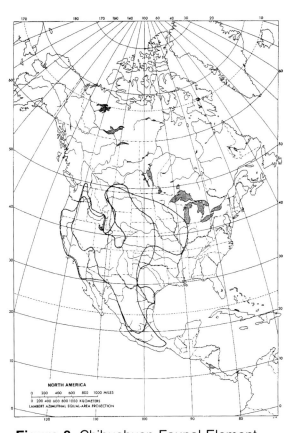

Figure 8. Chihuahuan Faunal Element

11

and Least Weasel have been found from Alaska to Arkansas (Kurtén and Anderson 1980). Both the Ermine and Wolverine, along with the Canada Lynx, have fossil records from Beringia as well as Colorado, Idaho and Wyoming indicating that they survived in two isolated refugia. In North America, Pleistocene fossils of the Canada Lynx are restricted to the western part of the continent.

The Moose also appears to have evolved recently from its European conspecies. Fossil evidence suggests that, for most of the Wisconsinan, the North American species was in Beringia and moved south of the ice sheet only in the postglacial period.

An unusual member of this element is the Red Squirrel whose fossil record suggests a closer affinity with the Eastern Forest Faunal Element than the Cordilleran Faunal Element. Its fossils are known only from the Appalachian states of eastern North America (Kurtén and Anderson 1980). I offer two explanations for this anomalous pattern. First, given the upland habitat and arboreal habit of this squirrel, its fossil record is expected to be quite poor. Fossil remains may yet be discovered in the west and midwest. Second, the Red Squirrel may not have occupied western mountain or Great Plains boreal refugia during the Wisconsinan. If true, then this squirrel has apparently successfully "escaped" from the eastern forests and occupied boreal and mountain habitats typical of the Boreal-Cordilleran fauna.

It appears that most members of the Boreal-Cordilleran element survived in the forested mountain areas of the western and eastern United States along with island refugia of boreal forest in what is now the Great Plains. At the end of the Wisconsinan, members of this element migrated north with the boreal and mountain forests but also remained in the higher-altitude mountain regions. Five members of the element also survived in Beringia, immigrating southwards to Alberta from Alaska and the Yukon.

Eastern Forest Faunal Element

Two species of bats — Northern Long-eared and Red — are the sole representatives in Alberta of the Eastern Forest Element. The Lower Mississippi and Central Lowlands of the eastern United States form the centre of distribution for this faunal element (Fig. 5). Although I placed the Woodchuck into the Boreal Faunal Element, its distribution could also be interpreted as being of a more northerly member of the Eastern Forest Element (cf. Hoffmann and Jones 1970). Members of this element apparently survived in the temperate hardwood forests during the Wisconsinan and have immigrated into Alberta from the south and east.

Campestrian Faunal Element

Ten species have ranges which are largely delimited by the Great Plains with a centre of distribution in the prairies of Nebraska, Kansas, and eastern Colorado (Fig. 6). Most of these species are limited to grassland ecosystems and do not range into mountainous habitats or eastern hardwood forests. The Thirteen-lined Ground Squirrel is a notable exception with a distribution extending eastwards through the Great Lakes States. The fossil record for this species extends far to the east with specimens from Pennsylvania and Virginia. These fossils suggest that parkland environments existed well eastward of their present range during the Wisconsinan glaciation.

Most of these species have their greatest fossil record around the centre of their current distribution. A number of species (e.g., White-tailed Jack Rabbit and Richardson's Ground Squirrel) had ranges that reached into southern New Mexico and Eastern Texas, well south of their current distribution. The Pronghorn has an excellent fossil record from southern California; again, far south of its current range in the west. Botanical evidence suggests that these areas had cooler summers and greater annual rainfall than at present. Temperate grasslands probably shifted south in response to pluvial conditions associated with glaciation. With postglacial warming and drying, mammals of the Campestrian Element have migrated northwards and westwards into Alberta out of their refugia on the southern Great Plains.

Great Basin Faunal Element

Five species of Albertan mammals have a centre of distribution in the northern Great Basin or Wyoming Basin (Fig. 7). Species from this element are usually associated with sagebrush or rock outcrops. The Northern Pocket Gopher is an exception; it prefers foothill meadows, natural grasslands, and cultivated fields. It has recently expanded its range in response to opening of land for settlement.

Members of this element apparently inhabited refugia in the sagebrush communities which occupied the Snake River Plain and Columbia Plateau of the northern Great Basin and also in similar communities in the Wyoming Basin (Kurtén and Anderson 1980). Nuttall's Cottontail, Northern Pocket Gopher, and the Sagebrush Vole all have Wisconsinan-age fossils from these areas. Fossils of all members of the Great Basin Element have also been collected in southeast New Mexico and/or on the Edwards Plateau of central Texas, areas considerably south and east of the current ranges of most members of the Great Basin Element. Plant remains from the New Mexico sites indicate the area was covered by a mixture of sagebrush grasslands and desert grasslands. Unlike today, cool summers and mild winters with ample precipitation were apparently the norm in New Mexico.

Low-lying passes, occupied by sagebrush communities, in eastern and northeastern Idaho were likely the principal routes of immigration of the Great Basin mammalian fauna out of the Snake River and Columbia Plateau refugia onto the Great Plains (Hoffmann and Jones 1970). Once on the plains, these species migrated north with the sagebrush grasslands into southern Alberta.

Chihuahuan Faunal Element
The Chihuahuan Faunal Element is represented in Alberta by two species, both rodents. This faunal element is centred in the deserts east of the continental divide in northern Mexico (Fig. 8). Wisconsinan-age fossils of the Western Harvest Mouse have been collected in sites from California to New Mexico and Texas, south to northeastern Mexico and as far east as Missouri (Kurtén and Anderson 1980). Fossils of the Ord's Kangaroo Rat are mostly from the Edwards Plateau north to the panhandle in Texas and west to central New Mexico. Remains have also been found in southeast Idaho but these may be post-Wisconsinan.

According to Armstrong (1972) both the Ord's Kangaroo Rat and the Western Harvest Mouse have spread northwards through the Wyoming

Basin and have crossed into domains more typical of the Great Basin and Campestrian Faunal Elements. The dispersal route through the Wyoming Great Basin coincides with the one used by the eastward-dispersing members of the Great Basin Faunal Element.

Ecological Biogeography
According to the classification of Hagmeier (1966), Alberta has three of the 35 faunal provinces found in North America: Western Canadian (Boreal), Montanian (Mountain), and Saskatchewanian (Plains) (Fig. 9). On a continental scale, the size and abundance of faunal provinces appears to be correlated with topographic and air mass diversity. In North America there is a trend for numerous but small provinces in the structurally

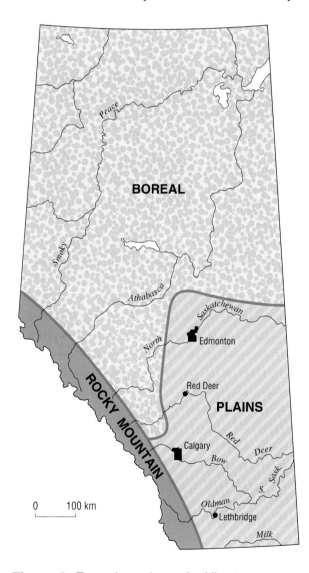

Figure 9. Faunal provinces in Alberta.

complex American Southwest with fewer and larger provinces towards both the north and east. The flat interior of North America, dominated by relatively few air masses has the largest and fewest provinces. Thus, the structurally and climatically diverse state of California has seven faunal provinces while the much larger area that includes southern North Dakota, South Dakota, Nebraska, and Kansas is covered by one faunal province.

Alberta's three provinces compares to four provinces in each of British Columbia, Montana, and Manitoba, and two in Saskatchewan. The topographic diversity of British Columbia and Montana contribute to their higher number of provinces. Manitoba, although not topographically complex, is at a meeting place of four different air masses (Polar Continental, Arctic Continental, Temperate Continental, and Temperate Maritime) and thus, perhaps surprisingly, has a greater number of faunal provinces than the more topographically complex Alberta. Saskatchewan fits the general North American pattern; it is topographically uniform and dominated by only two air masses (Arctic Continental and Temperate Continental). Thus, it has only two faunistic provinces. Alberta would be much like Saskatchewan in terms of faunal provinces were it not for the presence of the Rocky Mountains. The mountains add an element of structural diversity to the region and increase the number of faunal provinces to three.

Boreal Faunal Province

The Boreal Faunal Province is the largest of the three faunal provinces that occur in Alberta. It encompasses almost the entire northern half of Alberta and is similar to Soper's (1964) Canadian life zone and Hagmeier's (1966) Western Canadian mammal province. Characteristic mammals of this province include: Masked Shrew, Water Shrew, Arctic Shrew, Northern Long-eared Bat, Woodchuck, Northern Flying Squirrel, Taiga Vole, Meadow Jumping Mouse, Arctic Fox, Fisher, River Otter, Black Bear, Canada Lynx, Moose, and Barren-ground Caribou. These animals are derived from four faunal elements: Arctic, Boreal, Boreal-Cordilleran, and Eastern Forest, showing that animals from a diversity of refugia were able to recolonize postglacial boreal forest environments successfully.

This faunal province encompasses five ecoregions (cf. Strong and Leggat 1981) in Alberta: Boreal Mixedwood, Boreal Foothills, Boreal Uplands, Boreal Northlands and Boreal Subarctic. The area is characterized floristically by mixed forests. The modal forest occupying the central part of the boreal in Alberta is Aspen Poplar and Balsam Poplar. White Spruce replaces Balsam Poplar in the north, and in the highlands Black Spruce/peatmoss form the climax communities. Towards the higher elevations in the west, in the Boreal Foothills and Boreal Uplands, Lodgepole Pine replaces Balsam Poplar in the drier sites while White and Black Spruce replace Poplar in more mesic to wet sites. Wetlands cover large areas in all the boreal forest ecoregions.

The boreal forest is a snow forest. The growing season is warmer and longer (mean=1100 growing degree days) in the boreal forest than the mountains but winters are colder. Growing season precipitation is about the same for both provinces. Winter is the limiting season for all permanent mammalian residents in the Boreal Faunal Province and all show adaptations to this relatively long, cold, and snowy period. For example, all the shrews, mice, and voles do not hibernate but stay active under the relatively deep and soft snowcover in the forest. Both the Woodchuck and Black Bear avoid winter by hibernating through this season. Other animals such as the lynx and Caribou show morphological adaptations of their limbs which allow them to conserve energy as they move across the snow. Lynx have large, well furred paws which distribute their weight over a large surface. Similarly the Caribou have wide hooves which allow them to walk over hard-packed snow, and these hooves are used as shovels to reveal edible plants hidden under the snowpack.

Rocky Mountain Faunal Province

This is the smallest faunal province in Alberta, occupying only the mountainous areas. It forms part of Hagmeier's (1966) Montanian mammal province and includes Soper's (1964) Arctic-Alpine and Hudsonian-Canadian Life Zones. Characteristic mammals include: Pika, Yellow-pine Chipmunk, Hoary Marmot, Golden-mantled Ground Squirrel, Bushy-tailed Woodrat, Long-tailed Vole, Water Vole, Western Jumping Mouse, Mountain Goat, and Bighorn Sheep.

This faunal province encompasses three ecoregions: Montane, Subalpine, and Alpine. Due to its high elevation, this province has the lowest growing season temperatures in Alberta and generally has the shortest frost-free period. However, the greater influence of the warmer Pacific air masses means that winter temperatures are higher than those of the boreal forest. The short, cool summers (mean=800 growing degree days) limit the development of broad-leaved deciduous trees and thus mixedwood forests are not as common in the mountains as in the boreal forest. Mountain forests are dominated by conifers. The area is characterized by Douglas Fir in dry lower valleys, Lodgepole Pine and Engelmann Spruce in mid-to-high forest sites and by a variety of evergreen and deciduous shrubs, krummholz Whitebark Pine, and cryptogams above treeline.

Like the Boreal Faunal Province, mammals in the Rocky Mountain Province are particularly limited by the winter conditions. Chipmunks, marmots, and ground squirrels, all avoid winter by hibernation. Small microtine rodents remain active under the snow pack in areas of relatively deep snow accumulation. Mountain Goat and Bighorn Sheep are elevational migrants, moving out of their summer range in the open, high mountain meadows to more sheltered lower-elevation sites during the winter.

Plains Faunal Province

That portion of Hagmeier's (1966) Saskatchewanian mammal province that is found in Alberta is roughly comparable to the Plains Faunal Province as defined in this work. This province also includes Soper's (1964) Transition Parkland, Transition Prairie, and Upper Sonoran Life Zones. Characteristic mammals include: Prairie Shrew, Western Small-footed Bat, Nuttall's Cottontail, White-tailed Jack Rabbit, Richardson's Ground Squirrel, Thirteen-lined Ground Squirrel, Franklin's Ground Squirrel, Northern Pocket Gopher, Olive-backed Pocket Mouse, Ord's Kangaroo Rat, Northern Grasshopper Mouse, Prairie Vole, Sagebrush Vole, Badger, and Pronghorn.

This faunal province covers four ecoregions in Alberta: Short Grass, Mixed Grass, Fescue Grass, and Aspen Parkland. Due to its southerly latitude and relatively low elevation, this province has the warmest and longest growing season (mean=1300 growing degree days) of the three faunal provinces found in Alberta. Winters are relatively warm due to both a high frequency of chinooks and a greater influence of Continental Tropical air masses. Winter precipitation is low due to the dry air masses, and chinooks frequently remove the snow cover, both of which contribute to a low soil moisture recharge. Consequently, vegetation is dominated by grass communities. The most drought-tolerant grasses, Blue Grama and Spear, are found in the relatively arid southeast. At higher elevations towards the west there is greater precipitation and cooler summer temperatures. Tall grass communities of Rough Fescue and Parry Oatgrass become predominant. Towards the north the arctic airmass becomes more important, leading to cooler summer temperatures and a shorter growing season. Aspen Poplar along with Rough Fescue become the dominant vegetation. The Aspen Parkland has greater, late growing season precipitation than the grasslands which "reduces moisture stress on vegetation, and is likely critical to survival of aspen" (Strong and Leggat 1981).

Unlike the boreal and mountain faunas, where there is considerable overlap in species occurring in both regions, mammals of the grasslands tend to be more strongly restricted to this faunal province. These animals are adapted to drought, high temperatures, and frequent fires. A large proportion of the mammals are burrowers. The burrows have a more stable temperature regime and higher humidity which not only allows the animals to escape the daytime heat and but also provides a warmer shelter at night. Many of the rodents are nocturnal, thereby avoiding daytime weather extremes as well as predation by diurnal raptors. The rodents are often more lightly coloured than closely related forest-dwelling species, the coloration either increasing albedo or serving as camouflage.

Conclusion

In summary, the Albertan mammalian fauna shows a relatively complex history modified by current environmental conditions. Species which survived in refugia in the arctic ecosystems of the Canadian Arctic Islands and Alaska almost meet with species whose centre of dispersal was in the deserts of northern Mexico. While we will never know all the details of the postglacial migration of mammals back into the province, the equiformal progressive area analysis coupled with what is known from the fossil record allows us to identify some broad patterns in this history. Eight distinct faunal elements now occur in the province, each faunal element having its own history correlated with patterns of the Wisconsinan glaciation.

Three faunal provinces occur in Alberta. Each province is occupied by a group of animals adapted to the generally prevailing environmental conditions and specifically adapted to microhabitats within each province. The provinces contain a complex of animals from a number of faunal elements. Although historical factors determine the origins of Alberta's mammals, current distributions in the province are tied to available habitats. These distributions will continue to shift as habitats are modified by human activity and other factors.

Acknowledgments

I would like to thank Hugh Smith for providing the initial manuscript on which this biogeographical study was based. Dr. Bruce McGillivray provided the opportunity to undertake this project and assisted greatly in the earlier drafts of this chapter. Dr. Jim Burns, in addition to significantly improving this chapter through his extensive editorial comments on both style and content, also assisted in preparing the final versions of the figures.

Ross I. Hastings
Curator, Biogeography
and Non-vascular Plants,
Provincial Museum of Alberta

Species Accounts

Key to the Orders of Mammals Found in Alberta

1. Forelimbs modified as wings; large U-shaped gap between
   premaxillae and upper middle incisors . . . . Chiroptera (p. 34)
   Forelimbs not modified as wings; if present, premaxillary gap not
   U-shaped and upper incisors absent 2

Myotis lucifugus (Chiroptera)

U-shaped gap

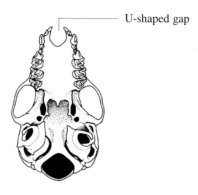

2. Feet modified as cloven hooves with 2 or 4 toes; upper incisors
   absent (except Suidae — pigs); antlers or horns normally present
   (except Suidae) in males of all species and in females of many
   species . . . . Artiodactyla (p. 199)
   Feet not modified as above; upper incisors present 3

3. Feet modified as single hoof or toe; 6 upper incisors each with
   central enamel pit; large diastema in front of cheek teeth . . . . Perissodactyla (p. 221)
   Feet with 4-5 toes; 2, 4, or 6 upper incisors with no enamel pits . . . 4

4. Skull with first pair of incisors long, curved, chisel-like; diastema
   between incisors and cheek teeth 5
   Skull with first pair of incisors unlike above; diastema variable but
   almost never large 6

5. Skull with 2 upper incisors, usually pigmented orange or orange-
   red . . . . Rodentia (p. 64)
   Skull with 4 upper incisors, 2 larger ones in front of 2 smaller
   ones, unpigmented . . . . Lagomorpha (p. 55)

6. Canines inconspicuous; unworn-to-moderately-worn teeth with dark
   red pigmentation on cusp tips; molar teeth with W-shaped
   occlusal surface; eyes small; rostrum long, slender . . . . Insectivora (p. 19)
   Canines conspicuous; diastema usually absent (except Ursidae —
   bears); molar occlusal surfaces either blade-like for shearing or
   flat/cuspidate for grinding . . . . Carnivora (p. 149)

Order: Insectivora

Members of the Order Insectivora are found in North America, northern South America, Europe, Asia, and Africa. The fossil record for this Order extends back to the Cretaceous period, the time of the dinosaurs. There are approximately 391 recognized species worldwide (Anderson and Jones 1984).

Only the shrew family, Soricidae, is represented in Alberta. Seven species of shrews are known to occur in the province. Each species is small with a long, pointed nose, low braincase, and small ears and eyes. The pelage is short and dense.

Key to the Shrews (Insectivora)

1. Unicuspids 3 and 5 extremely small, may not be visible from side view . . . . *Sorex hoyi* (p. 32)

   Unicuspids 3 and 5 "normal" size, all 5 unicuspids visible from side view 2

2. Unicuspid 3 smaller than unicuspid 4 3

   Unicuspid 3 larger or the same size as unicuspid 4 5

3. Total length greater than 130 mm; pelage strongly bicolored—black on the back, silver-grey on the belly; fringe of fine, stiff hairs on feet . . . . *Sorex palustris* (p. 28)

   Total length shorter than 130 mm; pelage brownish, not bicolored . . 4

4. Medial tine on upper incisor large, extending into dark orange pigmentation; more than four friction pads on hind toes . . . . *Sorex monticolus* (p. 24)

   Medial tine on upper incisor small, barely reaching dark orange pigmentation; four or fewer friction pads on hind toes . . . . *Sorex vagrans* (p. 26)

Sorex monticolus   *Sorex vagrans*

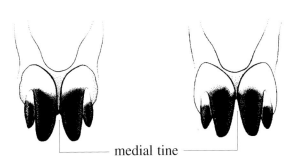

————— medial tine —————

5. Pelage frequently tricolored—dark on back, lighter on sides, and lighter still on belly; skull robust . . . . *Sorex arcticus* (p. 30)

   Pelage brownish; skull delicate 6

6. Unicuspid toothrow length greater than 2.2 mm; terminal tail tuft may be darker on upper surface . . . . *Sorex cinereus* (p. 20)

   Unicuspid toothrow length less than 2.3 mm; terminal tail tuft uniform color, not dark . . . . *Sorex haydeni* (p. 22)

MASKED SHREW
Sorex cinereus

IDENTIFYING CHARACTERS

This is a long-tailed, grayish brown shrew with a terminal tail tuft that is faintly dark. The unicuspid toothrow is generally longer than 2.2 mm and the skull has a long, narrow rostrum.

The dental formula is I 1/1, U 5/0, P 1/2, M 3/3 x 2 = 32.

DISTRIBUTION

The Masked Shrew is found throughout northern Alberta south to the eastern portion of the Red Deer River and along the mountains and foothills to Waterton Lakes National Park. It is absent from the arid grasslands of the southeast.

HABITAT

This species occupies a variety of habitats from damp meadows, to uplands, to deadfall in coniferous, deciduous, and mixed forests.

STATUS

Common to very common.

SIMILAR SPECIES

Prairie Shrews are slightly smaller with a shorter tail and paler pelage. The most reliable character for separating the two species is the length of the unicuspid toothrow. This toothrow in the Prairie Shrew is shorter than 2.3 mm. The terminal tuft on the tail is not dark. The skull is flatter with a shorter rostrum (Junge and Hoffmann 1981).

Dusky Shrews are larger and the third unicuspid is smaller than the fourth.

Pygmy Shrews are approximately the same size and color but are easily identified by the fact that in the Pygmy Shrew the third and fifth unicuspids are extremely small and are not visible when viewed from the side.

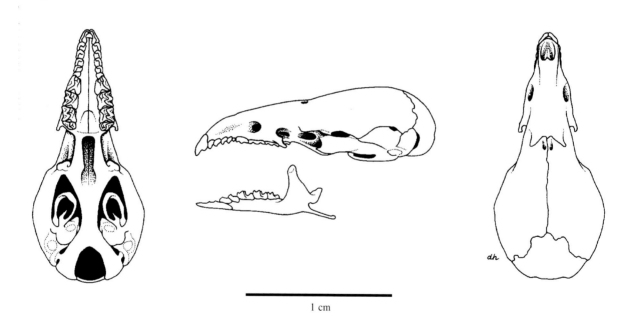

1 cm

Measurements

Sex		Weight (g)	Total Length (mm)	Tail (mm)	Hindfoot (mm)	Ear (mm)
Male, Female and Unsexed (N=53)	Mean	4.0	94.1	39.4	12.2	7.7
	Range	2.4-7.0	81-116	35-49	11-13	6-10

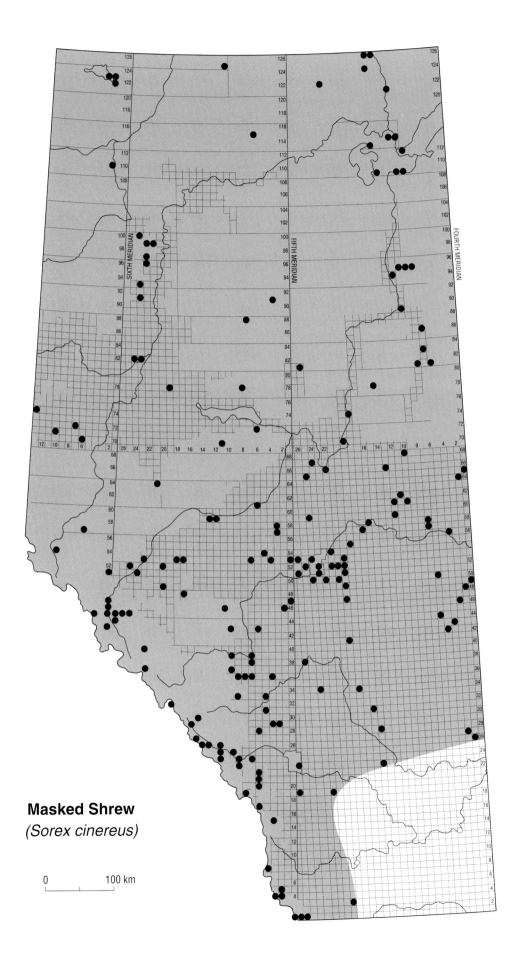

Masked Shrew
(Sorex cinereus)

0   100 km

PRAIRIE SHREW
Sorex haydeni

IDENTIFYING CHARACTERS

No one character can be used with confidence to separate this species from the Masked Shrew. This is one of the smallest shrews in Alberta. It is brown to dark brown on the back, grayish white below. The terminal tail tuft is not noticeably dark.

The skull is small and delicate with a short rostrum and flattish profile. The length of the unicuspid toothrow is less than 2.3 mm. The cheek teeth are relatively large. The short, broad rostrum has a slight downward hook. The dental formula is I 1/1, U 5/0, P 1/2, M 3/3 x 2 = 32.

DISTRIBUTION

This shrew is found in southeastern Alberta, from the United States border north to Smoky Lake and St. Paul and from the Saskatchewan border west to Edmonton, Pigeon Lake, Calgary, and Milk River. One specimen has been reported from Beaverlodge in northwestern Alberta (van Zyll de Jong 1980).

HABITAT

From the arid grasslands to the parklands this species finds suitable habitat in dense vegetation, shrubby areas, and meadows.

STATUS

Uncommon.

SIMILAR SPECIES

Masked Shrews are slightly larger with a longer tail. The terminal tuft on the tail is dark. The length of the unicuspid toothrow is greater than 2.2 mm.

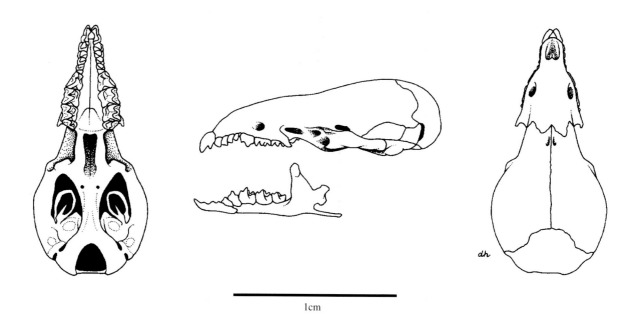

1cm

Measurements

Sex		Weight (g)	Total Length (mm)	Tail (mm)	Hindfoot (mm)	Ear (mm)
Male, Female and Unsexed (N=17)	Mean	3.3	82.5	31.9	11.1	7.7
	Range	2.5-4.9	77-94	28-35	10-12	7-8

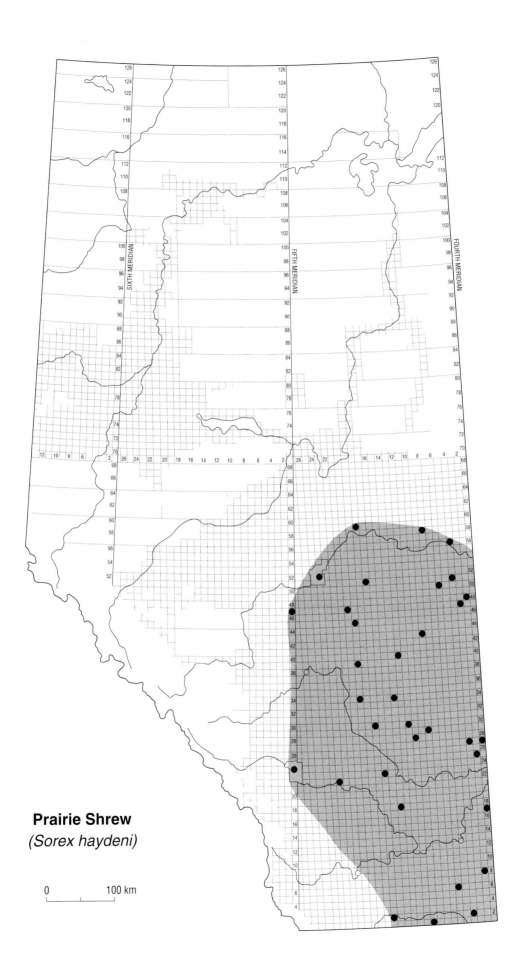

Prairie Shrew

(Sorex haydeni)

0   100 km

23

DUSKY SHREW
Sorex monticolus

IDENTIFYING CHARACTERS

The Dusky Shrew is a small-to-medium-sized shrew, grayish brown on the back, sometimes with a reddish tinge, and the belly is smoky gray. The brown tail is darker above but the tip is not black.

The skull is relatively short and broad. The medial tine of the upper incisors extends well down in the zone of orange pigmentation (see key to the shrews, p. 19). The third unicuspid is smaller than the fourth. The dental formula is I 1/1, U 5/0, P 1/2, M 3/3 x 2 = 32.

DISTRIBUTION

Found throughout the province.

HABITAT

The Dusky Shrew is widely distributed because it tolerates a variety of habitats, from arid grasslands to damp meadows, to northern bogs, to areas along alpine streams. Most frequently these shrews occur where there is dense cover.

STATUS

Common in all but the grassland areas, uncommon in the latter.

SIMILAR SPECIES

Wandering Shrews are slightly smaller. The medial tines on the upper incisors are smaller. The feet are smaller.

Masked Shrews are smaller. The third unicuspid is larger than the fourth.

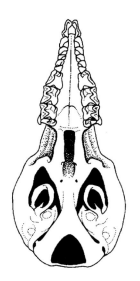 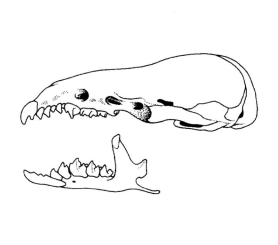 

1 cm

Measurements

Sex		Weight (g)	Total Length (mm)	Tail (mm)	Hindfoot (mm)	Ear (mm)
Males (N=18)	Mean	5.7	108.2	44.8	12.9	7.6
	Range	4.4-7.6	102-115	41-50	12-14	6-10
Females (N=23)	Mean	6.3	108.0	44.6	12.9	7.7
	Range	4.6-9.8	101-120	38-50	11-15	6-10

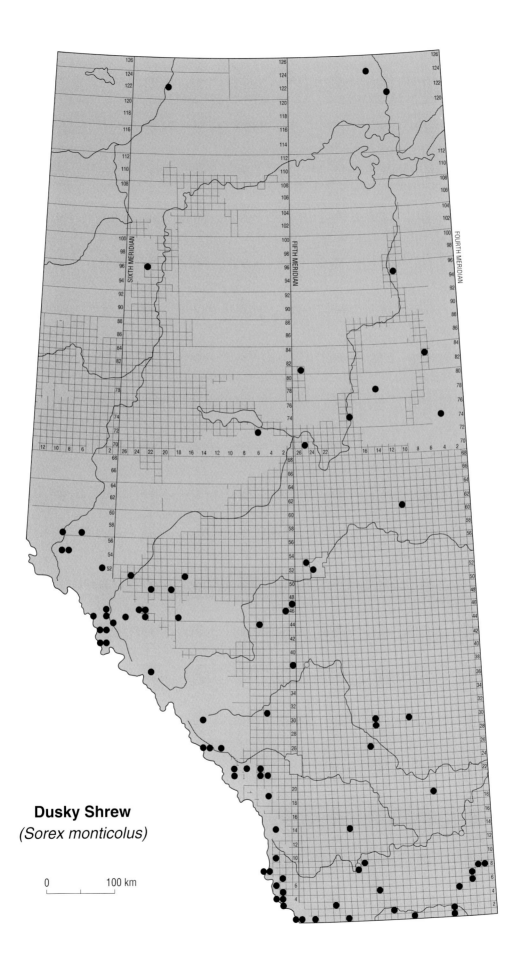

Dusky Shrew

(Sorex monticolus)

0   100 km

WANDERING SHREW
Sorex vagrans

IDENTIFYING CHARACTERS

The Wandering Shrew's pelage is grayish brown on the back and smoky gray on the belly. Although very similar externally to some other species, this shrew is identified by the short medial tines of the upper incisors (see Key to the Shrews, p. 19), and by the four or fewer friction pads on the toes of the hindfoot.

The skull is delicate without distinguishing features. The third upper unicuspid is smaller than the fourth. The dental formula is I 1/1, U 5/0, P 1/2, M 3/3 x 2 = 32.

DISTRIBUTION

This species has been found in only three sites in the West Castle area of southwestern Alberta.

HABITAT

Specimens were collected along a mountain stream in a coniferous forest.

STATUS

Not known at this time, probably rare.

SIMILAR SPECIES

Dusky Shrews are slightly larger. The medial tines on the upper incisors extend well into the orange pigmentation. There are more than four friction pads on the toes of the hindfeet. The feet of the Dusky Shrew are slightly larger.

Masked Shrews are smaller. The third unicuspid is larger than the fourth.

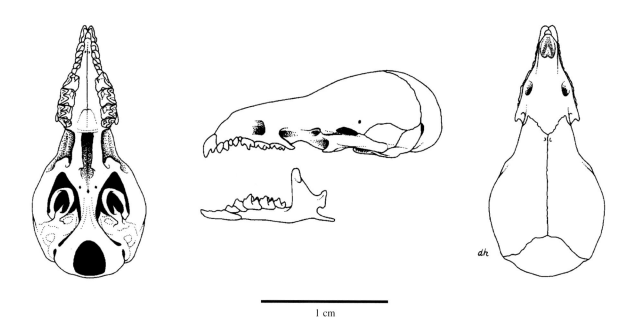

1 cm

Measurements

Sex		Weight (g)	Total Length (mm)	Tail (mm)	Hindfoot (mm)	Ear (mm)
Male, Female and Unsexed (N= 7)	Mean	5.2	100.1	45.6	13.5	7.9
	Range	4.3-7.7	92-110	42-56	13-14	6-10

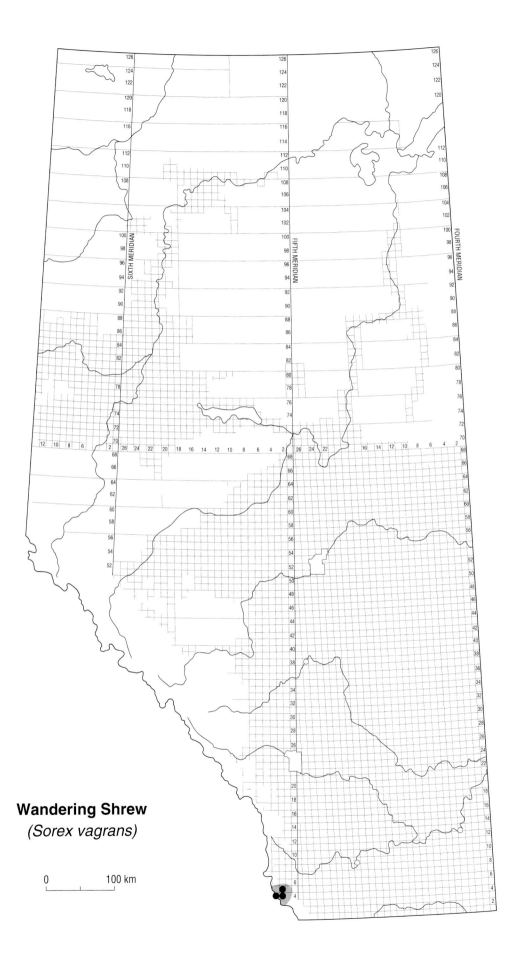

Wandering Shrew

(Sorex vagrans)

0   100 km

WATER SHREW
Sorex palustris

IDENTIFYING CHARACTERS

The distinctly bicolored pelage of this large shrew is dark, almost blue-black on the back and white or silver-gray on the belly. The feet are white. The hindfeet are large and have a fringe of stiff hairs along the toes. The tail is long and sharply bicolored.

The skull is large and robust for a shrew. Some individuals may have a sagittal crest. The teeth are large and the third unicuspid is smaller than the fourth. In older individuals the upper incisors are more down-turned and hooked than in younger animals. The dental formula is I 1/1, U 5/0, P 1/2, M 3/3 x 2 = 32.

DISTRIBUTION

The Water Shrew is found throughout the northern forests and parklands south to approximately 52° N in the east and throughout the mountains and foothills to Waterton Lakes National Park in the west.

HABITAT

Water Shrews are seldom found away from water. Creeks, ponds, and lakes where there are overhanging banks or branches to provide cover are suitable locations for these shrews.

STATUS

These shrews are considered uncommon. However, this may reflect more on the ability of the collector than on the abundance or scarcity of the shrews. Some collectors are able to collect good numbers while others collect very few specimens.

SIMILAR SPECIES

Arctic Shrews are smaller, have a tricolored pelage, lack the fringe of fine hairs on the toes, and the third unicuspid is larger than the fourth.

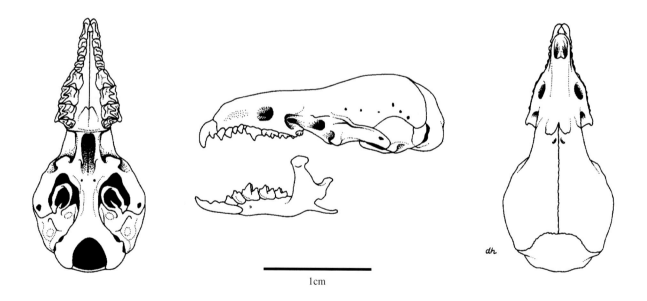

1cm

Measurements

Sex		Weight (g)	Total Length (mm)	Tail (mm)	Hindfoot (mm)	Ear (mm)
Male, Female and Unsexed (N= 33)	Mean	13.2	148.0	68.6	19.6	8.4
	Range	8.2-19.4	132-160	43-86	17-21	5-10

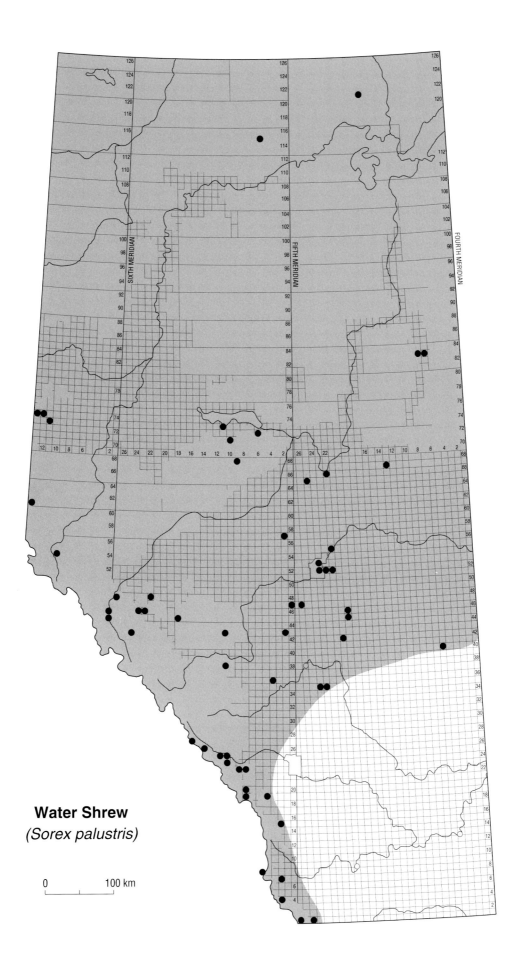

Water Shrew
(Sorex palustris)

0   100 km

ARCTIC SHREW
Sorex arcticus

IDENTIFYING CHARACTERS

The Arctic Shrew is relatively large and has a distinct seasonal pelage coloration. The summer pelage is grayish brown on the sides, slightly darker on the back, and dirty gray on the belly. There may be a hint of a rust or orange around the head and shoulders. The winter pelage is dark brown on the back with grayish brown sides and a smoky gray belly. This is the only Alberta shrew that has a distinctly tricolored pelage.

The skull is relatively large and robust. The third unicuspid is larger than the fourth. The dental formula is I 1/1, U 5/0, P 1/2, M 3/3 x 2 = 32.

DISTRIBUTION

The Arctic Shrew is found throughout the northern forests and parklands south to 52° N in the east and Turner Valley in the west. It has not been acquired in the mountains.

HABITAT

Damp meadows, aspen groves, black spruce-larch bogs, deadfall, lodgepole pine-aspen forest.

STATUS

Relatively common.

SIMILAR SPECIES

Water Shrews are larger, have a distinctly bicolored pelage, and the third unicuspid is smaller than the fourth. The feet have rows of fine hairs along the toes.

Dusky Shrews are smaller, the pelage color is more uniform, and the third unicuspid is smaller than the fourth.

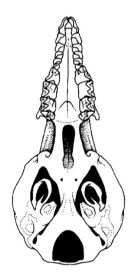 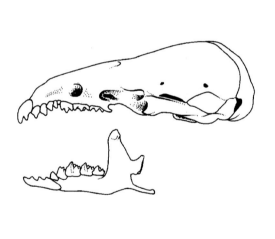 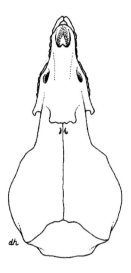

1 cm

Measurements

Sex		Weight (g)	Total Length (mm)	Tail (mm)	Hindfoot (mm)	Ear (mm)
Males (N=20)	Mean	8.2	110.8	40.7	14.2	7.9
	Range	6.2-10.2	104-123	38-45	14-15	6-10
Females (N=20)	Mean	8.4	107.8	41.1	13.8	7.3
	Range	5.9-10.9	99-119	38-46	12-18	4-9

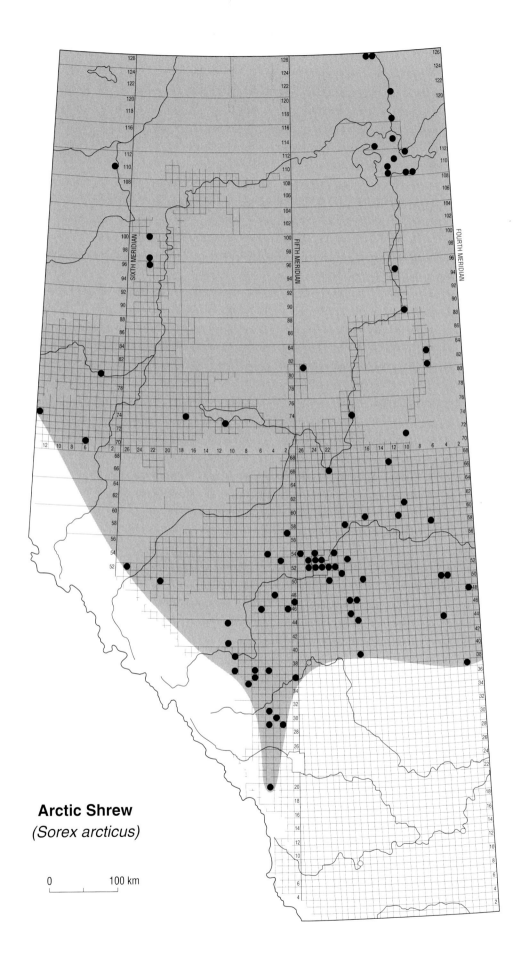

Arctic Shrew

(Sorex arcticus)

0   100 km

PYGMY SHREW
Sorex hoyi

IDENTIFYING CHARACTERS

Pygmy Shrews are smoky brown on top and lighter on the belly. Externally unremarkable, this shrew is distinguished from other shrews by the fact that the upper unicuspids 3 and 5 are extremely small and are not visible from the side.

The skull is relatively flat and low-crowned with a short rostrum. Unicuspids 3 and 5 are disc-like. The dental formula is I 1/1, U 5/0, P 1/2, M 3/3 x 2 = 32.

DISTRIBUTION

The Pygmy Shrew occurs in the mountains and foothills south to Racehorse Creek and throughout the boreal and parkland forests south to the Battle River. There are no confirmed records of this species from the Waterton Lakes area.

HABITAT

Dry, upland coniferous and deciduous forests.

STATUS

As this species is only taken occasionally in traplines, its true status is difficult to determine. At this time it is considered uncommon.

SIMILAR SPECIES

Masked Shrews are impossible to separate from Pygmy Shrews based on external characters. However, the Masked Shrew's five unicuspid teeth are readily seen in lateral view.

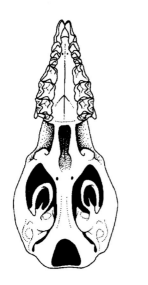
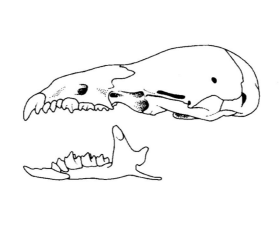

1 cm

Measurements

Sex		Weight (g)	Total Length (mm)	Tail (mm)	Hindfoot (mm)	Ear (mm)
Male, Female and Unsexed (N= 20)	Mean	3.3	88.1	29.4	10.7	6.6
	Range	2.7-5.1	83-95	25-33	10-11	5-9

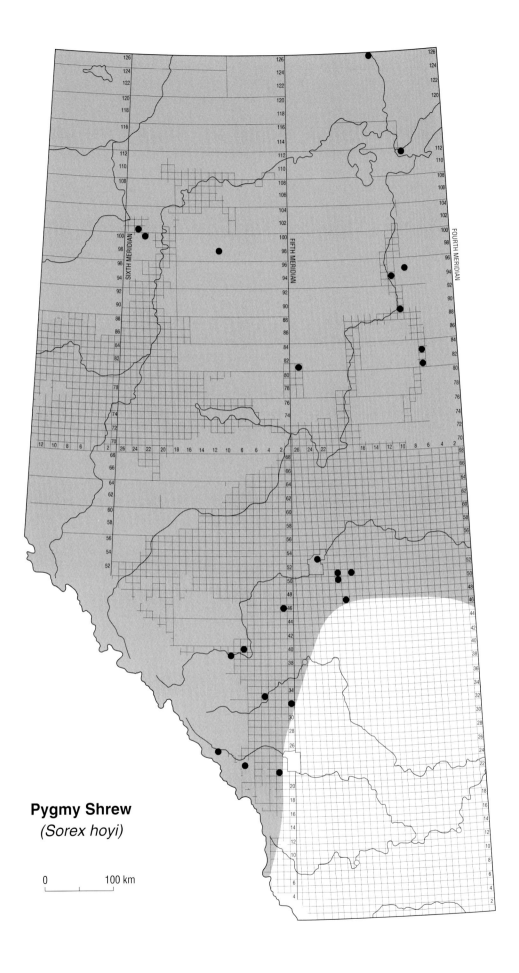

Pygmy Shrew
(Sorex hoyi)

0   100 km

33

Order: Chiroptera

This Order is the only group of mammals that has evolved true flight. The forelimbs have been modified by the elongation of the digits into supports for a thin skin membrane that permits these animals to fly. Bats are widely distributed throughout tropical and temperate areas. They are present everywhere except in extremely cold regions (Antarctica, the Arctic) and a few isolated, remote islands.

Bats evolved during the early Eocene, approximately 50 million years ago. Today over 900 species of bats are recognized worldwide (Anderson and Jones 1984).

The nine species of bats found in Alberta are placed in the family Vespertilionidae. This family has over 300 species and is found in most areas of the world.

Vespertilionid bats are usually small, insect feeders. They roost in caves, hollow trees, buildings, or rock crevices. Some species hibernate, others migrate from temperate areas to milder climates during the winter.

Key to the Bats (Chiroptera)

1. Pelage frosted 2
   Pelage brownish, lacking any frosting 4

2. Weight greater than 30 g; total length greater than 130 mm; cream-colored ruff around neck, cream-colored spots at wrist joint on underside of wing; pelage frosted or hoary; ears small, roundish, thick at edge, black . . . . *Lasiurus cinereus* (p. 52)
   Weight less than 20 g; total length less than 120 mm; lacks cream-colored neck ruff; pelage dark brown or black or orange-red 3

3. Pelage black or dark brown with silver-tipped hairs . . . . *Lasionycteris noctivagans* (p. 46)
   Pelage orange-red or brick-red . . . . *Lasiurus borealis* (p. 50)

4. Ears long, greater than 16 mm 5
   Ears short, less than 16 mm 8

5. Total length greater than 105 mm; weight greater than 15 g; pelage glossy brown; upper premolar long, half length of canine . . . . *Eptesicus fuscus* (p. 48)
   Total length less than 105 mm; weight less than 15 g 6

6. Calcar keeled . . . . *Myotis ciliolabrum* (p. 44)
   Calcar not keeled 7

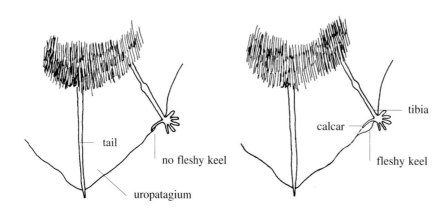

7. Pelage light brown with dark patch at shoulders; ears and flight
    membranes black; ears 18-22 mm long . . . . *Myotis evotis* (p. 40)

    Pelage medium to dark brown; ears and flight membranes dark
    brown; ears 17-19 mm long . . . . *Myotis septentrionalis* (p. 38)

8. Calcar with a fleshy keel . . . . *Myotis volans* (p. 42)

    Calcar without a fleshy keel . . . . *Myotis lucifugus* (p. 36)

LITTLE BROWN BAT
Myotis lucifugus

IDENTIFYING CHARACTERS

This is a medium-sized bat (weighs up to 12 g). The pelage has a glossy sheen and ranges from dark brown to reddish brown to pale brown. The ears and flight membranes are dark brown to black. The ears, when laid forward, reach the nose. The tragus tapers from a relatively wide base to a rounded, blunt tip. Specimens from the grasslands are lighter colored than those from forested areas.

The skull is slightly triangular in shape with a globose braincase and a short rostrum. The slope from the rostrum to the forehead may rise gently or abruptly. The dental formula is I 2/3, C 1/1, P 3/3, M 3/3 x 2 = 38.

DISTRIBUTION

Found in suitable habitat throughout the province.

HABITAT

Old buildings that allow entry and are situated near both trees and water are primary areas for nursery colonies. Caves are used for hibernating sites.

STATUS

Common to very common.

SIMILAR SPECIES

Northern Long-eared Bats have a duller pelage, longer ears, and a long, narrow tragus.

Long-legged Bats have shorter, rounder ears, a keeled calcar, and wings with more heavily furred undersides.

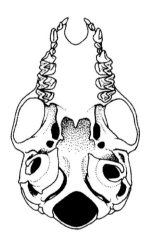 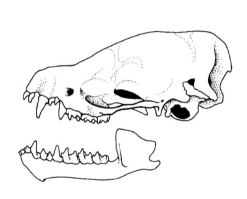 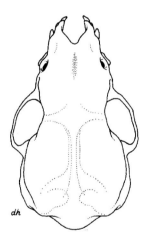

1 cm

Measurements

Sex		Weight (g)	Total Length (mm)	Tail (mm)	Hindfoot (mm)	Ear (mm)
Males (N=20)	Mean	9.4	89.6	38	10.9	14.3
	Range	7.0-10.6	82-97	34-41	10-12	12-16
Females (N=20)	Mean	9.3	90.5	39.8	11.9	15.2
	Range	6.6-11.8	82-94	37-46	11-13	15-16

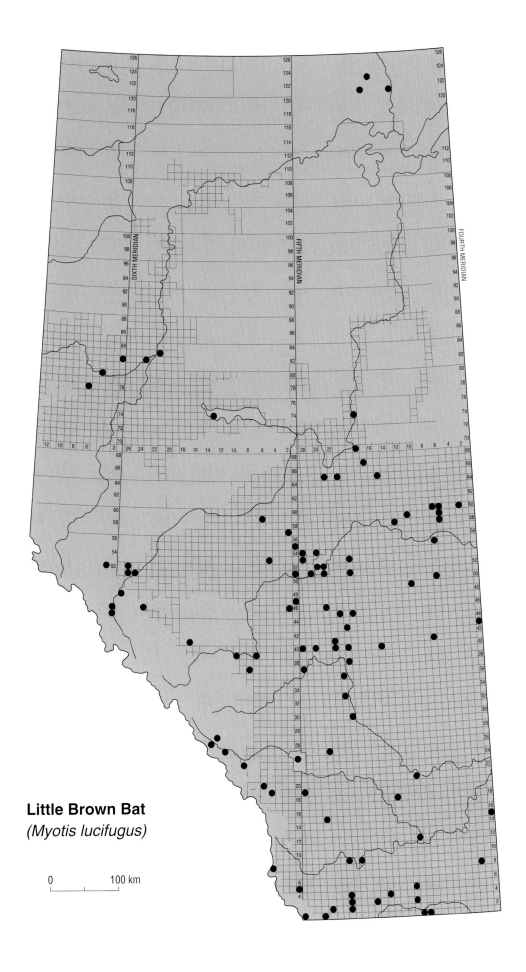

Little Brown Bat
(Myotis lucifugus)

0   100 km

NORTHERN LONG-EARED BAT
Myotis septentrionalis

IDENTIFYING CHARACTERS

This is a medium-sized (weighs up to 9 g) brown bat with long ears (up to 19 mm in length) and a uniformly narrow tragus. The pelage is smoky brown on the back and lighter brown on the belly. The flight membranes and ears are dark brown.

The skull is long and narrow with a globose braincase. The rostrum slopes gently to the forehead. The dental formula is I 2/3, C 1/1, P 3/3, M 3/3 x 2 = 38.

DISTRIBUTION

This bat is found throughout the northern forested areas south to Cadomin and Edmonton and possibly Cold Lake.

HABITAT

Mixed and coniferous forests. Hibernates in caves.

STATUS

Widely distributed throughout the northern forests, probably uncommon.

SIMILAR SPECIES

Long-eared Bats have longer and darker ears, and the pelage is lighter with dark shoulder patches.

Little Brown Bats have shorter ears, a wider tragus, and a glossier pelage.

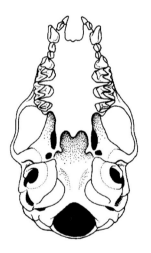 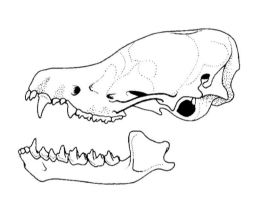 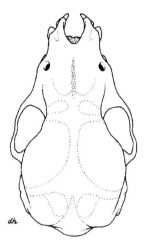

1 cm

Measurements

Sex		Weight (g)	Total Length (mm)	Tail (mm)	Hindfoot (mm)	Ear (mm)
Males (N=40)	Mean	6.6	92.9	40.9	10.4	17.8
	Range	5.7-7.8	86-99	38-46	10-11	17-18
Females (N=10)	Mean	7.4	94.3	43.0	10.6	18.2
	Range	6.0-9.7	86-101	38-48	10-11	17-19

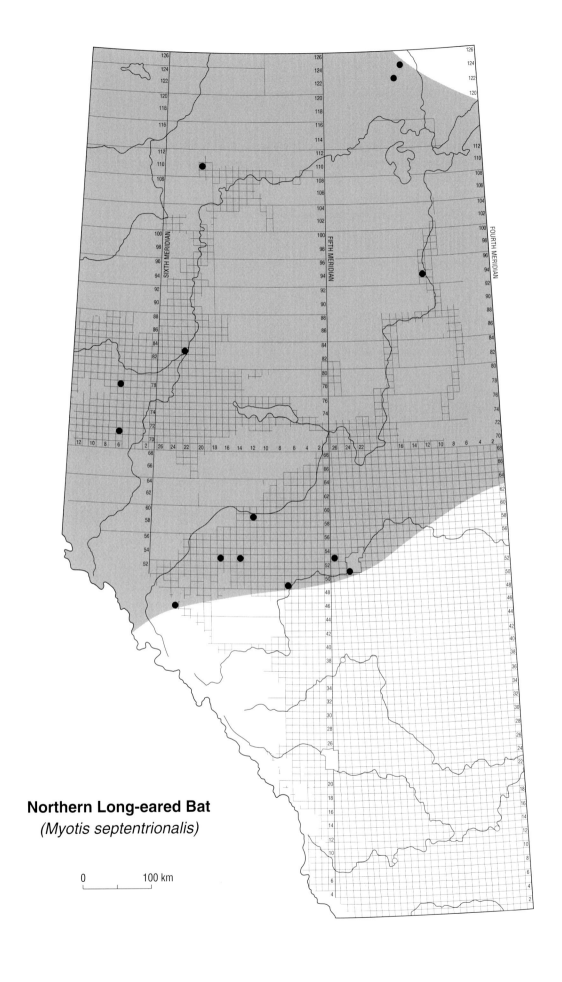

Northern Long-eared Bat
(Myotis septentrionalis)

0   100 km

LONG-EARED BAT
Myotis evotis

IDENTIFYING CHARACTERS

Among Alberta bats, this species has the longest ears (usually longer than 19 mm). When laid forward they extend well past the nose. The ears and flight membranes are strikingly black in comparison to the light brown-colored pelage. There is a dark patch at the shoulders.

The skull is delicate with a globose braincase, gently sloping forehead, and a long, tapered rostrum. The dental formula is I 2/3, C 1/1, P 3/3, M 3/3 x 2 = 38.

DISTRIBUTION

This bat is found in the mountains from Jasper south to Waterton and on the grasslands as far north as Trochu.

HABITAT

River valleys and coulees where rock outcrops provide shelter are suitable habitat for this species. It will occasionally occupy buildings.

STATUS

Uncommon on the grassland, rare in the mountains.

SIMILAR SPECIES

No other Alberta bat has ears as long as this species.

Northern Long-eared Bats are larger and darker. The ears are not as long.

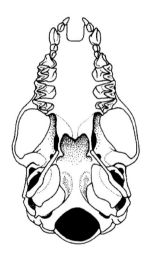 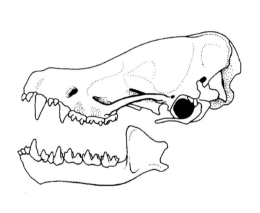 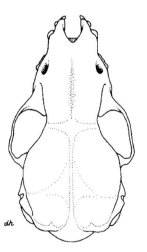

1 cm

Measurements

Sex		Weight (g)	Total Length (mm)	Tail (mm)	Hindfoot (mm)	Ear (mm)
Males (N=8)	Mean	6.6	91.9	42.0	10.6	19.8
	Range	5.1-7.5	85-96	40-45	10-12	18-21
Females (N=11)	Mean	7.6	97.5	44.3	10.5	20.8
	Range	6.4-9.3	92-105	40-49	10-12	19-22

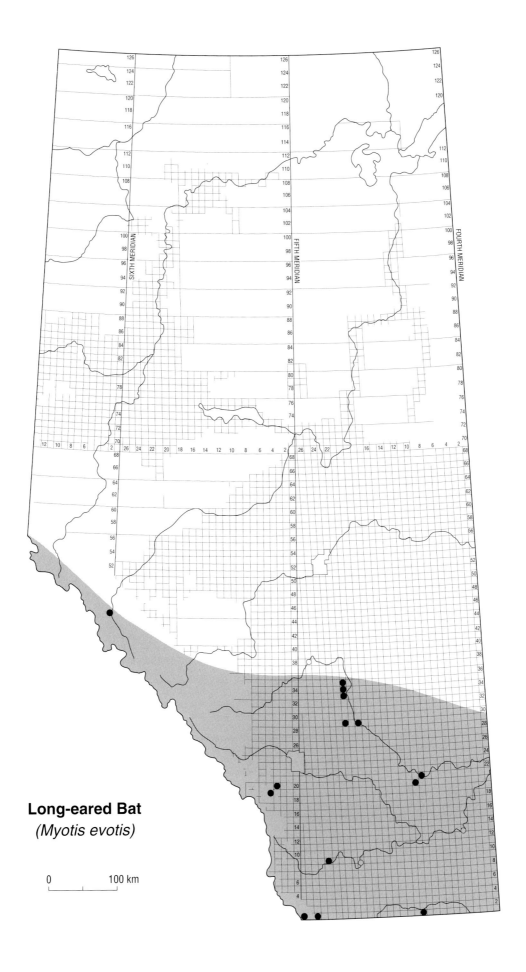

Long-eared Bat

(Myotis evotis)

0   100 km

41

LONG-LEGGED BAT
Myotis volans

IDENTIFYING CHARACTERS

This medium-sized (weighs up to 9 g), brown bat is characterized by having a keeled calcar, short, rounded ears, and a light covering of fur extending onto the underside of the wing. The pelage varies from light to medium reddish brown; the ears and flight membranes are black. Specimens from the grassland areas are lighter-colored than those from the forested areas.

The braincase is globose with a fairly steep forehead. The rostrum is short and broad. The dental formula is I 2/3, C 1/1, P 3/3, M 3/3 x 2 = 38.

DISTRIBUTION

The Long-legged Bat is a western and southern bat and is found from Spirit River in the north, south along the mountains in the west, and eastward along the Milk River.

HABITAT

Rocky outcrops along the Milk River and caves in the mountains.

STATUS

This bat occurs in reasonable numbers in local situations. Throughout its Alberta range it is best described as sporadically common to scarce.

SIMILAR SPECIES

Little Brown Bats lack a keeled calcar, have longer ears, and little or no fur on the underside of the wings.

Northern Long-eared Bats have much longer ears and the calcar lacks a keel.

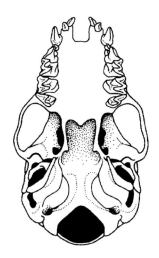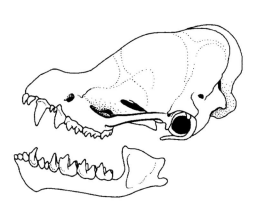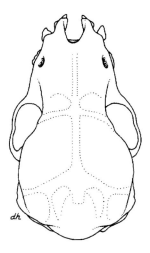

1 cm

Measurements

Sex		Weight (g)	Total Length (mm)	Tail (mm)	Hindfoot (mm)	Ear (mm)
Males (N=20)	Mean	7.4	97.1	41.7	10.0	13.2
	Range	5.8-9.1	90-103	37-44	9-11	8-15
Females (N=7)	Mean	8.3	97.6	43.4	9.7	13.9
	Range	7.2-9.5	95-101	40-46	8-11	12-16

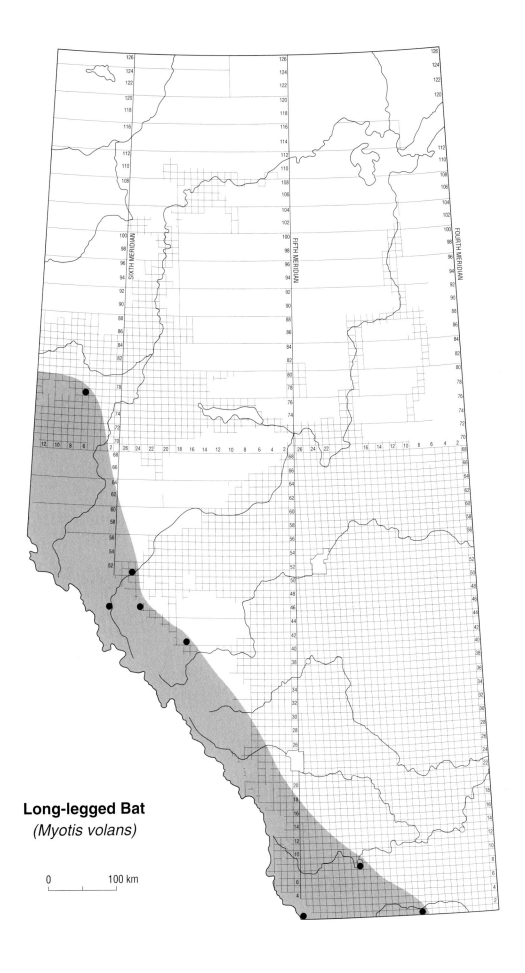

Long-legged Bat
(Myotis volans)

0   100 km

43

WESTERN SMALL-FOOTED BAT
Myotis ciliolabrum

IDENTIFYING CHARACTERS

Small size (weighs up to 7 g) and light brown or tan pelage are sufficient to set this bat apart from other Alberta bats. There is a dark band across the muzzle and eyes. The ears and flight membranes are dark brown. The calcar is keeled.

The skull is delicate with a long, narrow rostrum and a globose, gently sloped braincase. The teeth are relatively small. The dental formula is I 2/3, C 1/1, P 3/3, M 3/3 x 2 = 38.

DISTRIBUTION

This bat is found only on the grasslands. It occurs as far north as Rumsey and south of the Red Deer River. It occurs as far west as Lethbridge.

HABITAT

Rocky outcrops and crevices in badland areas.

STATUS

In some areas of the grasslands (e.g., Dinosaur Provincial Park), this species is common. Generally, throughout its Alberta range it is uncommon.

SIMILAR SPECIES

Long-eared Bats are larger with much longer ears. The calcar is not keeled.

Little Brown Bats are much larger, darker, and lack a keeled calcar.

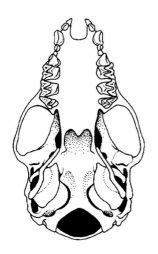 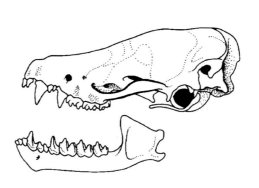 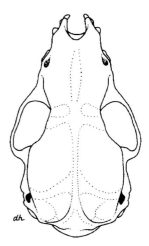

1 cm

Measurements

Sex		Weight (g)	Total Length (mm)	Tail (mm)	Hindfoot (mm)	Ear (mm)
Males (N=13)	Mean	5.3	84.8	38.1	9.1	14.8
	Range	4.1-7.1	80-88	35-39	8-10	14-16
Females (N=12)	Mean	6.0	88.8	41.3	8.8	15.3
	Range	4.7-7.0	85-91	39-42	8-9	15-17

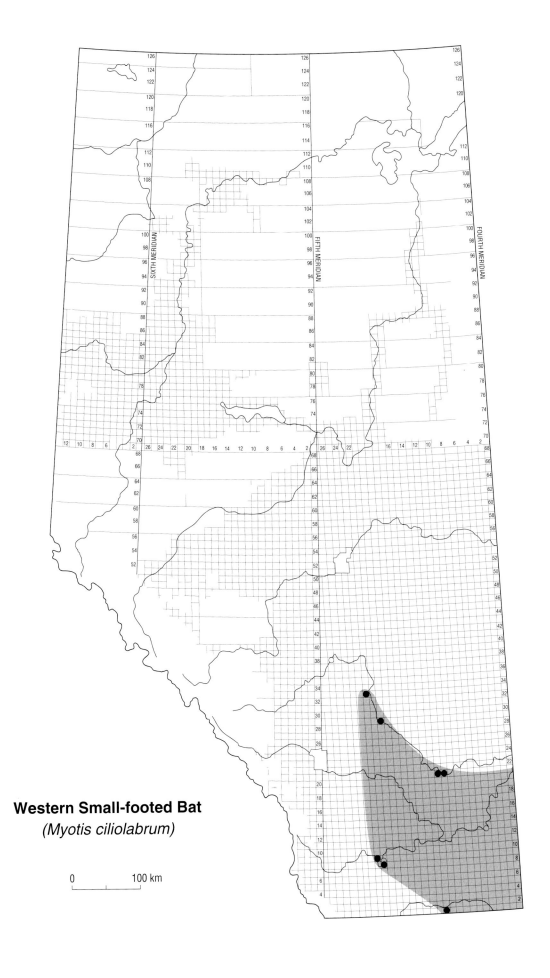

Western Small-footed Bat
(Myotis ciliolabrum)

0   100 km

SILVER-HAIRED BAT
Lasionycteris noctivagans

Chiroptera: Vespertilionidae

(plate 2)

IDENTIFYING CHARACTERS

The Silver-haired Bat is the only Alberta bat that looks black. The pelage is dark brown or black with white- or silver-tipped hairs, hence a silvery or frosted appearance. This bat is moderately large (weighs up to 13 g). The ears are short and roundish. The flight membranes and ears are black. The tail portion of the flight membrane is partially furred.

The skull is robust with a relatively low crown. The rostrum is broad and short. The first upper incisor is bilobed, the lower incisors are trilobed. There are only two upper premolars. The first one (P3) is small, the other (P4) is molar-like in size. The dental formula is I 2/3, C 1/1, P 2/3, M 3/3 x 2 = 36.

DISTRIBUTION

This bat is found throughout the southern three-quarters of the province. It occurs as far north as Kemp River in the west to Fort McMurray in the east. In southern Alberta this species occurs as a spring and fall migrant.

HABITAT

This is essentially a woodland bat. It has been found roosting in woodpecker holes and behind loose bark. It rarely enters buildings.

STATUS

Roosts are rarely found and, as a result, single individuals are most frequently encountered. By the numbers of individuals that have been turned in to wildlife offices for rabies testing, this bat is considered common.

SIMILAR SPECIES

Red Bats and **Hoary Bats** are the only other "frosted-looking" bats in Alberta. Both of these bats are more brightly colored and are larger than the Silver-haired Bat, which is the only dark or black-bodied bat in this region.

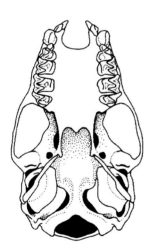 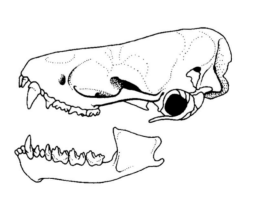 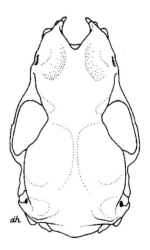

1 cm

Measurements

Sex		Weight (g)	Total Length (mm)	Tail (mm)	Hindfoot (mm)	Ear (mm)
Females (N=22)	Mean	9.9	100.1	39.9	10.0	15.1
	Range	5.7-13.7	92-111	36-46	7-12	10-18

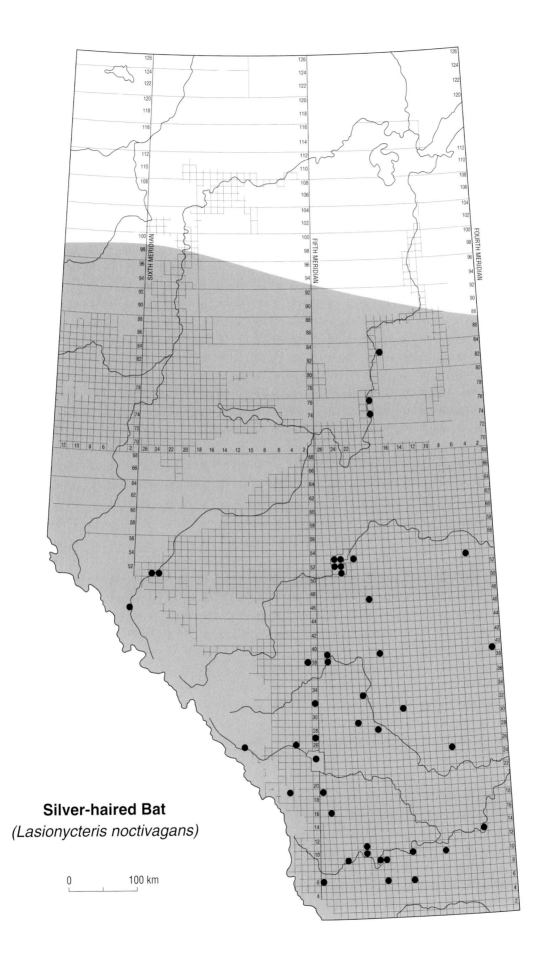

Silver-haired Bat
(Lasionycteris noctivagans)

0   100 km

47

BIG BROWN BAT
Eptesicus fuscus

IDENTIFYING CHARACTERS

This is a large brown bat (weighs up to 29 g) with a glossy pelage. The pelage varies from pale brown to reddish brown. The flight membranes and ears are black. The ears are relatively large, although they do not reach the nose when laid forward. They are ovoid in shape. The calcar is keeled. The muzzle is broad.

The skull is massive with a short, broad rostrum. In profile, the skull is relatively flat. There is only one upper premolar and it is large, approximately half the length of the canine. A sagittal crest may be evident in some individuals. The dental formula is I 2/3, C 1/1, P 1/2, M 3/3 x 2 = 32.

DISTRIBUTION

The Big Brown Bat is found throughout the province, except for the northwestern corner.

HABITAT

Buildings that allow access are probably the principal habitat in which these bats are found. They also occupy caves and crevices.

STATUS

Relatively common. It is, however, vulnerable to habitat loss through the destruction of older buildings.

SIMILAR SPECIES

The Big Brown Bat can be separated from other brown bats by its large size, glossy pelage, keeled calcar, large, ovoid ears, and broad muzzle. No other brown bat is as large.

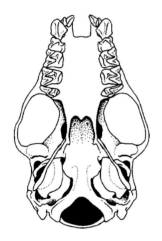 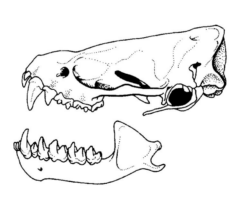 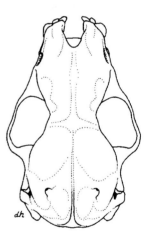

1 cm

Measurements

Sex		Weight (g)	Total Length (mm)	Tail (mm)	Hindfoot (mm)	Ear (mm)
Males (N=15)	Mean	19.9	116.0	46.0	12.5	17.7
	Range	15.8-28.4	109-129	37-51	11-15	13-20
Females (N=20)	Mean	22.2	119.2	48.9	12.7	18.5
	Range	15.6-29.6	112-128	44-59	11-14	16-20

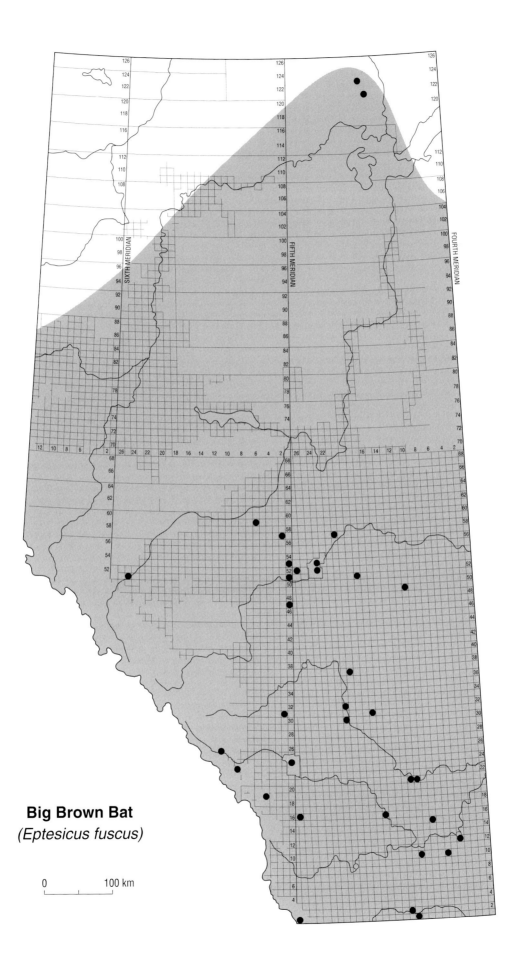

Big Brown Bat
(Eptesicus fuscus)

0   100 km

49

RED BAT
Lasiurus borealis

IDENTIFYING CHARACTERS

This is a colorful, medium sized (weighs up to 12 g) bat. The pelage varies from dull brick-red to yellow-brown. Males are more brightly colored than females. Both have numerous white hairs sprinkled throughout the pelage so that they have a frosted or hoary appearance. Fur extends onto the wing and tail membranes. The ears are short and roundish.

The skull is short and broad with an elevated cranium. The rostrum is very short. The upper incisors and premolars are reduced in number. The dental formula is I 1/3, C 1/1, P 1/2, M 3/3 x 2 = 30.

DISTRIBUTION

Four specimens have been collected in Alberta: two from Enchant, one from Calgary, and one from the Writing-on-Stone Provincial Park area (Saunders 1990).

HABITAT

Open forested areas or farm shelter belts.

STATUS

This bat is an accidental wanderer to the province.

SIMILAR SPECIES

No other bat has such a brightly colored pelage.

Hoary Bats are larger and browner.

Silver-haired Bats appear black.

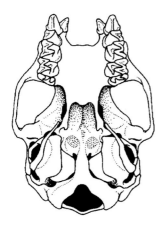 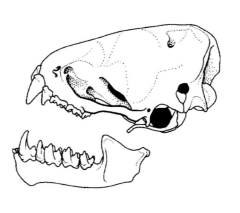 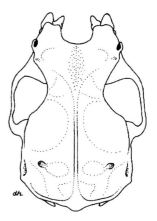

1 cm

Measurements

Sex		Weight (g)	Total Length (mm)	Tail (mm)	Hindfoot (mm)	Ear (mm)
Males	Mean	10.6 *(N=5)*	102.7 *(N=12)*	43.2 *(N=9)*	7.9 *(N=12)*	10.6 *(N=6)*
	Range	8.6-12.5 *(N=5)*	94-114 *(N=12)*	40-46 *(N=9)*	7-9 *(N=12)*	9-13 *(N=6)*
Females	Mean	--	107 *(N=1)*	49 *(N=1)*	7 *(N=1)*	9 *(N=1)*

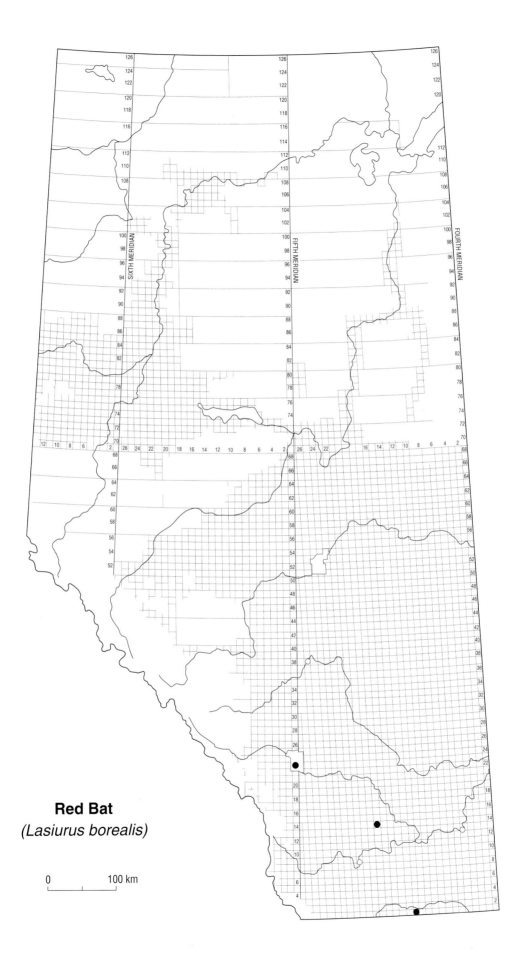

Red Bat

(Lasiurus borealis)

0   100 km

HOARY BAT
Lasiurus cinereus

IDENTIFYING CHARACTERS

The Hoary Bat is the largest (weighs up to 35 g) and most distinctively colored bat in Alberta. The pelage is essentially brown but numerous white or gray hairs give a 'hoary' or frosted appearance. There is a cream-colored ruff around the neck. The tail and underside of the wings are well furred. There are cream-colored patches at the thumbs. The black, round ears are relatively thick and small.

The skull has an extremely short rostrum and high cranium. There are only two upper incisors and the upper P3 is extremely small. The dental formula is I 1/3, C 1/1, P 2/2, M 3/3 x 2 = 32.

DISTRIBUTION

Most of the records of these bats have occurred in the fall. It is believed that this bat can be found throughout all but the northwest portion of the province during the summer.

HABITAT

Trees in both coniferous and deciduous forests provide suitable habitat for this species.

STATUS

Relatively common. As it is a solitary bat, large numbers are never encountered, but every year there are several reports of these bats.

SIMILAR SPECIES

None.

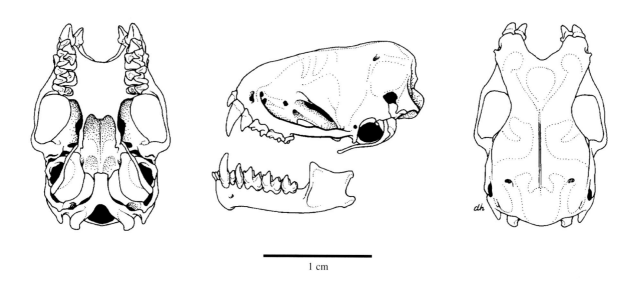

1 cm

Measurements

Sex		Weight (g)	Total Length (mm)	Tail (mm)	Hindfoot (mm)	Ear (mm)
Females (N=7)	Mean	34.0	136.3	57.4	12.5	17.7
	Range	32.6-35.7	132-143	52-62	12-14	15-20

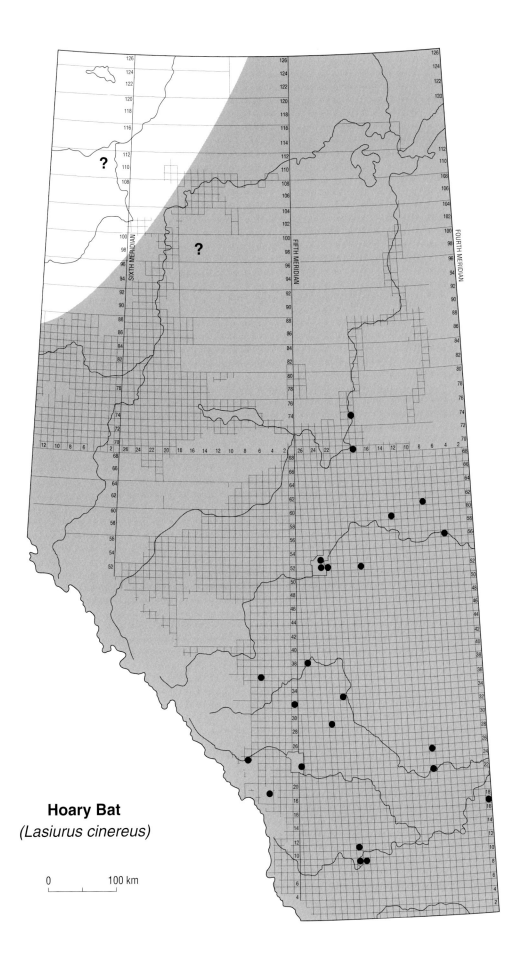

Hoary Bat

(Lasiurus cinereus)

0   100 km

Order: Lagomorpha

This widely distributed Order consists of two families, Ochotonidae and Leporidae, with approximately 60 species recognized (Anderson and Jones 1984). The general characteristics of the Order include a short or even rudimentary tail, fenestrate skull, first upper incisors with a deep groove on the front surface, and small, peg-like second upper incisors directly behind the first. There is a large diastema between the incisors and cheek teeth.

Both families of the Order occur in Alberta. The family Ochotonidae has one species and the family Leporidae is represented by three species.

Key to Pikas, Hares, and Rabbits (Lagomorpha)

1. Weight less than 200 g; ears short and rounded; hindlegs not
   noticeably longer than forelegs; no visible tail . . . . *Ochotona princeps* (p. 56)
   Weight greater than 750 g; ears and hindlegs long; tail short but
   visible 2

2. At any season pelage brownish gray, rusty patch on nape of neck;
   hindfoot less than 105 mm . . . . *Sylvilagus nuttallii* (p. 58)
   Pelage seasonally variable, white in winter, brownish in summer,
   no rust on nape of neck; hindfoot long, greater than 105 mm 3

3. Weight greater than 2.0 kg; ears long, greater than 90 mm . . . . *Lepus townsendii* (p. 62)
   Weight less than 2.0 kg; ears less than 90 mm . . . . *Lepus americanus* (p. 60)

PIKA
Ochotona princeps

Lagomorpha: Ochotonidae

(plate 2)

IDENTIFYING CHARACTERS

The Pika is a small, squat-bodied animal with short legs, small feet with furred soles, no tail, and short, round, well furred ears. The grayish pelage is soft. The back is dark gray with rust-colored shoulders and head. The belly is silvery gray.

The skull is narrow with relatively large auditory bullae. The rostrum is short. The grooved upper incisors have a notch on the front cutting edge. The second incisors, situated directly behind the first incisors, are small and peg-like. The upper P2 is also small. The dental formula is I 2/1, C 0/0, P 3/2, M 2/3 x 2 = 26.

DISTRIBUTION
Found throughout the Rocky Mountains in Alberta.

HABITAT
Rock slides and talus slopes in the alpine zone.

STATUS
Common in the mountains of Alberta.

SIMILAR SPECIES
None.

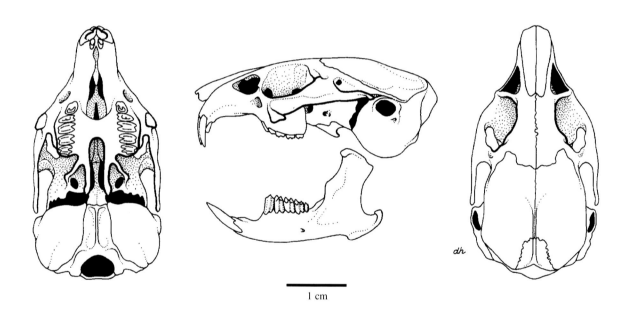

1 cm

Measurements

Sex		Weight (g)	Total Length (mm)	Hindfoot (mm)	Ear (mm)
Males (N=8)	Mean	139.7	178.0	29.4	23.5
	Range	119.3-157.0	161-191	27-31	22-27
Females (N=6)	Mean	136.4	165.4	29.5	24.2
	Range	118.2-159.5	159-175	28-31	22-28

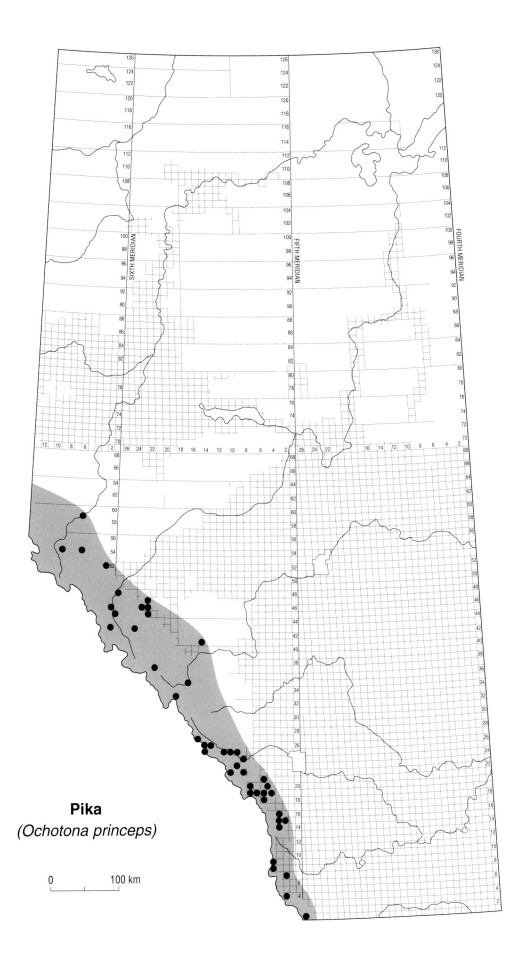

Pika
(Ochotona princeps)

0   100 km

NUTTALL'S COTTONTAIL
Sylvilagus nuttallii

IDENTIFYING CHARACTERS

This small Alberta rabbit has a long, soft, and grayish pelage. The back is darker than the sides. There is a rufous patch on the nape of the neck. The rump is gray and the belly is white. The back portion of the thighs is rufous. The tops of the feet are dirty white. The ears are short (up to 75 mm in length). The tail is short and is gray on top and white underneath. The pelage is the same color in all seasons.

The skull is typically lagomorph with a narrow, high-arched braincase and a medium-length, tapered rostrum. The upper M3 is peg-like. The dental formula is I 2/1, C 0/0, P 3/2, M 3/3 x 2 = 28.

DISTRIBUTION

The grasslands of southeastern Alberta, from the international border north to the Red Deer River, from the Saskatchewan border to the Calgary area. It has not been recorded in the Waterton Lakes National Park area. There are unconfirmed reports that this species occurs as far north as Red Deer but there are no specimens to substantiate this claim.

HABITAT

River bottomlands, rocky valley sides, and areas of scrub bush on the grasslands.

STATUS

Common in southern Alberta.

SIMILAR SPECIES

Immature **Snowshoe Hares** in summer pelage may be mistaken for this cottontail, but the lack of a rufous nape patch and larger hindlegs and longer ears separate the two species. Snowshoe Hares are extremely rare in the habitat of the cottontail.

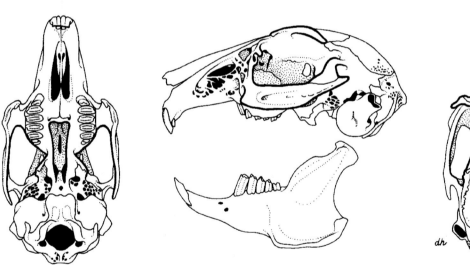
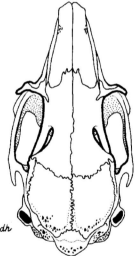

5 cm

Measurements

Sex		Weight (g)	Total Length (mm)	Tail (mm)	Hindfoot (mm)	Ear (mm)
Males (N=8)	Mean	978.3	384.5	40.3	97.1	64.5
	Range	791.4-1110	364-451	33-50	94-102	55-72
Females (N=6)	Mean	1167.7	399.8	45.2	97.2	62.2
	Range	928.8-1428.5	393-428	37-57	91-100	59-70

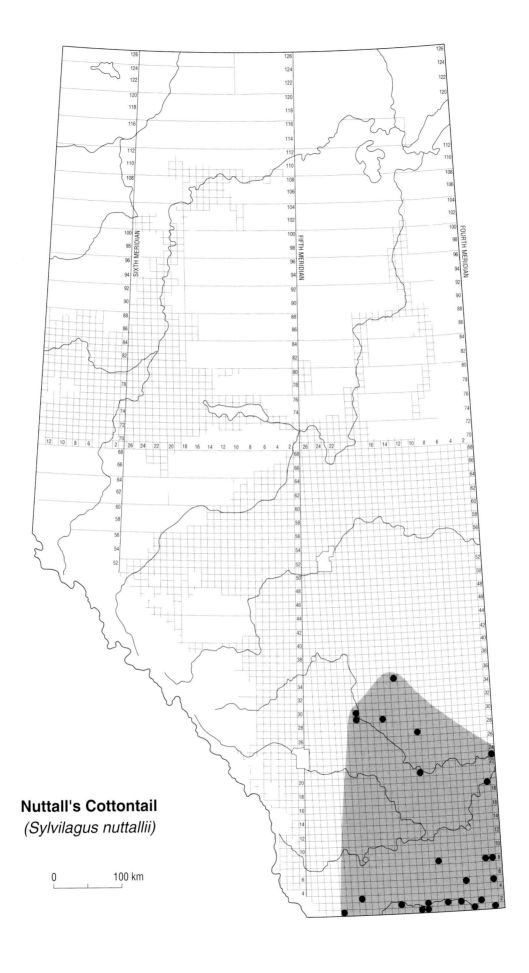

Nuttall's Cottontail
(Sylvilagus nuttallii)

0   100 km

SNOWSHOE HARE
Lepus americanus

IDENTIFYING CHARACTERS

This is a medium-sized hare (up to 1.8 kg) with moderately long ears (up to 90 mm), large hindfeet, and a small tail shaped like a powder-puff. The pelage is long and soft and the color varies seasonally. In summer the pelage is some shade of brown and in winter it is whitish. The summer pelage on the back is brown, on the head ochraceous brown, and white on the belly. The winter pelage is white with dark hairs sprinkled throughout. The tail is white in all seasons. The ears have a black border at the tip.

The skull is long and narrow with elongate supra-orbital processes that are not fused. The front upper incisors have a deep medial groove, the back incisors are small and peg-like. The cheek teeth are grooved on both the inside and outside edges. The dental formula is I 2/1, C 0/0, P 3/2, M 3/3 x 2 = 28.

DISTRIBUTION

The Snowshoe Hare is found throughout the northern forests and parklands. It occurs in the mountains and foothills south to Waterton Lakes National Park. Specimens have been obtained in the Cypress Hills in times past but there are no recent records of their occurrence in that region.

HABITAT

This is an animal of the forest. It prefers forests and shrubby areas and occurs in open areas only rarely and only if a quick route to brushy cover is available.

STATUS

Generally this hare is common. The population is, however, subject to periods of high numbers and low numbers. During the low periods few, if any, individuals may be encountered.

SIMILAR SPECIES

White-tailed Jack Rabbits are much larger, with longer ears and hindlegs, and they occur in open areas.

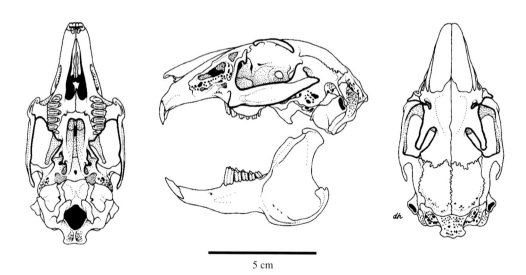

5 cm

Measurements

Sex		Weight (kg)	Total Length (mm)	Tail (mm)	Hindfoot (mm)	Ear (mm)
Males (N=11)	Mean	1.31	426.3	32.7	129.4	74.3
	Range	1.1-1.5	400-445	22-50	113-140	65-90
Females (N=10)	Mean	1.56	457.5	42.4	133.2	77.3
	Range	1.2-1.8	420-518	30-84	115-146	70-90

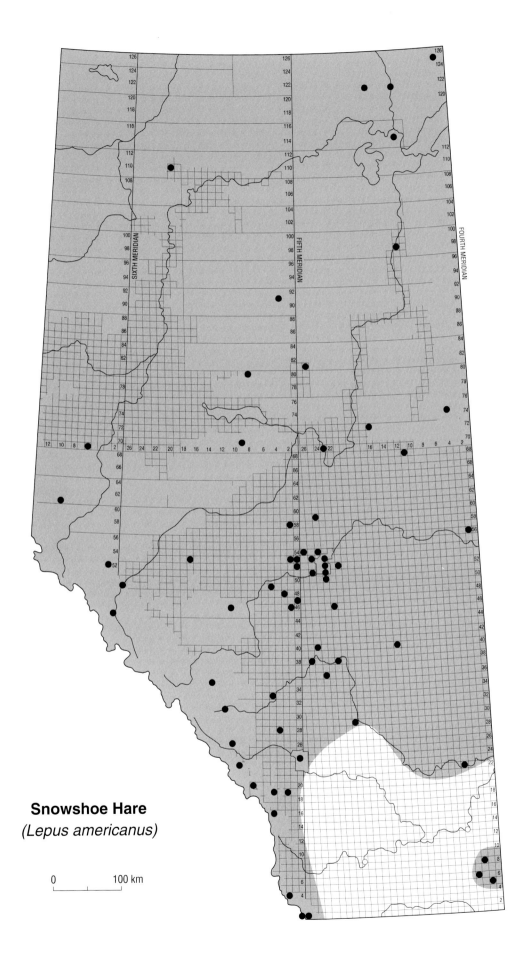

Snowshoe Hare
(Lepus americanus)

0   100 km

WHITE-TAILED JACK RABBIT
Lepus townsendii

IDENTIFYING CHARACTERS

This is the largest member of the hare and rabbit family (weighs up to 4 kg) in Alberta. This open-country animal has long, black-tipped ears and long hind legs. The pelage is long and soft and is seasonally variable. In summer, it is grayish brown along the back and sides, the feet and belly are white, and the ears are brown with black tips. The tail is short and white at any season but, in the summer pelage, a narrow brown stripe is present on the top surface. The winter pelage is entirely white except for the black-tipped ears.

The skull is large and is characterized by a network of lattice-like openings, or fenestrae, in the maxillary and occipital bones. The supraorbital processes are elongate. The first upper incisors have a deep medial groove. The second upper incisors, placed directly behind the first incisors, are small and peg-like. The cheek teeth have lateral grooves. The dental formula is I 2/1, C 0/0, P 3/2, M 3/3 x 2 = 28.

DISTRIBUTION

The White-tailed Jack Rabbit is a prairie resident. Its centre of distribution is in the grassland areas of the province. It occurs as far north as Dapp. The western boundary almost parallels 114° W in the north to just west of Calgary and to Waterton townsite in the south.

HABITAT

Open grasslands in the south and open meadows in the north.

STATUS

The jack rabbit is common on the grasslands. It is less common farther north. It is considered rare in the Waterton area (Nielsen 1973).

SIMILAR SPECIES

Snowshoe Hares are smaller overall with shorter ears and legs.

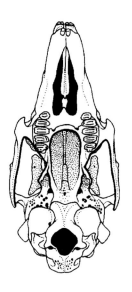 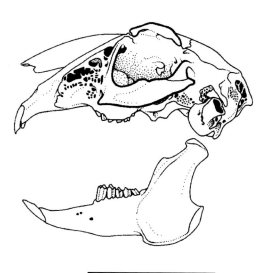 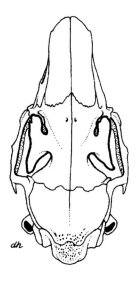

5 cm

Measurements

Sex		Weight (kg)	Total Length (mm)	Tail (mm)	Hindfoot (mm)	Ear (mm)
Males (N=13)	Mean	3.02	593.2	89.7	146.4	101.4
	Range	2.7-3.7	555-635	80-110	138-161	92-111
Females (N=9)	Mean	3.46	600.3	86.8	143.4	99.0
	Range	2.9-4.1	568-640	74-109	133-155	95-110

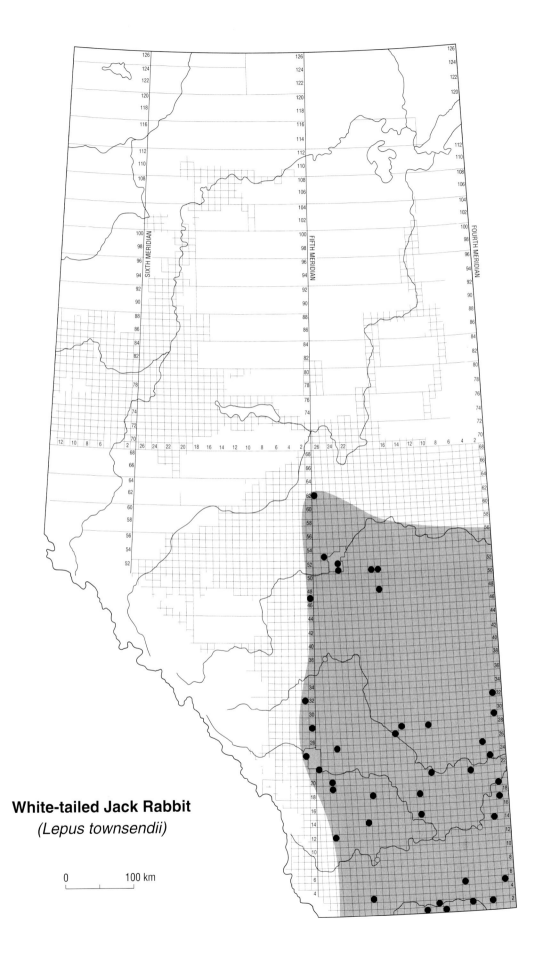

White-tailed Jack Rabbit

(Lepus townsendii)

0   100 km

Order: Rodentia

The Order Rodentia has a worldwide distribution (except Antarctica), with more families (50) and more species (over 1700) than any other Order (Anderson and Jones 1984). Those rodents now found in New Zealand were introduced by Europeans. Rodents are characterized by two upper and two lower, ever-growing incisors that work together in such a way that a chisel-sharp cutting edge is maintained. Canine teeth are absent. This results in a wide diastema between the incisors and the cheek teeth.

The 39 species of rodents in Alberta are placed into eight families. They range in size from the 11 g pocket mouse to the 30 kg beaver. Many have a direct economic impact on human activities.

Key to the Rodents (Rodentia)

1. Pelage with long, coarse guard hairs; back, sides, head, and tail
    covered with hard, sharp quills . . . . *Erethizon dorsatum* (p.146)
    Pelage soft, not covered with quills 2

2. Tail large, scaly, hairless, flattened dorso-ventrally; pelage soft and
    glossy; hindfeet large (longer than 150 mm) and webbed . . . . *Castor canadensis* (p.104)
    Tail not flat; hind feet shorter than 150 mm 3

3. External, fur-lined cheek pouches 4
    Without external cheek pouches 6

4. Weight greater than 100 g; frontlegs same size as hindlegs; pelage
    lead-gray, soft, moult lines frequently present; tail stout, blunt-
    tipped; auditory bullae not inflated . . . . *Thomomys talpoides* (p. 98)
    Weight less than 100 g; tail sparsely haired or tail greater than 50
    percent of total length with bushy tip; auditory bullae inflated . . . 5

Thomomys talpoides **Dipodomys ordii**

auditory bullae

5. Tail greater than 100 mm, with bushy tip; hindlegs larger than frontlegs;
    dorsal pelage bright golden brown above . . . . *Dipodomys ordii* (p. 102)
    Tail less than 70 mm, sparsely haired, thin; hindlegs and frontlegs
    same size; dorsal pelage drab olive brown . . . . *Perognathus fasciatus* (p. 100)

6. Hindlegs considerably larger than frontlegs; tail greater than 50
    percent of body length, tapered, scaly 7
    Frontlegs and hindlegs equal in size; tail length variable relative to
    total length 8

7. Posterior portion of septum dividing the incisive foramina very thin; length of upper tooth row greater than 3.80 mm . . . . *Zapus princeps* (p. 144)

Posterior portion of the septum dividing the incisive foramina broad; length of upper tooth row less than 3.75 mm . . . . *Zapus hudsonius* (p. 142)

Zapus princeps   **Zapus hudsonius**

septum

8. Tail shorter than 50 percent of total length, well furred, may be bushy; prominent postorbital process on skull 9

Tail variable; skull lacks postorbital process 22

9. Weight 3 to 8 kg; body squat; tail short and bushy 10

Weight less than 1 kg, tail variable 12

10. Dorsal pelage grizzled brown, belly rusty brown, feet dark brown or black . . . . *Marmota monax* (p. 76)

Pelage yellowish brown or creamy brown, belly rusty orange or gray 11

11. Belly rusty orange; posterior border of nasal bones extends past premaxillary-frontal suture . . . . *Marmota flaviventris* (p. 78)

Belly grayish; nasal bones wide, posterior border forms straight line with premaxillary-frontal suture . . . . *Marmota caligata* (p. 80)

Marmota flaviventris   **Marmota caligata**

nasal   premaxillary-frontal suture

12. Alternating dark and light stripes along both sides of the back or over the entire back 13

Pelage essentially a solid color without alternating stripes 17

13. Total length less than 240 mm 14

Total length greater than 250 mm 16

14. Underside of tail bright orange or rust, belly white. . . . . *Tamias ruficaudus* (p. 74)

Underside of tail pale or dark orange, belly grayish. 15

15. Central dark stripe on back extends onto head; belly gray . . . . *Tamias minimus* (p. 70)
    Central dark stripe on back does not reach head; belly yellow-
    gray . . . . *Tamias amoenus* (p. 72)

16. Flank stripes wide, do not reach face, each of two white stripes
    bordered by two black stripes . . . . *Spermophilus lateralis* (p. 90)
    Alternating dark and light stripes over entire back extend onto
    head, light stripes narrow; light-colored spots occur in most dark
    stripes . . . . *Spermophilus tridecemlineatus* (p. 86)

17. Fold of loose skin between frontlegs and hindlegs; tail bushy,
    flattened dorso-ventrally . . . . *Glaucomys sabrinus* (p. 96)
    No fold of skin between frontlegs and hindlegs 18

18. Total length greater than 400 mm; pelage gray or black . . . . *Sciurus carolinensis* (p. 92)
    Total length less than 400 mm; pelage variable, not gray or black . . 19

19. Pelage reddish brown, white belly, frequently with a narrow black
    stripe between the belly and back . . . . *Tamiasciurus hudsonicus* (p. 94)
    Pelage sandy brown or bluish gray with a yellowish hue 20

20. Pelage sandy brown; tail slim . . . . *Spermophilus richardsonii* (p. 82)
    Pelage bluish gray; tail bushy 21

21. Rusty tinge on head, nose, and feet, belly rusty orange; tail 74-124
    mm long . . . . *Spermophilus columbianus* (p. 84)
    Head and feet gray; belly pale yellowish; tail long and bushy . . . . . *Spermophilus franklinii* (p. 88)

22. Total length greater than 300 mm 23
    Total length less than 200 mm 26

23. Pelage long and soft; tail well furred and bushy . . . . *Neotoma cinerea* (p. 112)
    Pelage coarse; tail long and without hair 24

24. Pelage glossy; tail flattened laterally; hindfeet larger than frontfeet;
    teeth prismatic . . . . *Ondatra zibethicus* (p. 130)
    Pelage coarse and flat; tail round; hindfeet small, similar in size to
    frontfeet; teeth cuspidate 25

prismatic teeth of **Ondatra zibethicus**   cuspidate teeth of **Rattus norvegicus**

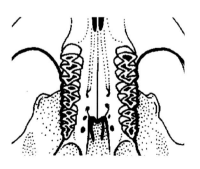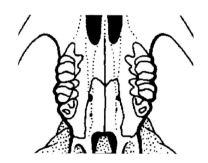

25. Tail robust, less than 50 percent of total length; pelage reddish
    brown . . . . *Rattus norvegicus* (p. 138)
    Tail slender, greater than 50 percent of total length; pelage dark
    gray or brown . . . . *Rattus rattus* (p. 136)

26. Ears conspicuous; pelage short; teeth cuspidate 27
    Tail length variable; ears and feet frequently hidden by long pelage;
    teeth prismatic 30

27. Tail short and stout; body chunky; coronoid process on mandible
    prominent . . . . *Onychomys leucogaster* (p. 110)
    Tail long and tapered; body gracile; coronoid process on mandible
    small 28

Onychomys leucogaster   **Peromyscus maniculatus**

coronoid process

28. Upper incisors deeply grooved . . . . *Reithrodontomys megalotis* (p. 106)
    Upper incisors not grooved 29

29. Pelage strongly bicolored; tail well furred; cheek teeth with two
    longitudinal rows of cusps . . . . *Peromyscus maniculatus* (p. 108)
    Pelage essentially uniform, slate gray or possibly white; tail appears
    scaly and hairless; cheek teeth with three longitudinal rows of
    cusps . . . . *Mus musculus* (p. 140)

30. Pelage buffy to pale gray with reddish dorsal stripe from forehead
    to base of tail, re-entrant angles equal in depth . . . . *Clethrionomys gapperi* (p. 114)
    Pelage without reddish dorsal stripe, re-entrant angles variable 31

31. Tail very short, rarely extending past the hind feet when legs
    outstretched 32
    Tail length variable but extending past the hind feet when legs
    outstretched 34

32. Pelage sandy brown . . . . *Lagurus curtatus* (p. 128)
    Pelage variable but some shade of reddish brown 33

33. Upper incisors deeply grooved; lower cheek teeth with re-entrant
    angles extremely deep on the inside, extremely shallow on the
    outside (see figure 10, p. 69). . . . . *Synaptomys borealis* (p. 134)
    Upper incisors without grooves; pelage reddish brown with tawny
    hindquarters . . . . *Lemmus sibiricus* (p. 132)

34. Total length greater than 185 mm 35
    Total length less than 185 mm 36

35. Rusty patch around nose; incisive foramen long and narrow along
    entire length; upper incisors do not extend past nasal bones . . . . . . *Microtus xanthognathus* (p. 122)
    No rusty patch around nose; incisive foramen flares at front; front
    of upper incisors extends past nasal bones . . . . *Microtus richardsoni* (p. 126)

Microtus xanthognathus   **Microtus richardsoni**

incisive foramen

36. Upper M2 with additional loop (5 loops) (see Fig. 10, p. 69) . . . . . . *Microtus pennsylvanicus* (p. 118)
    Upper M2 without additional loop (4 loops) (see Fig. 10, p. 69) 37

37. Tail long, 52-65 mm . . . . *Microtus longicaudus* (p.120)
    Tail shorter 25-40 mm 38

38. Pelage grizzled; re-entrant angles of equal depth . . . . *Microtus ochrogaster* (p. 124)
    Pelage grayish brown, feet light-colored; inner re-entrant angles
    deeper than outer angles . . . . *Phenacomys intermedius* (p. 116)

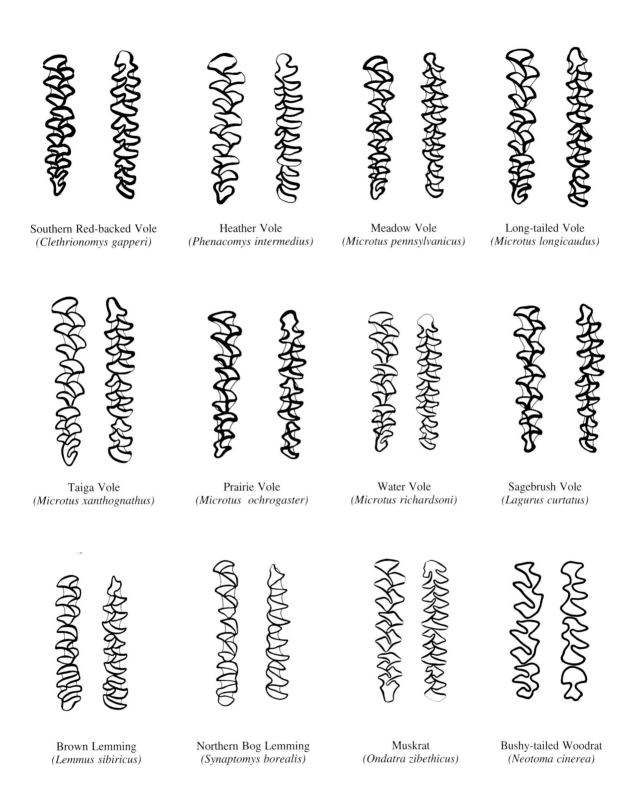

Southern Red-backed Vole
(Clethrionomys gapperi)

Heather Vole
(Phenacomys intermedius)

Meadow Vole
(Microtus pennsylvanicus)

Long-tailed Vole
(Microtus longicaudus)

Taiga Vole
(Microtus xanthognathus)

Prairie Vole
(Microtus ochrogaster)

Water Vole
(Microtus richardsoni)

Sagebrush Vole
(Lagurus curtatus)

Brown Lemming
(Lemmus sibiricus)

Northern Bog Lemming
(Synaptomys borealis)

Muskrat
(Ondatra zibethicus)

Bushy-tailed Woodrat
(Neotoma cinerea)

Figure 10. Molar tooth patterns of Alberta microtine rodents. Each diagram depicts the upper right (left diagram) and lower left (right diagram) teeth with the anterior toward the top. The non-microtine Bushy-tailed Woodrat is included for comparison. Drawings are not to scale.

LEAST CHIPMUNK
Tamias minimus

IDENTIFYING CHARACTERS

The pelage pattern of the Least Chipmunk is typical of all the chipmunks found in Alberta; alternating dark and light stripes on a grayish body. In the Least Chipmunk the central dark stripe extends onto the head. The general body color is smoky gray suffused with pale rufous along the sides. The nape of the neck and the belly are gray. The tail is long and slender and the underside is pale orange.

The skull is small and delicate with very small postorbital processes. The rostrum is short. The cheek teeth are small and the upper P3 is extremely small and peg-like. The dental formula is I 1/1, C 0/0, P 2/1, M 3/3 x 2 = 22.

DISTRIBUTION

The Least Chipmunk is the most widely distributed chipmunk in the province. It occurs throughout the mountains and foothills, the northern forested areas, and south to the Red Deer River north of Dorothy. There is also a population in the Cypress Hills.

HABITAT

In the mountains, the Least Chipmunk is found in alpine meadows and in shrubby areas along the forest edge. In the remainder of the province, this chipmunk can be found inhabiting a variety of situations from brush-lined forests to rocky outcrops, to deadfall and brush piles.

STATUS

Common.

SIMILAR SPECIES

Yellow-pine Chipmunks are slightly larger and darker. Yellow-pine Chipmunks have a yellow-gray belly and Least Chipmunks have a gray belly. The underside of the tail is more orange or rust-colored in the Yellow-pine Chipmunk.

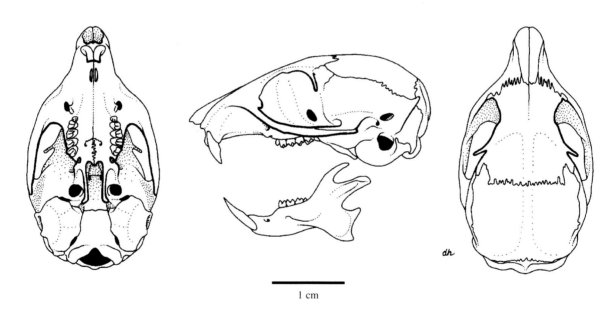

1 cm

Measurements

Sex		Weight (g)	Total Length (mm)	Tail (mm)	Hindfoot (mm)	Ear (mm)
Males (N=20)	Mean	43.6	210.5	92.9	31.9	15.8
	Range	31.0-50.7	200-225	79-103	30-38	13-19
Females (N=20)	Mean	51.5	214.4	95.1	32.1	16.1
	Range	43.2-63.2	202-228	83-105	30-35	12-19

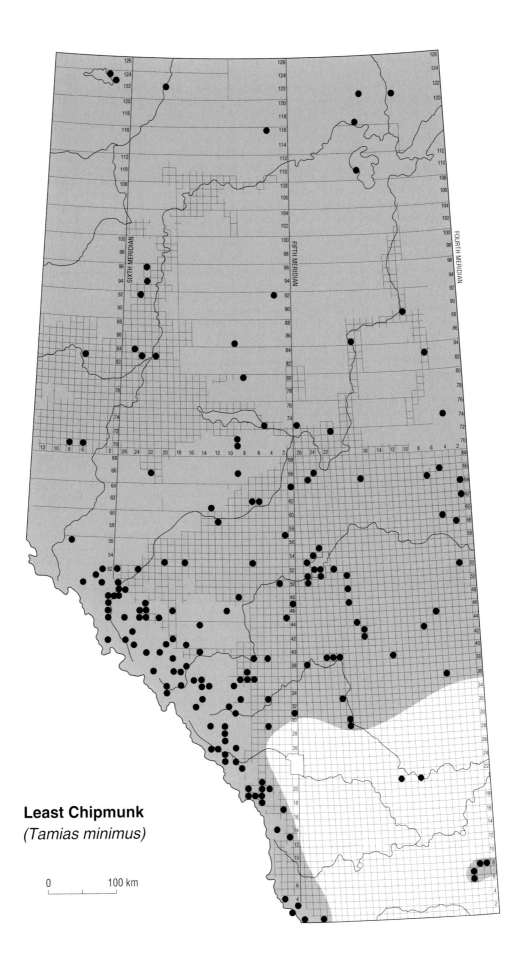

Least Chipmunk
(Tamias minimus)

0   100 km

YELLOW-PINE CHIPMUNK
Tamias amoenus

Rodentia: Sciuridae

IDENTIFYING CHARACTERS

The pelage of the Yellow-pine Chipmunk is grayish. The sides are rufous and this color extends onto the face. The belly is yellowish gray. The underside of the long, narrow, well furred tail is dark orange. The hindfeet are pale rufous. The central dark stripe does not extend onto the head but the other stripes reach the face.

The skull is ovate and the cranium is domed. The postorbital processes are small and poorly developed. The dental formula is I 1/1, C 0/0, P 2/1, M 3/3 x 2 = 22.

DISTRIBUTION

The Yellow-pine Chipmunk is distributed throughout the mountains from Waterton Lakes National Park north to the headwaters of the Smoky River. It is not evenly distributed in this region. The species appears to be absent in the northern part of Banff National Park and the southern part of Jasper National Park (Holroyd and Van Tighem 1983).

HABITAT

Found in forest openings and clearings from the subalpine zone to the valley floor.

STATUS

In the southern parts of its range this species is relatively common. It becomes less so in the northern portion, so much so that it is considered scarce in the north.

SIMILAR SPECIES

Least Chipmunks are smaller, the underside of the tail is paler, and the belly is gray.

Red-tailed Chipmunks are larger, the underside of the tail is redder, and the belly is more creamy-colored. The overall color is darker.

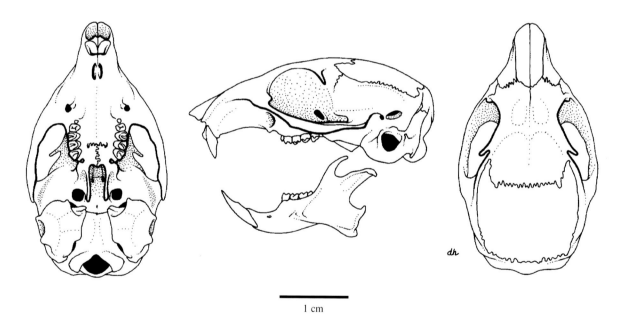

1 cm

Measurements

Sex		Weight (g)	Total Length (mm)	Tail (mm)	Hindfoot (mm)	Ear (mm)
Males (N=15)	Mean	51.4	209.4	89.7	31.4	18.1
	Range	44.0-56.2	195-219	71-103	28-33	15-21
Females (N=16)	Mean	60.8	211.7	90.5	32.2	16.0
	Range	48.7-89.0	187-230	66-105	26-34	14-20

72

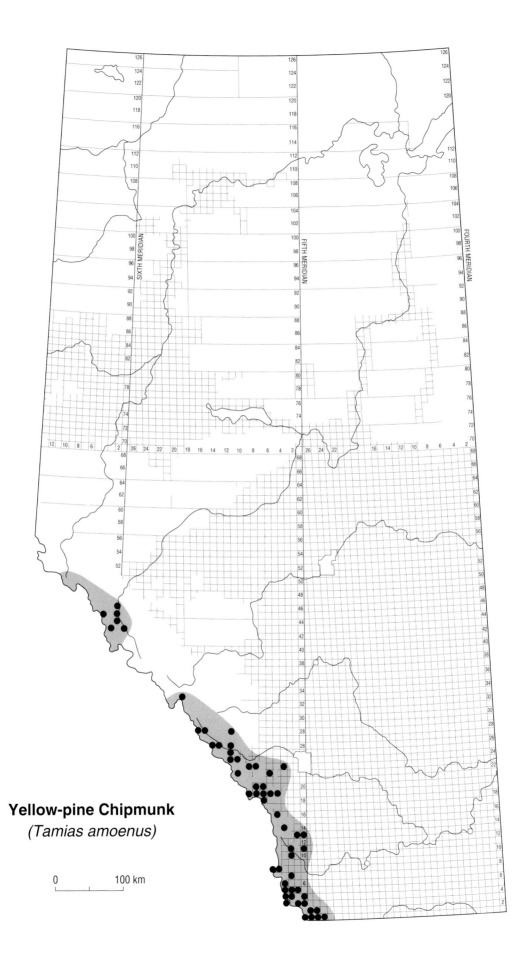

Yellow-pine Chipmunk

(Tamias amoenus)

0   100 km

RED-TAILED CHIPMUNK
Tamias ruficaudus

Rodentia: Sciuridae

IDENTIFYING CHARACTERS

The pelage of the Red-tailed Chipmunk is generally grayish on the back and rufous on the shoulders and sides, fading out on the hips. The rump is dark gray and the belly is gray. The underside of the tail is bright orange or rust .

The skull is ovate with a relatively short rostrum. The postorbital processes are long and slender. The dental formula is I 1/1, C 0/0, P 2/1, M 3/3 x 2 = 22.

DISTRIBUTION

This species occurs in a very small area of the province. It has been collected in Waterton Lakes National Park and on the northern periphery of the park on provincial lands.

HABITAT

The Red-tailed Chipmunk occupies mixed-wood and coniferous forests at elevations between 1500 and 2100 metres.

STATUS

Common within the limited Alberta range.

SIMILAR SPECIES

Least Chipmunks occur at higher elevations. The underside of the tail is pale orange.

Yellow-pine Chipmunks occur at lower elevations. The underside of the tail is dark orange.

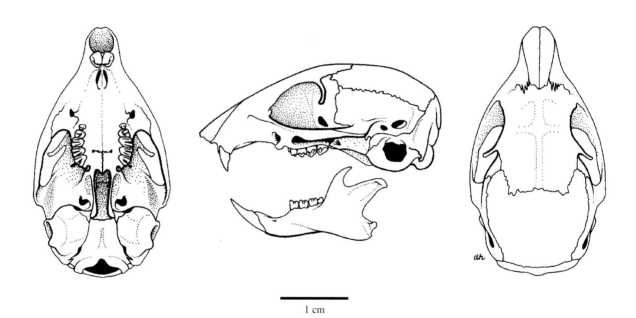

1 cm

Measurements

Sex		Weight (g)	Total Length (mm)	Tail (mm)	Hindfoot (mm)	Ear (mm)
Males	Mean	58.3 (N=2)	218.7 (N=14)	95.4 (N=13)	34.4 (N=14)	14.0 (N=1)
	Range	53.5-63.0 (N=2)	197-234 (N=14)	92-99 (N=13)	33-36 (N=14)	
Females	Mean	65.2 (N=2)	217.2 (N=5)	90.2 (N=5)	33.4 (N=5)	15.0 (N=1)
	Range	57.3-73.1 (N=2)	204-235 (N=5)	85-93 (N=5)	32-35 (N=5)	

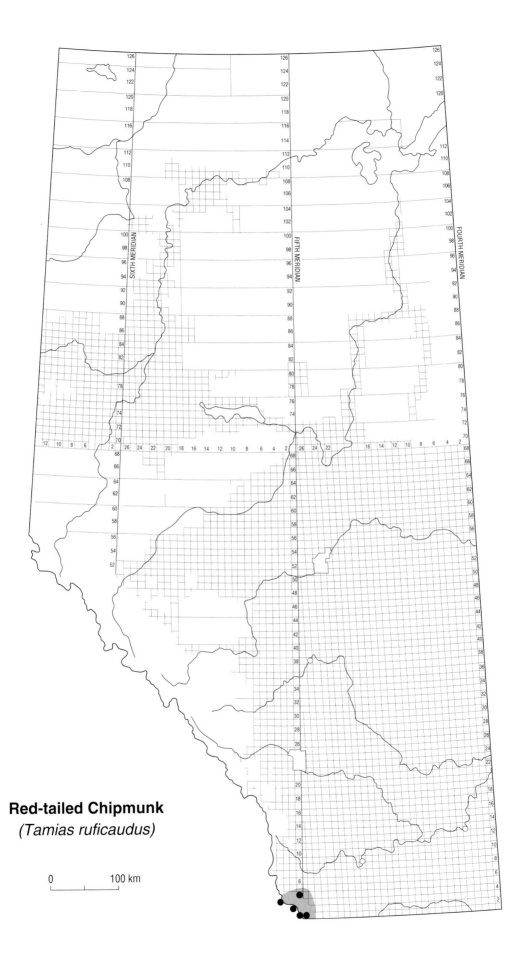

Red-tailed Chipmunk

(Tamias ruficaudus)

0   100 km

WOODCHUCK
Marmota monax

IDENTIFYING CHARACTERS

The Woodchuck is a chunky-bodied, short-legged animal. The upper parts are grizzled brown and the belly, chin, and throat are rusty brown. The shoulder area is golden brown and the rump is reddish brown. The tail is dark brown on both the top and underside. The feet are black as is the top of the head.

The skull has a flat profile. The rostrum is short and the postorbital processes project at right angles to the skull. The upper incisors lack pigmentation. The dental formula is I 1/1, C 0/0, P 2/1, M 3/3 x 2 = 22.

DISTRIBUTION

The Woodchuck is found throughout northern Alberta south to approximately Innisfail. The western edge of the range extends past Caroline north to Grande Cache.

HABITAT

River valleys, pastures, and rock piles.

STATUS

The Woodchuck is far from common even though it is widely distributed. Locally it may be fairly numerous but generally it is uncommon.

SIMILAR SPECIES

Yellow-bellied Marmots are much larger and lighter-colored, the tail is reddish brown and the feet are rusty brown. These marmots are found in southern Alberta, well outside the range of the Woodchuck.

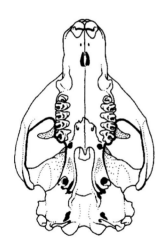 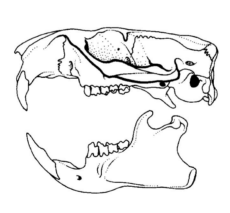 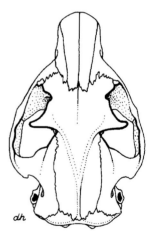

5 cm

Measurements

Sex		Weight (kg)	Total Length (mm)	Tail (mm)	Hindfoot (mm)	Ear (mm)
Males (N=6)	Mean	1.65	527.5	141.5	74.3	29.8
	Range	1.1-2.1	505-575	123-160	71-78	20-36
Females (N=8)	Mean	1.84	497.0	123.0	72.0	28.8
	Range	1.2-2.3	465-530	110-150	68-78	25-35

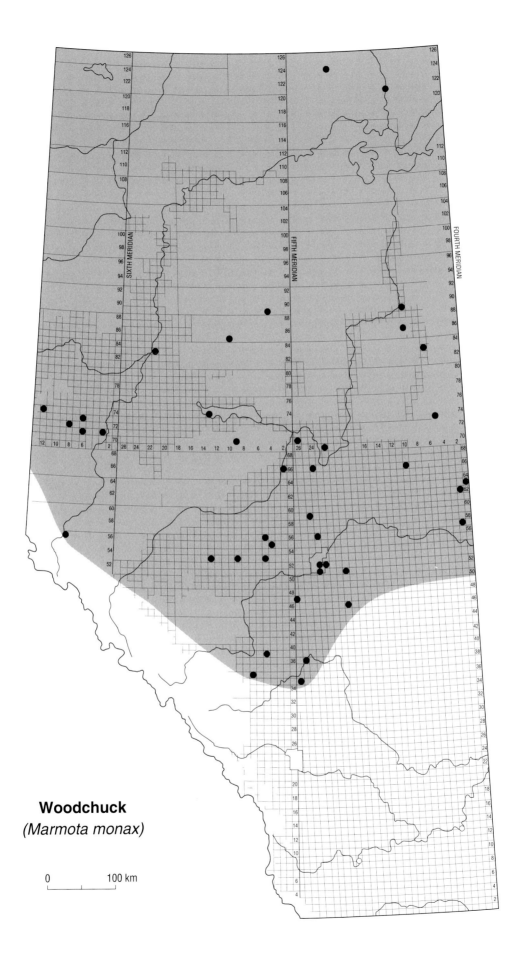

Woodchuck
(Marmota monax)

0   100 km

YELLOW-BELLIED MARMOT
Marmota flaviventris

IDENTIFYING CHARACTERS
The general color of this marmot is a frosted golden brown. The guard hairs are black with white tips and the underfur is two-toned: the bottom half is black, the top half is white. The forequarters are whitish or light-colored, the hindquarters are a dull cream or golden brown. The head is black. The belly is yellowish brown. The feet and legs are rusty orange. The bushy tail is brownish on top and black underneath.

The skull is robust. The nasal bones are narrow at the premaxillary suture line and extend past this line. The postorbital processes project slightly to the rear. The dental formula is I 1/1, C 0/0, P 2/1, M 3/3 x 2 = 22.

DISTRIBUTION
This marmot is still expanding its range in the province. At the present time it is found from Waterton Lakes National Park eastward along the Milk River and north to the southern end of the Porcupine Hills and Lake Newell. There are recent reports from the Calgary area (Depper 1989).

HABITAT
Found on rocky outcrops along the Milk River and in the Porcupine Hills.

STATUS
In some areas it occurs in sufficient numbers to be an agricultural pest. Overall, it is uncommon but with an increasing population.

SIMILAR SPECIES
Hoary Marmots are larger, and occur only in the mountains. In overall appearance, they are lighter-colored.

Woodchucks are smaller and occur much farther north. They are reddish brown.

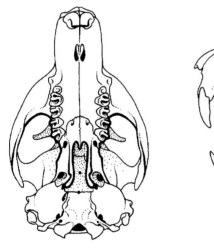 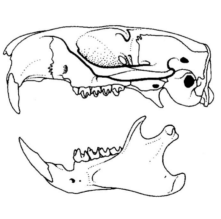 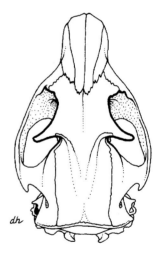

5 cm

Measurements

Sex		Weight (kg)	Total Length (mm)	Tail (mm)	Hindfoot (mm)	Ear (mm)
Males (N=4)	Mean	3.5 *(N=3)*	631.3	168.8	84.0	33.8
	Range	3.1-3.9 *(N=3)*	610-670	150-183	80-89	32-37
Females (N=3)	Mean	2.5 *(N=1)*	592.3	171.0	75.7	32.3
	Range		580-610	165-178	74-78	29-35

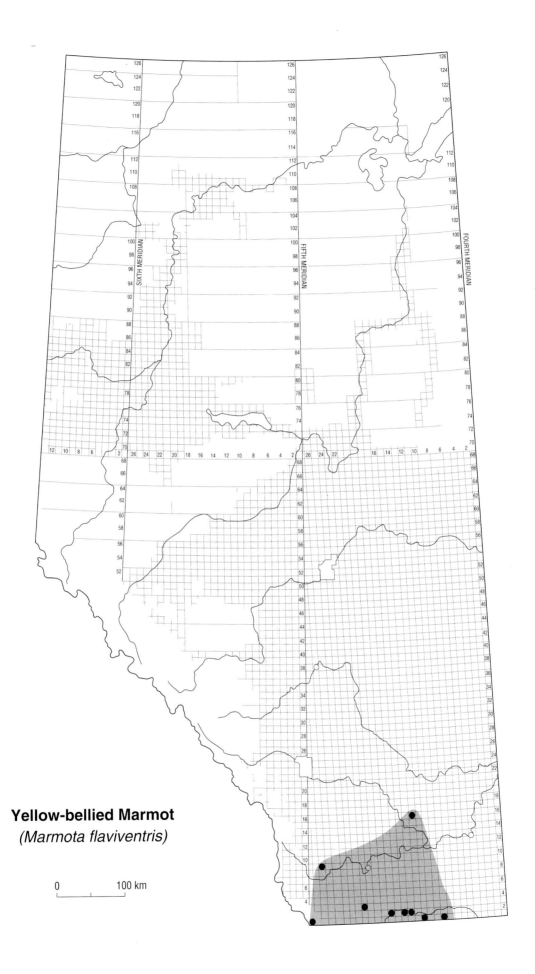

Yellow-bellied Marmot
(Marmota flaviventris)

0   100 km

79

HOARY MARMOT
Marmota caligata

Rodentia: Sciuridae

(plate 4)

IDENTIFYING CHARACTERS

This is the largest marmot in Alberta. The body is squat with short legs, a large head, short ears, and a relatively short, bushy tail. The pelage is two-toned. From the shoulders to mid-back the hairs are white with black tips. On the rump the hairs are creamy with black tips. The belly is grayish. The top of the tail is brownish, the underside is reddish brown. The feet and top of the head are black.

The skull is large and robust. The nasal bones are wide and at the posterior end they form a straight line at the premaxillary suture. The post-orbital processes project at right angles to the skull. The upper incisors have a pale pigmentation. The dental formula is I 1/1, C 0/0, P 2/1, M 3/3 x 2 = 22.

DISTRIBUTION

The Hoary Marmot is found in the mountains from Waterton Lakes National Park northward to the Torrens River area.

HABITAT

Alpine meadows, rock slides, and talus slopes.

STATUS

The Hoary Marmot is widely distributed in the mountains. It may be locally common but generally it is not abundant.

SIMILAR SPECIES

This is the only marmot that is found in the Alberta mountains north of Waterton.

Yellow-bellied Marmots are generally smaller and darker in appearance. The chin and throat are creamy yellow, the feet and legs rusty orange, and the belly is yellowish brown.

Woodchucks are much smaller and browner. They do not occur in the mountains.

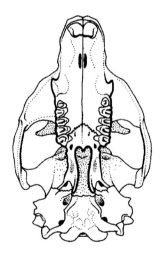 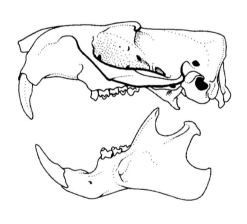 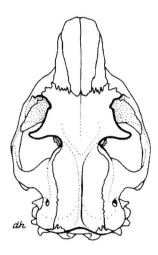

5 cm

Measurements

Sex		Weight (kg)	Total Length (mm)	Tail (mm)	Hindfoot (mm)
Males (N=8)	Mean	4.7 *(N=1)*	698.8	201.4	97.4
	Range		665-736	185-229	88-105
Females (N=3)	Mean	--	735.3	217.0	95.0
	Range	--	720-750	211-228	92-98

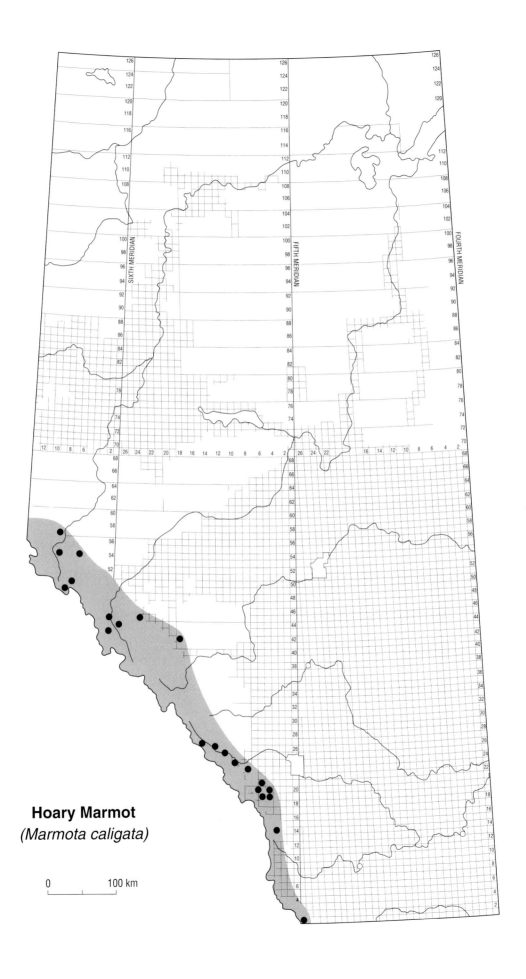

Hoary Marmot
(Marmota caligata)

0   100 km

RICHARDSON'S GROUND SQUIRREL
Spermophilus richardsonii

Rodentia: Sciuridae
(plate 4)

IDENTIFYING CHARACTERS

The Richardson's Ground Squirrel is a medium-sized rodent (weighs up to 610 g). The pelage is sandy brown, washed with buff, and speckled with darker hairs to give a mottled appearance to the back. The belly is lighter than the back. The ears are small and roundish, the eyes are large and placed high on the head, and the tail is well furred.

The skull is ovoid with prominent postorbital processes projecting perpendicularly from the skull. The temporal ridges are prominent and form a U-shape. The rostrum is relatively short and broad. The dental formula is I 1/1, C 0/0, P 2/1, M 3/3 x 2 = 22.

DISTRIBUTION

The Richardson's Ground Squirrel is found throughout the grasslands and parklands. It occurs as far north as the Athabasca area. The western boundary extends from Thunder Lake in the north, to the Ya Ha Tinda Ranch area northwest of Calgary, and the grasslands area of Waterton Lakes National Park.

HABITAT

This ground squirrel is found on the open grasslands and it can be especially numerous on overgrazed pasture lands. They also occur along roadside ditches, grain fields, and hay meadows.

STATUS

The Richardson's Ground Squirrel is common throughout its range. Because of control measures, there are many areas of the province where the number of ground squirrels is low.

SIMILAR SPECIES

Columbian Ground Squirrels are found only in the mountains and foothills. They can be distinguished by the rusty tinge to the head and feet and their bushier tail and larger size.

Franklin's Ground Squirrels are generally solitary. They are bluish gray in color with a longer, bushier tail. They are found in bushier areas.

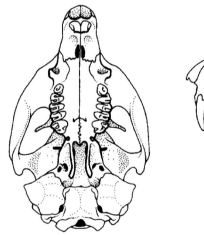 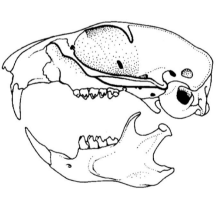 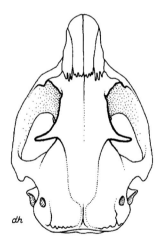

1 cm

Measurements

Sex		Weight (g)	Total Length (mm)	Tail (mm)	Hindfoot (mm)	Ear (mm)
Males (N=20)	Mean	359.5	309.3	78.7	46.9	12.0
	Range	271.7-609.0	279-332	66-92	41-50	10-15
Females (N=20)	Mean	332.5	292.8	71.9	44.2	13.5
	Range	273.2-375.0	284-306	62-78	42-46	12-14

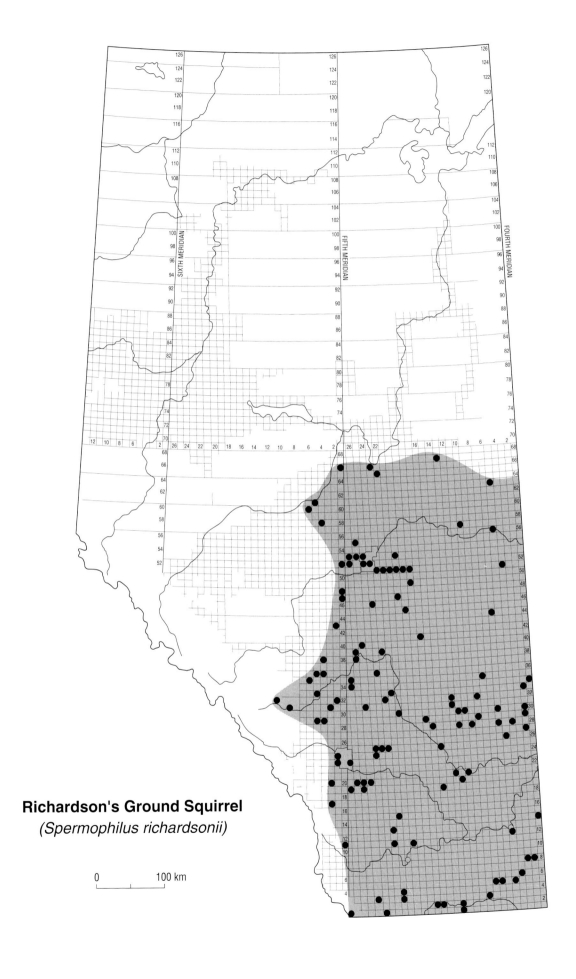

Richardson's Ground Squirrel

(Spermophilus richardsonii)

0   100 km

COLUMBIAN GROUND SQUIRREL
Spermophilus columbianus

Rodentia: Sciuridae

(plate 5)

IDENTIFYING CHARACTERS

The Columbian Ground Squirrel is large (weighs up to 821 g), with a stout body, short legs, and a medium-length, bushy tail. This ground squirrel is generally bluish gray with a yellowish or orange wash. The snout and feet are rusty orange, the cheeks bluish gray, and the back mottled yellowish gray. The tail is well furred and bluish gray.

The skull is robust with a relatively long rostrum. The temporal ridges converge to form a V-shape rather than a U-shape, as is found in other Alberta ground squirrels of comparable size. The dental formula is I 1/1, C 0/0, P 2/1, M 3/3 x 2 = 22.

DISTRIBUTION

The Columbian Ground Squirrel is found throughout the mountains and foothills from Waterton Lakes National Park in the south to the Wembley area in the north, and east as far as Longview and the Porcupine Hills.

HABITAT

Alpine meadows, valley bottomlands, pastures, and rocky slopes.

STATUS

This species is common throughout its range. Because of its diurnal habits, it is one of the most conspicuous mammals in mountain meadows.

SIMILAR SPECIES

Golden-mantled Ground Squirrels are the only other ground squirrels in the mountains. They are readily distinguished from the Columbian Ground Squirrel by the two broad white stripes on the back.

Richardson's Ground Squirrels and Columbian Ground Squirrels share their ranges in only a few places in Alberta. Richardson's is smaller and sandy brown.

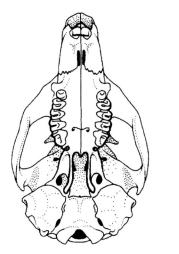 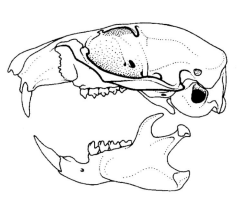 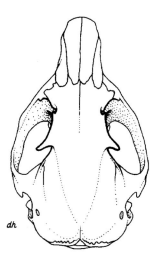

1 cm

Measurements

Sex		Weight (g)	Total Length (mm)	Tail (mm)	Hindfoot (mm)	Ear (mm)
Males (N=20)	Mean	544.8	362.4	101.3	51.7	19.1
	Range	394.3-820.6	330-388	75-116	48-55	16-27
Females (N=20)	Mean	476.5	357.8	106.8	50.4	17.7
	Range	275-629	333-385	90-124	46-53	15-22

84

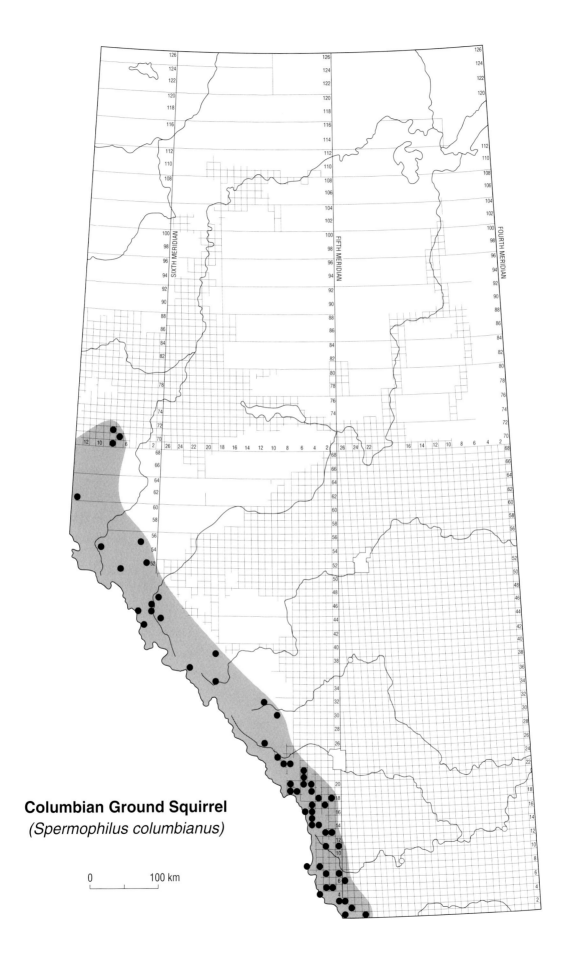

Columbian Ground Squirrel
(Spermophilus columbianus)

0   100 km

THIRTEEN-LINED GROUND SQUIRREL
Spermophilus tridecemlineatus

Rodentia: Sciuridae
(plate 5)

IDENTIFYING CHARACTERS

The Thirteen-lined Ground Squirrel is a slim-bodied, short-legged, striped ground squirrel. The alternating dark and light stripes of the pelage are distinctive among Alberta ground squirrels. The light-colored stripes and spots are buffy brown. There is a pale-colored, broken eye ring. The tail is well furred but narrow.

The skull appears delicate with very small postorbital processes. The rostrum is relatively long and tapered. The dental formula is I 1/1, C 0/0, P 2/1, M 3/3 x 2 = 22.

DISTRIBUTION

This ground squirrel is found throughout the aspen parkland belt as far north as the Cold Lake area and as far west as the Rocky Mountain House area. It is also found in extreme southern Alberta from Waterton east to the Cypress Hills and north along the Saskatchewan border to Empress. There is a region in south-central Alberta east of Calgary and south of the Red Deer River where this species has not been collected.

HABITAT

Along the edges of shrubby areas where the non-woody vegetation is dense, such as hay fields, and open pastures.

STATUS

Although loose colonies may occur in some areas, this ground squirrel is essentially solitary and as a result it seems to be not common. Generally, it can be classified as sporadic to common in some areas, absent or scarce in other areas.

SIMILAR SPECIES

Richardson's Ground Squirrels are larger and lack stripes.

Chipmunks are much smaller and darker in color.

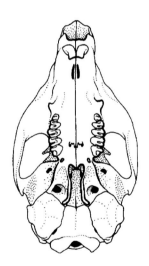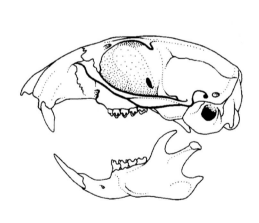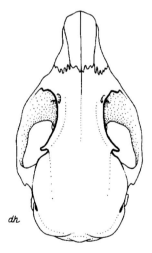

1 cm

Measurements

Sex		Weight (g)	Total Length (mm)	Tail (mm)	Hindfoot (mm)
Males	Mean	162.2 *(N=8)*	276.1 *(N=16)*	98.7 *(N=15)*	37.9 *(N=16)*
	Range	139.7-181.4 *(N=8)*	244-305 *(N=16)*	70-110 *(N=15)*	34-40 *(N=16)*
Females	Mean	179.4 *(N=6)*	276.9 *(N=16)*	92.1 *(N=14)*	38.4 *(N=15)*
	Range	142.0-201.6 *(N=6)*	258-295 *(N=16)*	80-110 *(N=14)*	35-46 *(N=15)*

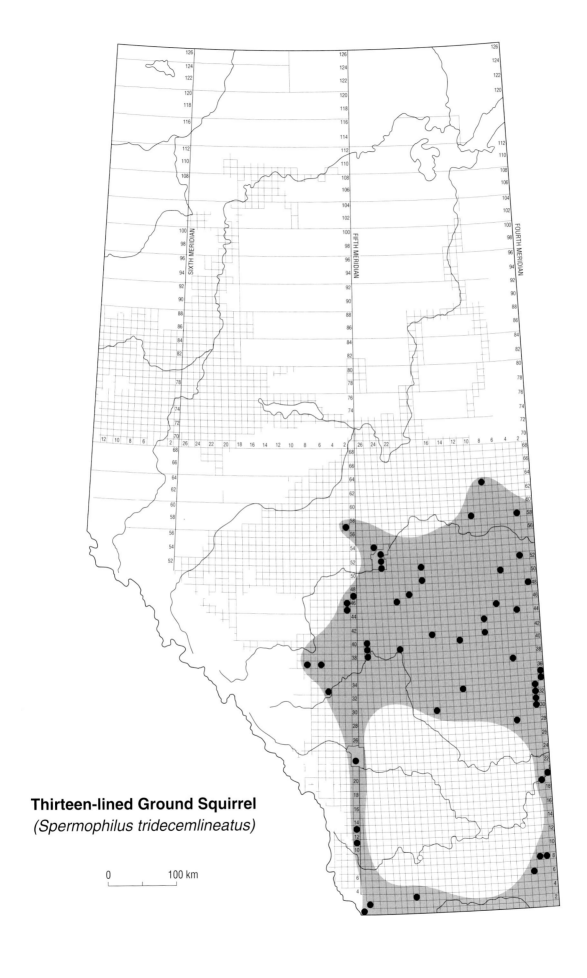

Thirteen-lined Ground Squirrel
(Spermophilus tridecemlineatus)

0   100 km

FRANKLIN'S GROUND SQUIRREL
Spermophilus franklinii

Rodentia: Sciuridae

(plate 5)

IDENTIFYING CHARACTERS

The Franklin's Ground Squirrel is a long-bodied, bushy-tailed, ground squirrel. The head is bluish gray; the body is tawny brown interspersed with black or dark-colored hairs that give a mottled or spotted look; the tail is long, bushy, and grayish; the belly is also grayish.

The skull is generally pear-shaped. The temporal ridges form a wide 'U' shape at the posterior end of the skull. The rostrum is long and appears narrow. The postorbital processes are slender and are directed rearward. The upper P3 is relatively small. The dental formula is I 1/1, C 0/0, P 2/1, M 3/3 x 2 = 22.

DISTRIBUTION

Found in much of the aspen parkland region. However, as agricultural practices have altered the landscape, previously inaccessible areas are now occupied. The range extends from Athabasca in the north to Edson in the west. There is a report of a colony of these ground squirrels from the Calgary area (R. Fisher, Alberta Animal Record Card).

HABITAT

The aspen parkland belt, especially along the forest edge, where there may be dense grasses.

STATUS

It is considered uncommon here but the status is difficult to determine. It may be numerous in some areas of the province but, because only small, loosely knit colonies are formed, it is not a conspicuous member of the mammal community and may go unreported.

SIMILAR SPECIES

Richardson's Ground Squirrels exist in colonies on the open grasslands. Their pelage is yellowish; the tail is shorter and not as bushy.

Columbian Ground Squirrels have a more rusty tone to the pelage. The ranges of the two species do not overlap.

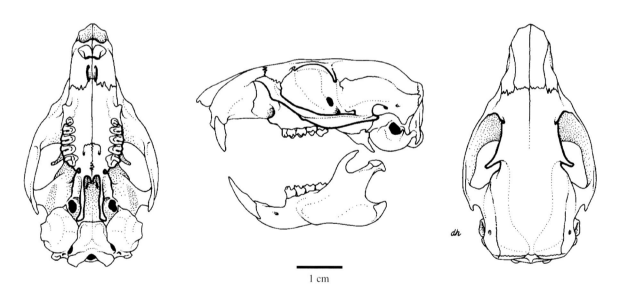

1 cm

Measurements

Sex		Weight (g)	Total Length (mm)	Tail (mm)	Hindfoot (mm)	Ear (mm)
Males (N=6)	Mean	440.4 *(N=1)*	384.8	135.5	55.0	16 *(N=1)*
	Range		372-412	113-153	53-58	
Females (N=12)	Mean	420.2 *(N=8)*	377.2	134.1	53.5	16.3 *(N=8)*
	Range	358.0-484.2 *(N=8)*	359-400	120-149	50-57	15-19 *(N=8)*

88

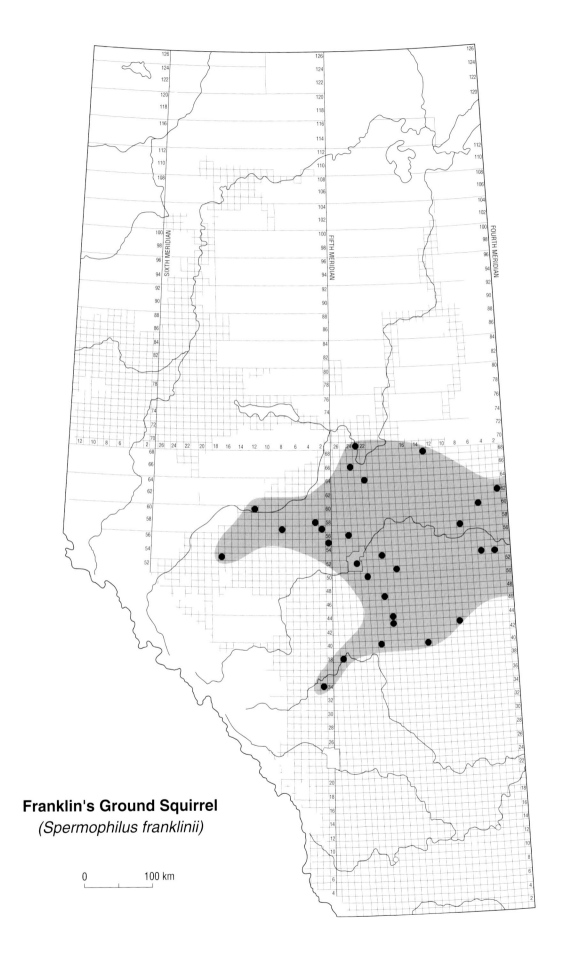

Franklin's Ground Squirrel

(Spermophilus franklinii)

0   100 km

GRAY SQUIRREL
Sciurus carolinensis

Rodentia: Sciuridae

(plate 6)

IDENTIFYING CHARACTERS

This is a large gray or black squirrel with a long, bushy tail. The pelage of the gray form is olive-gray sprinkled with black hairs. The large hindfeet are rufous-colored. In the black form the entire pelage is black. The ears are large.

The skull is large with a domed cranium and a relatively short rostrum. The postorbital processes are well developed and taper to a sharp point. The upper P3 is small and peg-like. The dental formula is I 1/1, C 0/0, P 2/1, M 3/3 x 2 = 22.

DISTRIBUTION

The only area of the province where this squirrel is well established is in the city of Calgary. There is one report of Gray Squirrels at Brooks (Bayer 1975), but no indication as to whether this is

a permanent population. Smith (1979) summarized reports of this species in the city of Edmonton and indicated that the individuals were from the Edmonton Valley Zoo.

HABITAT

Deciduous woodlands.

STATUS

The population in Calgary is still occupying new areas. It is not yet so common as to be a problem. At this time it is still novel enough to be commented on when observed.

SIMILAR SPECIES

Red Squirrels are smaller and redder.

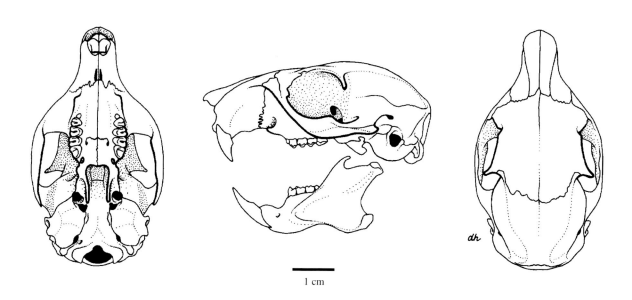

1 cm

Measurements

Sex		Weight (g)	Total Length (mm)	Tail (mm)	Hindfoot (mm)	Ear (mm)
Males (N=4)	Mean	463.1	474.0	225.3	64.8	28.8
	Range	378.5-537.2	424-500	200-246	62-66	24-33
Females (N=6)	Mean	460.4 *(N=5)*	467.2	223.7	66.3	28.7
	Range	291.1-645.5 *(N=5)*	426-510	203-238	62-69	24-31

92

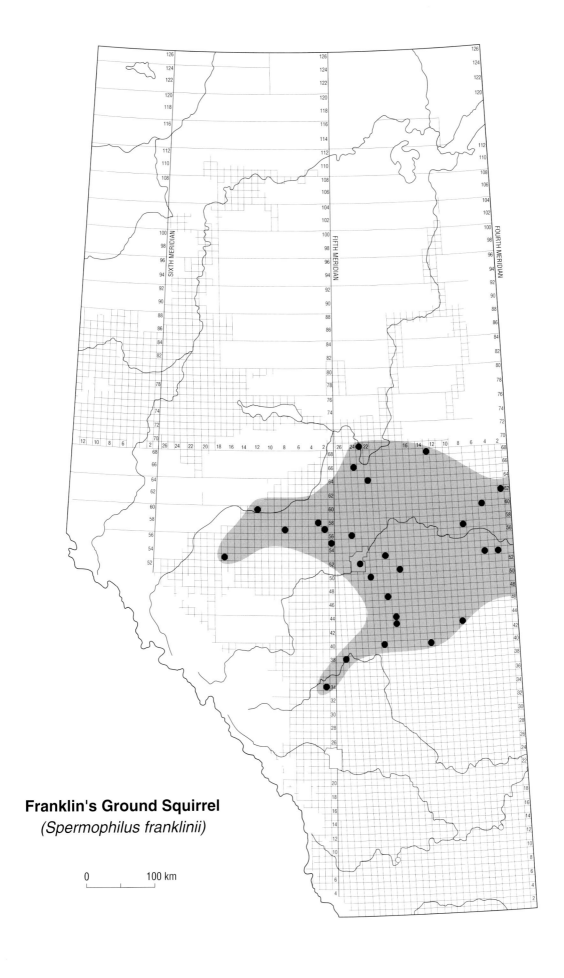

Franklin's Ground Squirrel
(Spermophilus franklinii)

0   100 km

GOLDEN-MANTLED GROUND SQUIRREL
Spermophilus lateralis

Rodentia: Sciuridae

(plate 6)

IDENTIFYING CHARACTERS

The Golden-mantled Ground Squirrel is a stout-bodied animal with two, broad, white stripes on either side of the back. The stripes are bordered in black and do not extend to the head area. The body is generally grayish on the back with the sides a lighter gray. The shoulders are rusty-colored. The face is sooty gray and the top of the head varies from gray to rust.

The skull is ovoid with a relatively short, broad rostrum. The postorbital processes are long and delicate. The zygomatic arches flare less widely than in other Alberta ground squirrels. The foramen magnum is roughly triangular. The dental formula is I 1/1, C 0/0, P 2/1, M 3/3 x 2 = 22.

DISTRIBUTION

The Golden-mantled Ground Squirrel is found throughout the Alberta mountains from Waterton Lakes National Park to the Kakwa and Torrens rivers area north of Jasper National Park.

HABITAT

This ground squirrel occupies a variety of habitats throughout its range, from rocky outcrops to open forests to dense shrubs.

STATUS

Generally considered common.

SIMILAR SPECIES

The chipmunks that occur in the mountains are all smaller. The stripes on the chipmunks extend onto the facial area. When running, chipmunks carry their tails in a vertical position.

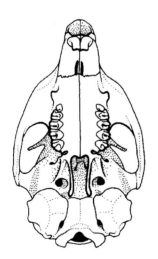 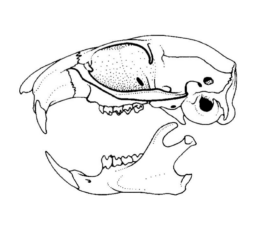 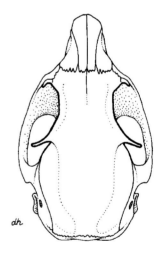

1 cm

Measurements

Sex		Weight (g)	Total Length (mm)	Tail (mm)	Hindfoot (mm)	Ear (mm)
Males	Mean	219.3 (N=5)	284.4 (N=16)	99.0 (N=16)	44.7 (N=16)	19.4 (N=5)
	Range	152.4-291.0 (N=5)	263-300 (N=16)	85-112 (N=16)	40-50 (N=16)	18-21 (N=5)
Females	Mean	222.0 (N=15)	278.8 (N=24)	92.2 (N=24)	43.8 (N=24)	21.9 (N=13)
	Range	172.0-377.6 (N=15)	248-305 (N=24)	60-114 (N=24)	40-47 (N=24)	20-24 (N=13)

90

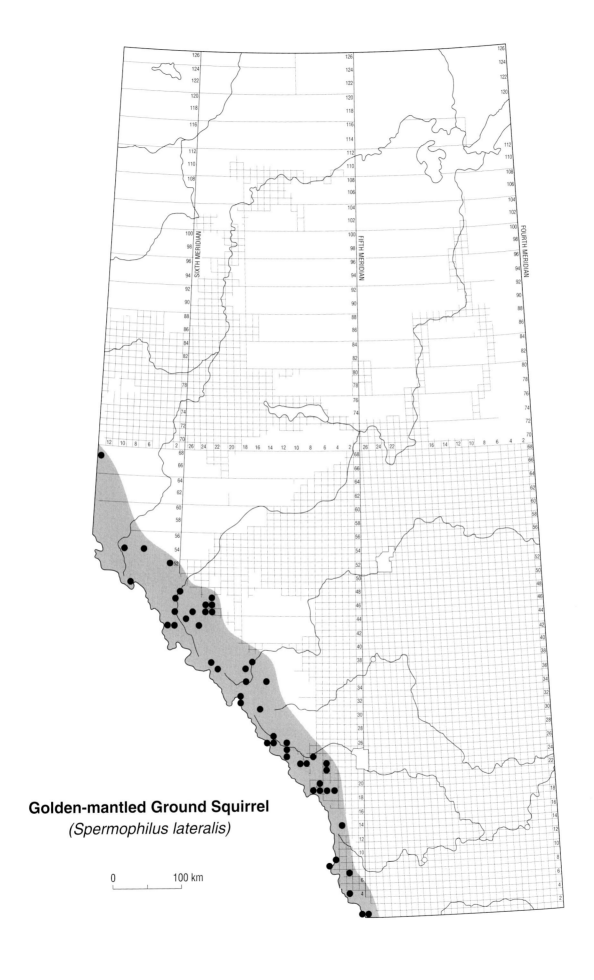

Golden-mantled Ground Squirrel
(Spermophilus lateralis)

0   100 km

GRAY SQUIRREL
Sciurus carolinensis

IDENTIFYING CHARACTERS

This is a large gray or black squirrel with a long, bushy tail. The pelage of the gray form is olive-gray sprinkled with black hairs. The large hindfeet are rufous-colored. In the black form the entire pelage is black. The ears are large.

The skull is large with a domed cranium and a relatively short rostrum. The postorbital processes are well developed and taper to a sharp point. The upper P3 is small and peg-like. The dental formula is I 1/1, C 0/0, P 2/1, M 3/3 x 2 = 22.

DISTRIBUTION

The only area of the province where this squirrel is well established is in the city of Calgary. There is one report of Gray Squirrels at Brooks (Bayer 1975), but no indication as to whether this is a permanent population. Smith (1979) summarized reports of this species in the city of Edmonton and indicated that the individuals were from the Edmonton Valley Zoo.

HABITAT

Deciduous woodlands.

STATUS

The population in Calgary is still occupying new areas. It is not yet so common as to be a problem. At this time it is still novel enough to be commented on when observed.

SIMILAR SPECIES

Red Squirrels are smaller and redder.

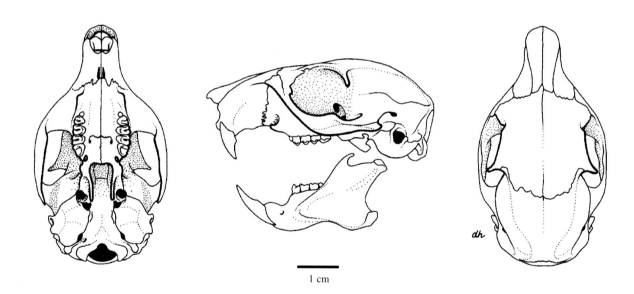

1 cm

Measurements

Sex		Weight (g)	Total Length (mm)	Tail (mm)	Hindfoot (mm)	Ear (mm)
Males (N=4)	Mean	463.1	474.0	225.3	64.8	28.8
	Range	378.5-537.2	424-500	200-246	62-66	24-33
Females (N=6)	Mean	460.4 *(N=5)*	467.2	223.7	66.3	28.7
	Range	291.1-645.5 *(N=5)*	426-510	203-238	62-69	24-31

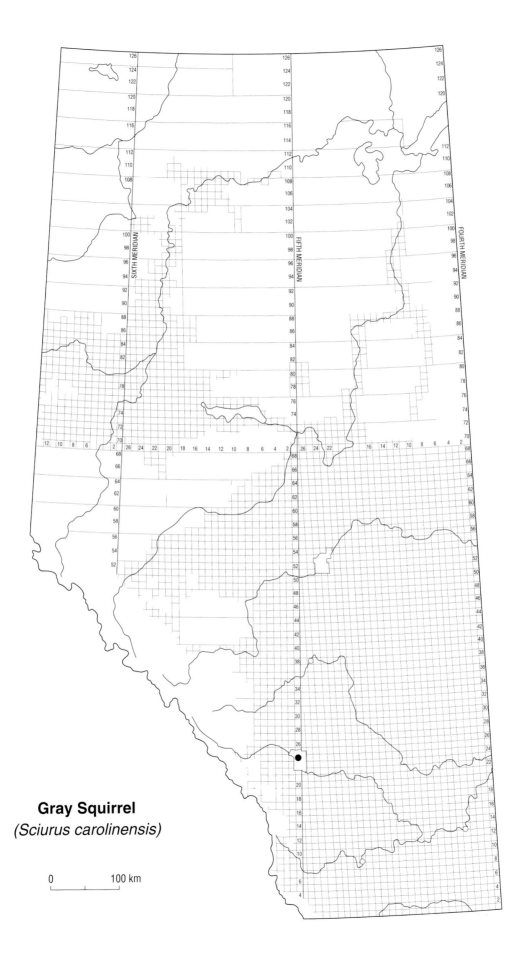

Gray Squirrel
(Sciurus carolinensis)

0   100 km

RED SQUIRREL
Tamiasciurus hudsonicus

IDENTIFYING CHARACTERS

This is a medium-sized member of the squirrel family. It is possibly the best known tree squirrel in Alberta. The pelage is generally olive-brown with a broad chestnut-red stripe along the midline of the back. The underside is gray or whitish. The tail is long and bushy and is the same color as the back. The sides of the tail have a black border.

The skull has a domed braincase and a short rostrum. The cheek teeth are relatively large and low-crowned. The upper P3 is frequently absent. If it is present it is extremely small and peg-like and is hidden by the crown of the upper P4. The dental formula is I 1/1, C 0/0, P 1/1 or 2/1, M 3/3 x 2 = 20 or 22.

DISTRIBUTION

Throughout most of northern and western Alberta. Absent from the grasslands. There is an introduced population in the Cypress Hills.

HABITAT

Coniferous and mixed wood forests.

STATUS

Common throughout its range.

SIMILAR SPECIES

Gray Squirrels occur only in the Calgary area. They are much larger with a longer, bushier tail. The pelage is either gray or black.

Northern Flying Squirrels are smaller and grayer. They have a flap of skin between the front- and hindlegs. The tail is flattened dorso-ventrally.

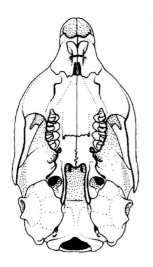 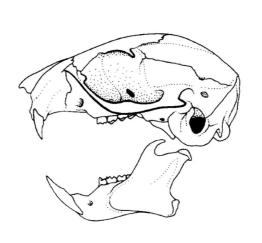 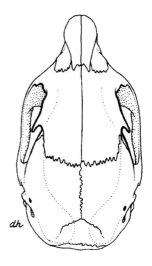

1 cm

Measurements

Sex		Weight (g)	Total Length (mm)	Tail (mm)	Hindfoot (mm)	Ear (mm)
Males (N=15)	Mean	226.7	321.9	122.3	48.2	25.4
	Range	185-258	308-338	111-131	44-51	21-29
Females (N=15)	Mean	235.9	320.3	125.5	47.1	26.3
	Range	195.7-330.5	306-336	112-140	42-52	18-36

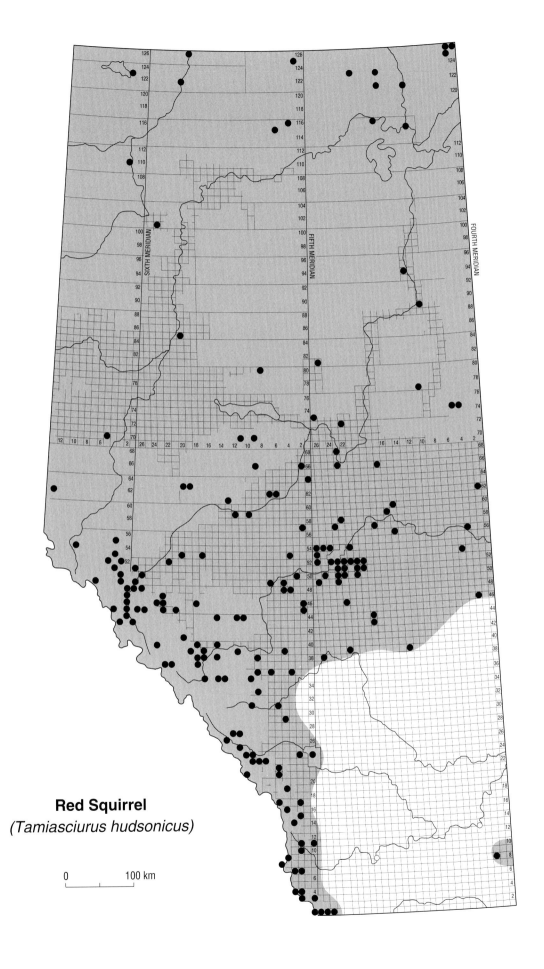

Red Squirrel
(Tamiasciurus hudsonicus)

0   100 km

NORTHERN FLYING SQUIRREL
Glaucomys sabrinus

Rodentia: Sciuridae

(plate 6)

IDENTIFYING CHARACTERS
The long, very soft pelage of this squirrel is grayish brown above and smoky gray below. The most conspicuous feature is the flap of skin, the patagium, that stretches between the front and rear feet, and the medium-length, flattened tail. Both features enable flying squirrels to glide between trees.

The skull is ovate with a short rostrum and small, thin postorbital processes. In profile, the skull is domed. The cheek teeth are small and relatively low-crowned. The upper P3 is small and peg-like. The dental formula is I 1/1, C 0/0, P 2/1, M 3/3 x 2 = 22.

DISTRIBUTION
Flying squirrels occur throughout the northern forests and parklands south to approximately the Battle River, the city of Red Deer, and the foothills west of Calgary, to Waterton Lakes National Park.

HABITAT
Coniferous and mixed wood forests. Trees with holes in which nests can be made are important requirements for these squirrels.

STATUS
Because this animal is nocturnal, it is rarely encountered and may be considered rare. It is, however, common in those areas where suitable habitat occurs.

SIMILAR SPECIES
Red Squirrels are the only other common tree squirrels in the province. The color, the diurnal habits, and lack of a flight membrane are characters that easily separate the two species.

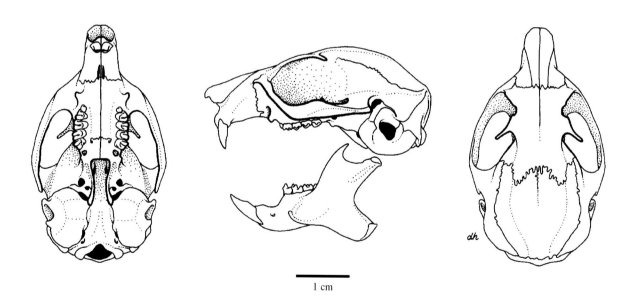

1 cm

Measurements

Sex		Weight (g)	Total Length (mm)	Tail (mm)	Hindfoot (mm)	Ear (mm)
Males (N=14)	Mean	151.6 *(N=5)*	314.8	142.1	40.6	24 *(N=2)*
	Range	132.9-165.0 *(N=5)*	292-341	120-159	32-45	22-24 *(N=2)*
Females (N=19)	Mean	153.3 *(N=8)*	326.9	145.2	41.8	24.1 *(N=8)*
	Range	100.2-198.8 *(N=8)*	304-358	124-162	38-48	21-26 *(N=8)*

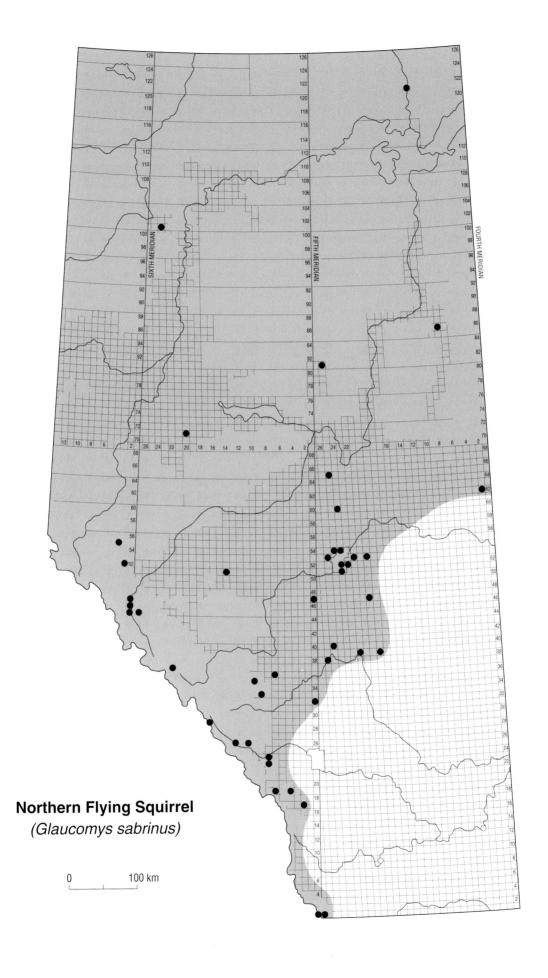

Northern Flying Squirrel
(Glaucomys sabrinus)

0   100 km

NORTHERN POCKET GOPHER
Thomomys talpoides

IDENTIFYING CHARACTERS

The pocket gopher is a stout-bodied, short-tailed, short-legged, burrowing rodent. It has a soft, dense steel-gray pelage. The head is large and the eyes and ears are small. The whitish tail is short and stocky with a blunt tip. External, fur-lined cheek pouches are present. The forefeet are large with long claws.

The skull is robust and angular. In older individuals temporal ridges are present. The rostrum is long. In profile view the skull is flat. The upper incisors are large and have an orange pigmentation on the anterior surface. The cheek teeth are teardrop shaped. The dental formula is I 1/1, C 0/0, P 1/1, M 3/3 x 2 = 20.

DISTRIBUTION

The distribution of the pocket gopher is disjunct. One population lives in the parkland region from as far north as Lac La Biche south to Trochu. The western border parallels the foothills extending into the mountains to Crowsnest and the Waterton area. A grassland population extends along extreme southern Alberta from the town of Milk River along the Milk River north to the Cypress Hills and north to Empress. Gophers are absent in south-central Alberta in an area east of Calgary, Drumheller, Oyen, and from Lethbridge north.

HABITAT

Native grasslands, hay meadows, roadside ditches, gardens, and alfalfa fields.

STATUS

Common. In many places it occurs in sufficient numbers to be considered a pest. Because it is a fossorial animal, many people will not be familiar with it, but the earth mounds it pushes up on lawns and in meadows are a familiar sight.

SIMILAR SPECIES

No other species should be mistaken for a pocket gopher. The combination of stout body, large head, short tail, long claws on the front feet, and external cheek pouches are found in no other native mammal. People who are not familiar with these animals frequently refer to them as moles because of the mounds of earth that are pushed up from their burrows. Moles are insectivores related to shrews and do not occur in Alberta.

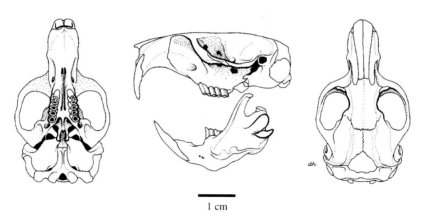

1 cm

Measurements

Sex		Weight (g)	Total Length (mm)	Tail (mm)	Hindfoot (mm)	Ear (mm)
Males (N=20)	Mean	148.9	223.8	55.9	28.9	7.6
	Range	117.5-180.7	205-244	44-67	27-31	6-10
Females (N=20)	Mean	143.3	221.0	58.1	28.8	7.2
	Range	115.2-204.8	205-246	43-70	26-31	6-9

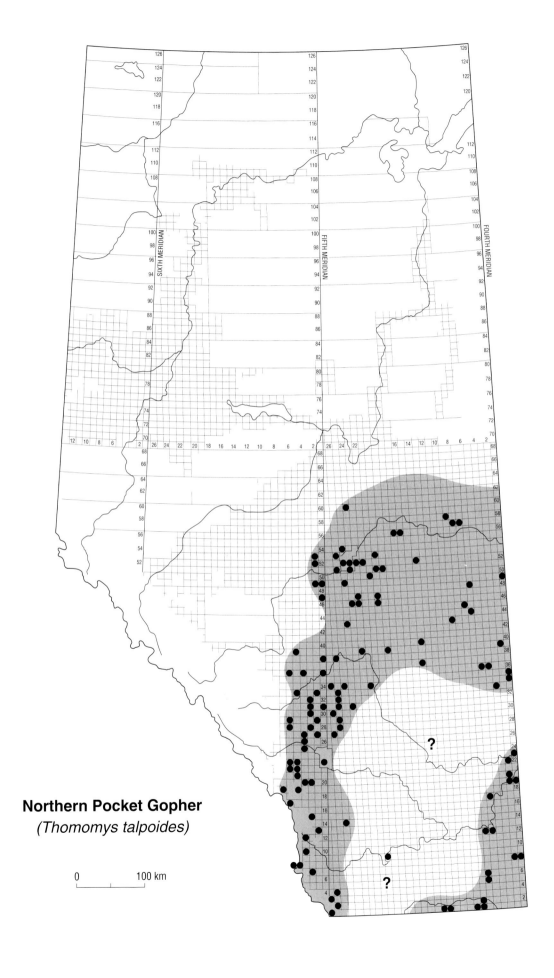

Northern Pocket Gopher

(Thomomys talpoides)

0   100 km

99

OLIVE-BACKED POCKET MOUSE
Perognathus fasciatus

IDENTIFYING CHARACTERS

This is one of the smallest mice in the province. The pelage is short, dark, sandy-brown on the back and white on the belly. There is a thin cream-colored line along the side. External cheek pouches are located on each side of the mouth. The tail is long and thin.

The skull is small and delicate with inflated auditory bullae. The nasal bones project past the upper incisors. The upper incisors have a shallow groove on the anterior surface. There are four cheek teeth. The dental formula is I 1/1, C 0/0, P 1/1, M 3/3 x 2 = 20.

DISTRIBUTION

The northern border of the range of this species is the Red Deer River; the western border is a line through Taber and Milk River.

HABITAT

Open grasslands, especially where there is sandy soil.

STATUS

Population density is variable, being more abundant in one area than another; typically, it is a scarce animal.

SIMILAR SPECIES

Western Harvest Mice are easily distinguished by their bicolored tail, slate gray pelage, three cheek teeth and lack of external cheek pouches.

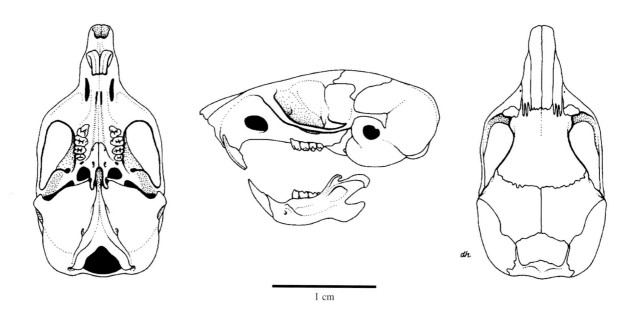

1 cm

Measurements

Sex		Weight (g)	Total Length (mm)	Tail (mm)	Hindfoot (mm)	Ear (mm)
Males (N=4)	Mean	11.8	123.0	58.3	16.5	7.3
	Range	11.0-13.7	112-130	51-64	15-18	7-8
Females (N=5)	Mean	10.8	127.8	60.2	17.2	7.3
	Range	10.1-12.4	125-132	58-63	16-18	7-8

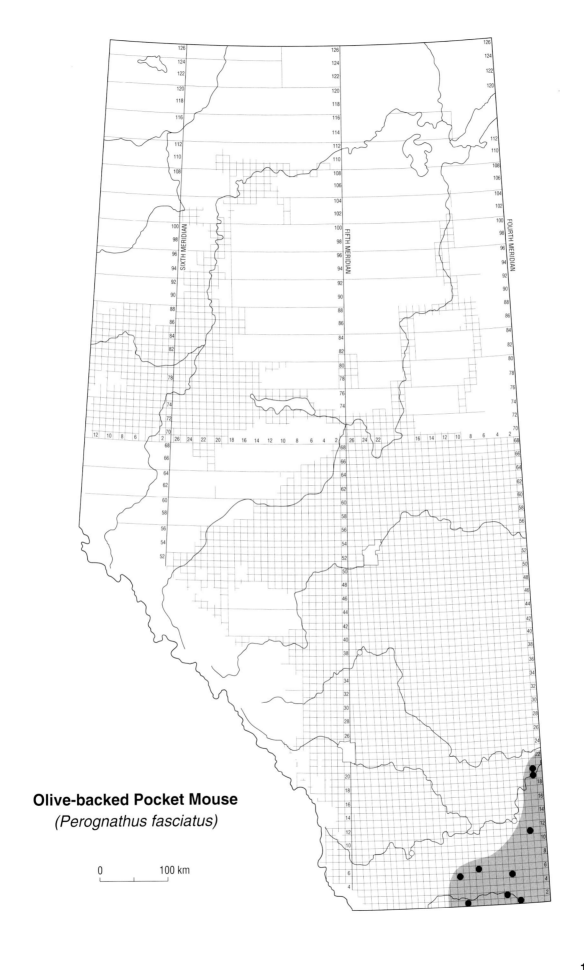

Olive-backed Pocket Mouse
(Perognathus fasciatus)

0   100 km

ORD'S KANGAROO RAT
Dipodomys ordii

Rodentia: Heteromyidae

(plate 7)

IDENTIFYING CHARACTERS

This attractive rodent is readily identified by its golden-brown back and white belly, the very long, well furred, tufted tail, very large hindlegs, large head, and external cheek pouches. The eyes are large and prominent.

The skull is unusual. The auditory bullae are extremely inflated, the zygomatic arches are small and thin, and the rostrum is long and narrow. The nasal bones extend well past the tightly curved upper incisors. The upper incisors are grooved. The dental formula is I 1/1, C 0/0, P 1/1, M 3/3 x 2 = 20.

DISTRIBUTION

In Alberta, Ord's Kangaroo Rats have a limited distribution. They occur south of the Red Deer River to just north of Hilda and from the Saskatchewan border to the military reserve at Suffield.

HABITAT

Sandy soil with a sparse grass cover.

STATUS

Uncommon. Distribution is extremely local and population density varies greatly.

SIMILAR SPECIES

The bright, contrasting pelage color, the long tail and hind legs, and relatively large head should not be mistaken for any other Alberta mammal.

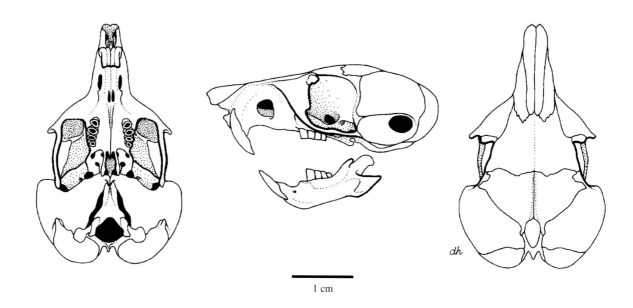

1 cm

Measurements

Sex		Weight (g)	Total Length (mm)	Tail (mm)	Hindfoot (mm)	Ear (mm)
Males (N=9)	Mean	73.1	252.6	143.7	41.3	12.5
	Range	71.1-79.6	201-265	140-154	39-43	11-14
Females (N=4)	Mean	71.7	254.0	146.8	42.8	13.5
	Range	50.7-74.0	206-275	144-150	41-45	10-19

102

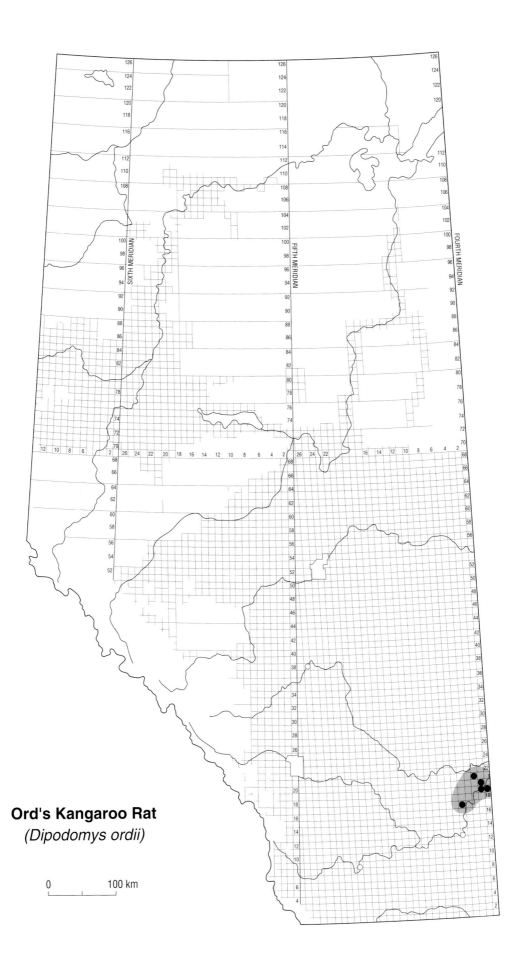

Ord's Kangaroo Rat

(Dipodomys ordii)

0   100 km

BEAVER
Castor canadensis

Rodentia: Castoridae

(plate 7)

IDENTIFYING CHARACTERS

The Beaver is a large, semi-aquatic rodent. It has short legs, a large head, small eyes and ears, large, webbed hindfeet, and a broad, flattened, scaly tail. The pelage consists of long, glossy guard hairs and short, dense underfur. The guard hairs vary from reddish brown to dark brown. The underfur is grayish.

The skull is massive with a relatively narrow braincase. The zygomatic arches are large. The auditory bullae are small but the long, bony auditory canal is prominent. The teeth are large. The upper incisors are heavily pigmented and do not extend past the nasal bones. The cheek teeth are squarish with a complex occlusal pattern. The dental formula is I 1/1, C 0/0, P 1/1, M 3/3 x 2 = 20.

DISTRIBUTION

Beavers are found throughout the province wherever there is suitable water.

HABITAT

Beavers require water: sloughs, rivers, creeks, and lakes with trees within easy access.

STATUS

Throughout the province, the Beaver can be considered common. However, there may be local situations where it is scarce or absent.

SIMILAR SPECIES

Muskrats are semi-aquatic rodents too, but they are smaller and have more rat-like tails that are laterally compressed, not flattened. The Beaver's large size and flat tail are distinctive.

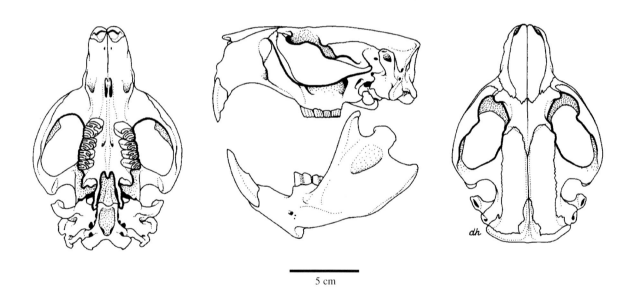

5 cm

Measurements

Sex		Weight (kg)	Total Length (mm)	Tail (mm)	Hindfoot (mm)	Ear (mm)
Males (N=7)	Mean	22.1 *(N=6)*	1112.9	347.3	187.6	37.2 *(N=6)*
	Range	15.9-30.0 *(N=6)*	1000-1260	283-500	178-200	32-42 *(N=6)*
Females (N=7)	Mean	22.3 *(N=4)*	1099.0	323.9	179.6	33.3
	Range	21.1-23.6 *(N=4)*	1015-1170	206-480	160-193	31-37

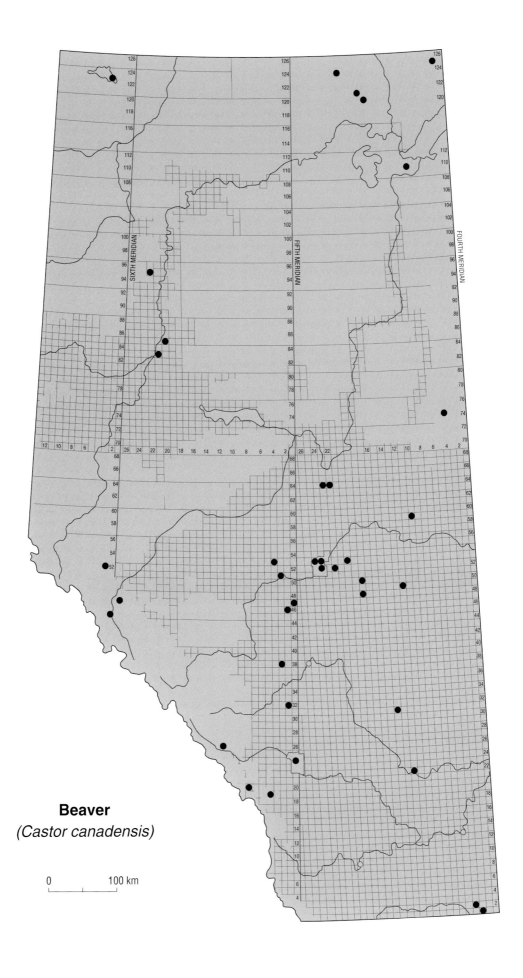

Beaver
(Castor canadensis)

0 ——— 100 km

WESTERN HARVEST MOUSE
Reithrodontomys megalotis

Rodentia: Cricetidae

IDENTIFYING CHARACTERS

The Western Harvest Mouse is a small, gray-colored mouse with a long, bicolored tail. The pelage is short, slate-gray on the back with a grayish belly. There is a contrasting dark stripe along the back.

The skull is delicate with a long, narrow rostrum. The nasal bones project past the upper incisors. The distinctive feature of this small mouse is the prominent groove on the anterior surface of the upper incisors. The dental formula is I 1/1, C 0/0, P 0/0, M 3/3 x 2 = 16.

DISTRIBUTION

This mouse has been collected at three locations in Alberta: Medicine Hat, Milk River (Haynes 1951, Moore 1952a), and the Pinhorn Grazing Reserve southwest of Manyberries. Two of these specimens are housed in the Zoology Museum, University of Alberta. The location of the third specimen is not known.

HABITAT

Open grassland.

STATUS

The Western Harvest Mouse is at the northernmost part of its range in Alberta. The status is difficult to assess on the basis of three specimens. It should be considered scarce.

SIMILAR SPECIES

House Mice are larger, with a uniformly colored pelage. The upper incisors are not grooved.

Olive-backed Pocket Mice are more colorful with slightly longer hindlegs, a tail that is not sharply bicolored, and external cheek pouches.

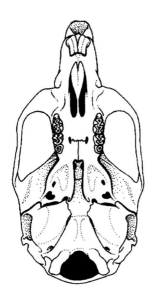 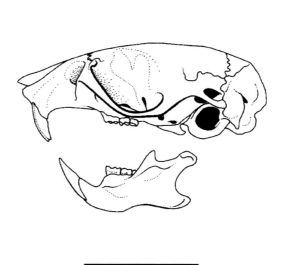 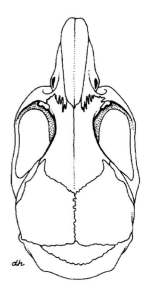

1 cm

Measurements

Sex		Weight (g)	Total Length (mm)	Tail (mm)	Hindfoot (mm)	Ear (mm)
Females (N=2)	Mean	14.6	142.5	62.5	15.5	12.5
	Range	13.0-16.2	138-147	62-63	14-17	12-13

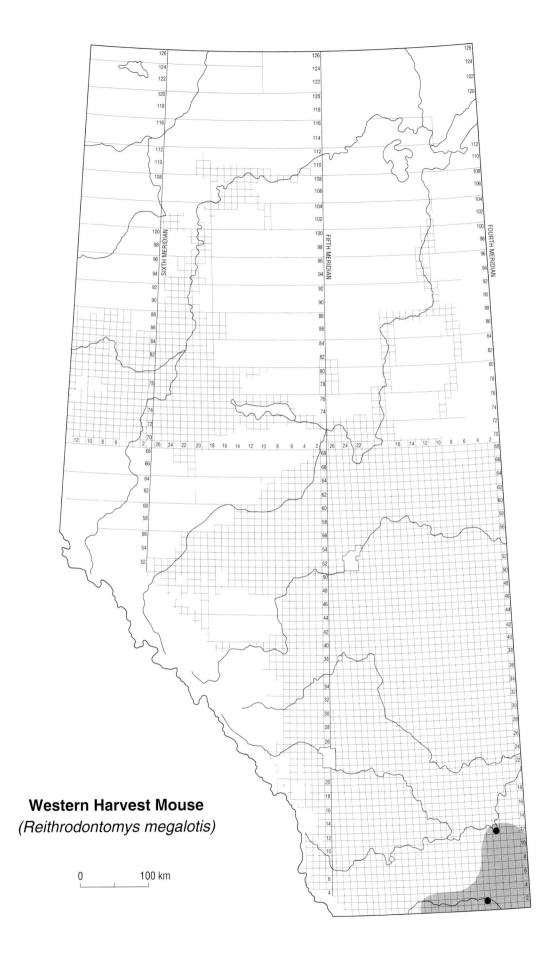

Western Harvest Mouse
(Reithrodontomys megalotis)

0   100 km

DEER MOUSE
Peromyscus maniculatus

IDENTIFYING CHARACTERS

The pelage ranges from slate-gray to golden-brown on the back with a white belly. The ears and eyes are large. The tail is long, well furred, and sharply bicolored. The feet are small and white in color.

The skull is slightly domed, smooth, and appears delicate. The bones of the zygomatic arch are slim and fragile. The coronoid process of the mandible is poorly developed. The cheek teeth are cuspidate with the cusps arranged in two longitudinal rows. The dental formula is I 1/1, C 0/0, P 0/0, M 3/3 x 2 = 16.

DISTRIBUTION

Found throughout the province.

HABITAT

This mouse is found in almost all habitats in the province from human habitations to open sand dunes, dense northern forests, alpine meadows, and open grasslands.

STATUS

Common. The Deer Mouse is likely the most abundant mammal in the province.

SIMILAR SPECIES

Northern Grasshopper Mice have a more robust body, a considerably shorter tail, and a larger coronoid process.

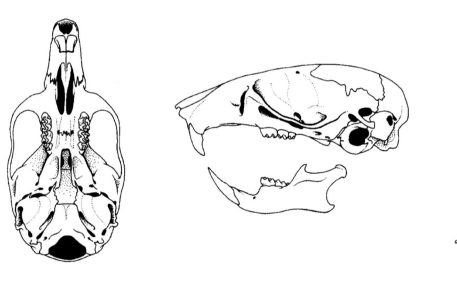 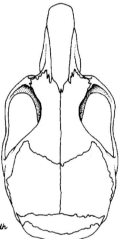

1 cm

Measurements

Sex		Weight (g)	Total Length (mm)	Tail (mm)	Hindfoot (mm)	Ear (mm)
Males (N=20)	Mean	23.1	164.0	74.3	20.1	19.4
	Range	20.1-26.4	141-181	58-88	18-22	16-23
Females (N=20)	Mean	24.9	166.3	75.3	19.8	19.9
	Range	20.0-36.3	151-182	56-92	18-22	16-22

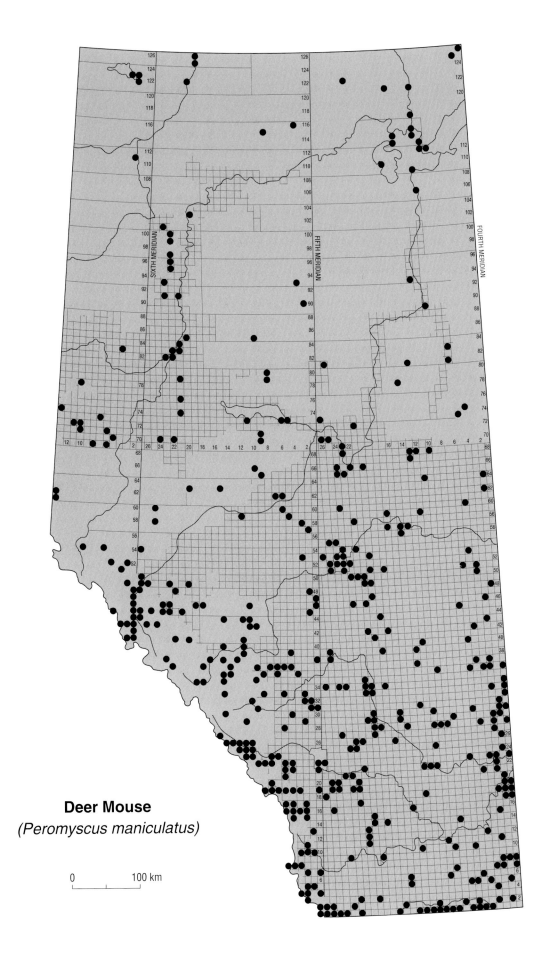

Deer Mouse
(Peromyscus maniculatus)

0   100 km

NORTHERN GRASSHOPPER MOUSE
Onychomys leucogaster

Rodentia: Cricetidae

IDENTIFYING CHARACTERS

This mouse has a chunky body and a short tail. The pelage is bicolored: pale sandy-brown on the back with a grayish head and a white belly. The short, stout, blunt-tipped tail is white. The ears are large and have a dark spot on the forward edge.

The skull is robust, relatively flat in profile, and smooth. The rostrum is relatively short and broad. The coronoid process of the mandible is well developed. The cheek teeth are relatively large. The dental formula is I 1/1, C 0/0, P 0/0, M 3/3 x 2 = 16.

DISTRIBUTION

The grasslands of southern Alberta, north to Compeer in the east, and west to Calgary and Lethbridge on the western edge of the range.

HABITAT

Open grasslands interspersed with sagebrush.

STATUS

Relatively common.

SIMILAR SPECIES

Deer Mice have a more gracile body and a much longer, bicolored tail. The coronoid process on the mandible is small and poorly developed.

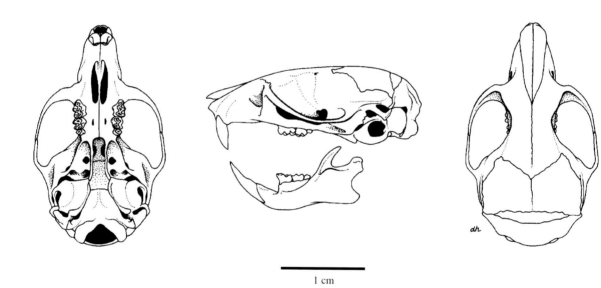

1 cm

Measurements

Sex		Weight (g)	Total Length (mm)	Tail (mm)	Hindfoot (mm)	Ear (mm)
Males (N=2)	Mean	31.0	126.5	34.5	20.5	15.5
	Range	29.7-32.2	125-128	34-35	20-21	15-16
Females (N=4)	Mean	34.2	138.5	35.5	20.8	15.8
	Range	24.7-42.9	129-147	34-38	20-21	14-17

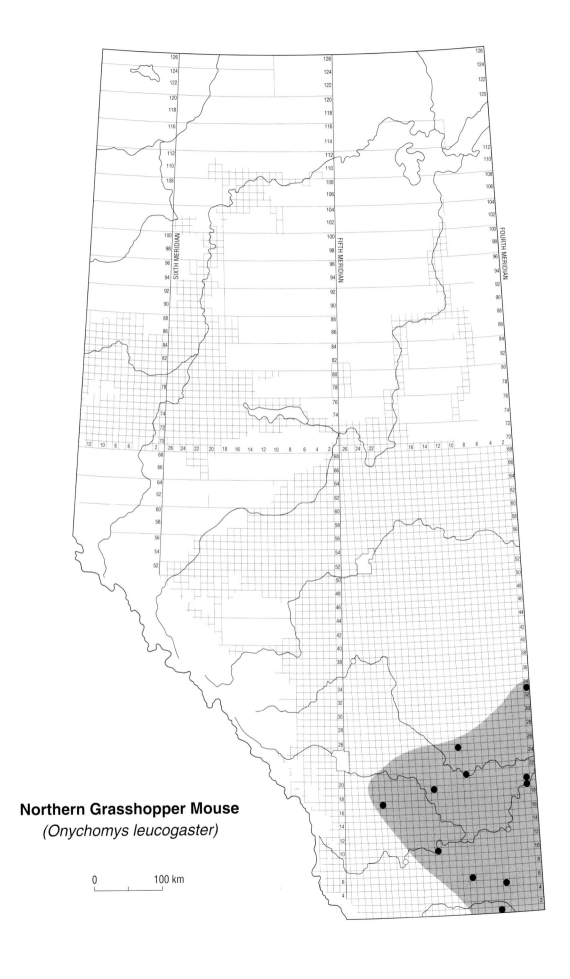

Northern Grasshopper Mouse
(Onychomys leucogaster)

0   100 km

BUSHY-TAILED WOODRAT
Neotoma cinerea

IDENTIFYING CHARACTERS

The Bushy-tailed Woodrat is a medium-sized rodent (weighs up to 530 g). The long, soft pelage is silver-gray on the back and sides and white on the belly and feet. The tail is long, well furred, and bushy and is a reliable character for distinguishing this species. There is a large scent gland on the belly. The eyes and ears are large and the face tapers sharply to the nose. The vibrissae are long.

The skull is not as robust as in rodents of comparable size. The rostrum is long and narrow. The cheek teeth are rooted, and unworn teeth have high crowns. The occlusal surfaces are prismatic. The dental formula is I 1/1, C 0/0, P 0/0, M 3/3 x 2 = 16.

DISTRIBUTION

The Bushy-tailed Woodrat is widely distributed throughout the mountains. It occurs north to Brownvale in the Peace River area. It is also found along the Milk River and north to the Cypress Hills. Skeletal remains have been found along the South Saskatchewan River at Sandy Point but no live animals are known from this area. Extralimital specimens have been taken at Edmonton, Leduc, Ponoka, and Strathmore. They may have been accidentally transported to these sites, but proof is lacking.

HABITAT

In the mountains, woodrats are found among rock slides, in caves, and crevices. Along the Milk River they inhabit rocky outcrops. In the mountains and foothills, vacant buildings are frequently used.

STATUS

Common throughout the mountains and the Milk River.

SIMILAR SPECIES

None. Its long, bushy tail, silver-gray fur, long pointed nose, and large eyes and ears are like no other Alberta mammal.

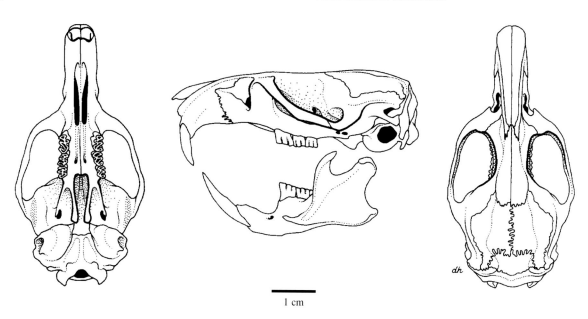

1 cm

Measurements

Sex		Weight (g)	Total Length (mm)	Tail (mm)	Hindfoot (mm)	Ear (mm)
Males	Mean	354.3 (N=11)	389.1 (N=24)	168.2 (N=23)	46.9 (N=24)	34.2 (N=10)
	Range	211.1-526.1 (N=11)	300-450 (N=24)	105-215 (N=23)	41-52 (N=24)	27-38 (N=10)
Females	Mean	315.8 (N=5)	381.9 (N=14)	161.5 (N=14)	44.3 (N=14)	32.8 (N=5)
	Range	263-341.3 (N=5)	335-400 (N=14)	112-181 (N=14)	40-47 (N=14)	31-34 (N=5)

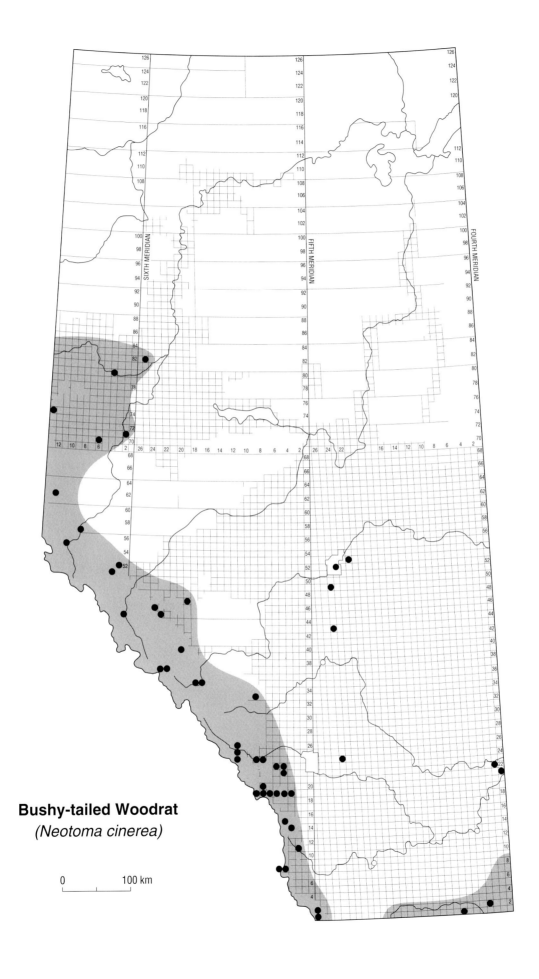

Bushy-tailed Woodrat

(Neotoma cinerea)

0   100 km

113

SOUTHERN RED-BACKED VOLE
Clethrionomys gapperi

Rodentia: Cricetidae

(plate 8)

IDENTIFYING CHARACTERS

The bright, chestnut-brown color of the pelage along the back readily distinguishes this vole from other Alberta species. The sides and rump are grayish brown and the belly is gray. Some individuals are very dark. The ears are large. The tail is bicolored and well furred.

The skull is smooth and less angular than in other voles. The cheek teeth are relatively small and the inner and outer re-entrant angles are equal in depth. The cheek teeth in adults become rooted. The dental formula is I 1/1, C 0/0, P 0/0, M 3/3 x 2 = 16.

DISTRIBUTION

The Southern Red-backed Vole is found throughout most of the forested areas of Alberta. It is absent from the grasslands but is found in the forested parts of the Cypress Hills.

HABITAT

This vole is found in a variety of forested habitats from dry uplands to the edges of moist meadows.

STATUS

This is one of the most common and abundant small rodents in those regions of the province where it is found.

SIMILAR SPECIES

Meadow Voles are much larger and darker. The upper M2 has an extra posterior loop.

Heather Voles have a darker pelage, light colored feet, and deep re-entrant angles on the cheek teeth.

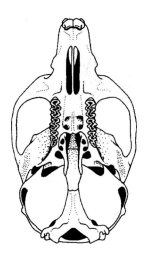 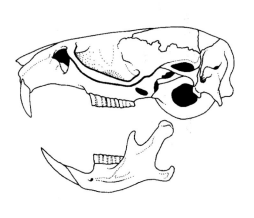 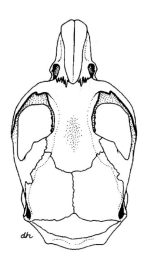

1 cm

Measurements

Sex		Weight (g)	Total Length (mm)	Tail (mm)	Hindfoot (mm)	Ear (mm)
Males (N=20)	Mean	22.9	133.0	36.8	18.2	16.6
	Range	20.3-28.9	123-153	30-41	15-20	13-21
Females (N=20)	Mean	24.4	131.9	36.0	17.7	16.8
	Range	18.7-31.6	122-145	30-44	15-19	13-21

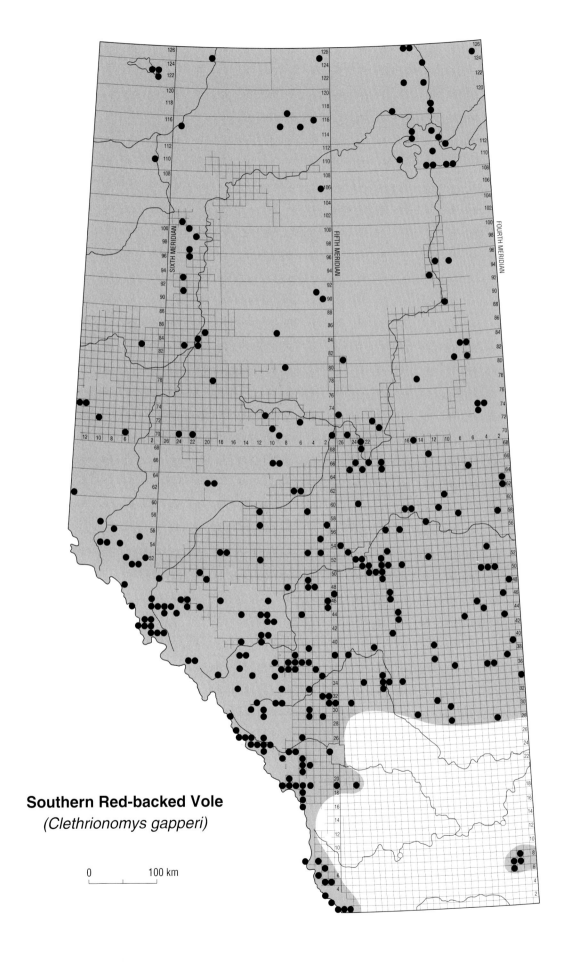

Southern Red-backed Vole
(Clethrionomys gapperi)

0   100 km

HEATHER VOLE
Phenacomys intermedius

IDENTIFYING CHARACTERS

The Heather Vole is a chunky-bodied, short-tailed, short-legged rodent. The pelage is long and lax, reddish brown on the back and gray on the belly. The tail is moderately long and the feet are light colored — white or grayish. This latter character is diagnostic.

The skull is less angular than in other voles. The cheek teeth are the most diagnostic features. They are rooted in adults and the inner re-entrant angles are deeper than the outer angles. The dental formula is I 1/1, C 0/0, P 0/0, M 3/3 x 2 = 16.

DISTRIBUTION

The Heather Vole is an inhabitant of the northern forest and mountain areas. It is absent from the parklands and grasslands.

HABITAT

Damp subalpine meadows to rocky talus slopes to shrubby areas along lakes.

STATUS

In the mountains, the Heather Vole is common. It is considerably less common in the forested regions.

SIMILAR SPECIES

Meadow Voles have an extra posterior loop on the upper M2, the feet are darker, and the cheek teeth are not rooted.

Northern Bog Lemmings have grooved upper incisors, the cheek teeth are not rooted, and the tail is very short.

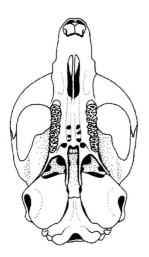 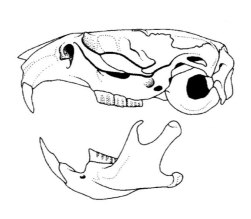 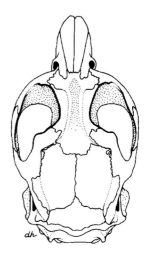

1 cm

Measurements

Sex		Weight (g)	Total Length (mm)	Tail (mm)	Hindfoot (mm)	Ear (mm)
Males (N=10)	Mean	29.6	131.2	28.2	17.9	14.3
	Range	23.6-36.1	116-144	21-37	16-20	11-16
Females (N=23)	Mean	31.2	140.7	33.2	17.8	14.3
	Range	21.5-45.5	124-158	27-40	16-20	11-20

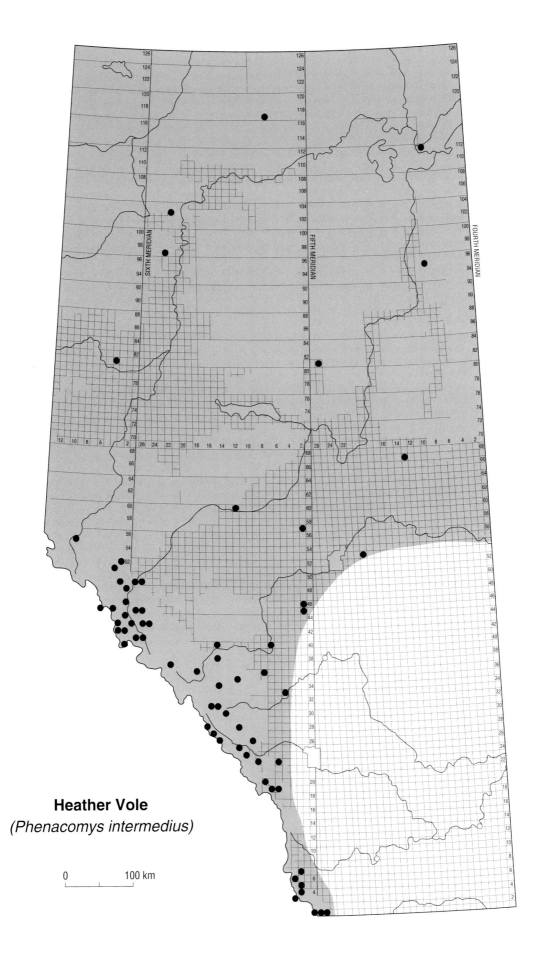

Heather Vole

(Phenacomys intermedius)

0   100 km

MEADOW VOLE
Microtus pennsylvanicus

IDENTIFYING CHARACTERS
This is a relatively large vole (weighs up to 50 g and total length up to 175 mm). The pelage is long and loose. The basic color is reddish brown, darker on the back and lighter on the sides. The belly is lead-gray. The tail is moderately long, about twice the length of the hind foot, and is bicolored.

The skull is angular with a long rostrum. The re-entrant angles of the cheek teeth are of approximately equal depth. The diagnostic character is an extra loop on the upper M2. The dental formula is I 1/1, C 0/0, P 0/0, M 3/3 x 2 = 16.

DISTRIBUTION
Found throughout the province in suitable habitat.

HABITAT
Open, grassy, moist meadows.

STATUS
Common, even abundant in some years.

SIMILAR SPECIES
Long-tailed Voles have a tail which is considerably longer. The upper M2 has no extra posterior loop.

Prairie Voles have a salt and pepper pelage, and are smaller. The upper M2 has no extra posterior loop.

Heather Voles are smaller with lighter-colored feet. Re-entrant angles are deep. Cheek teeth are rooted. The upper M2 has no extra posterior loop.

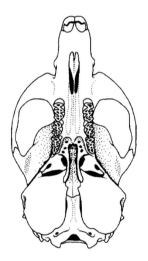 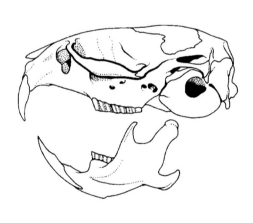 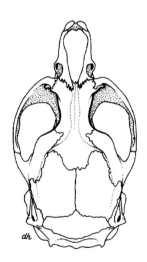

1 cm

Measurements

Sex		Weight (g)	Total Length (mm)	Tail (mm)	Hindfoot (mm)	Ear (mm)
Males (N=20)	Mean	31.5	144.9	37.9	17.9	14.7
	Range	19.1-42.7	122-172	29-46	14.5-20	11-18
Females (N=20)	Mean	30.5	139.1	37.3	17.6	14.4
	Range	22.0-49.2	123-176	21-49	15-21	12-17

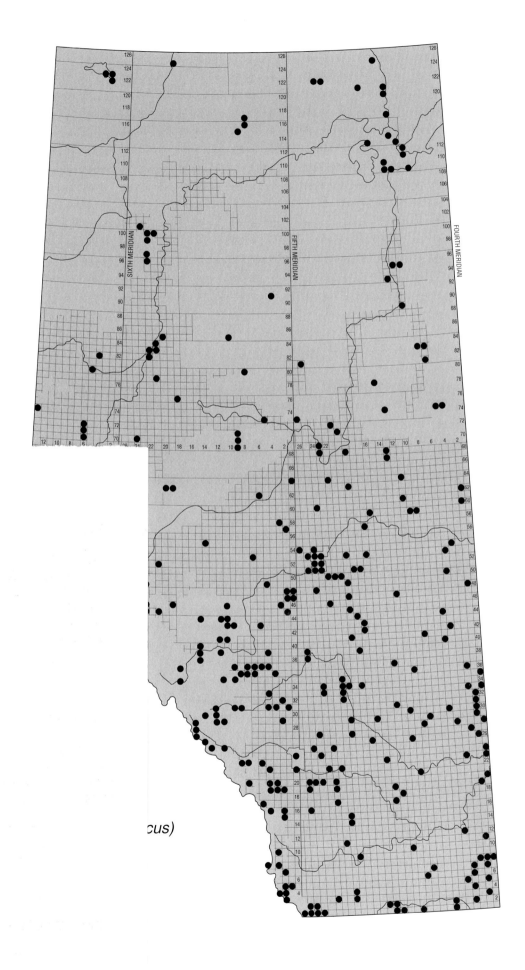

cus)

119

LONG-TAILED VOLE
Microtus longicaudus

IDENTIFYING CHARACTERS

The pelage is grayish brown with a red tinge on the back. The sides are a lighter shade of brown and the belly is dirty gray. The tail is well furred, bicolored, and very long for a vole.

The upper M2 has four loops or triangles. In the Meadow Vole the upper M2 has five loops or triangles. The dental formula is I 1/1, C 0/0, P 0/0, M 3/3 x 2 = 16.

DISTRIBUTION

The Long-tailed Vole is found throughout the mountains and on the grasslands parallel to the Milk River and into the Cypress Hills.

HABITAT

Damp alpine meadows and damp upland meadows on the grasslands.

STATUS

In the mountain regions this species is relatively common. On the grasslands it is very scarce.

SIMILAR SPECIES

Meadow Voles have a shorter tail and an extra loop on the upper M2. These two species are difficult to distinguish by external appearance.

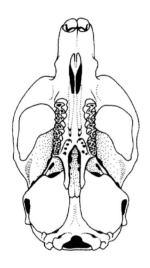 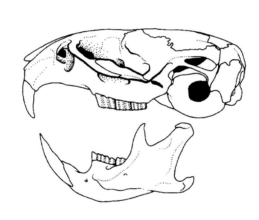 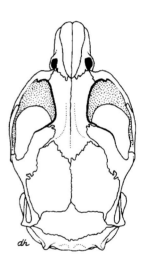

1 cm

Measurements

Sex		Weight (g)	Total Length (mm)	Tail (mm)	Hindfoot (mm)	Ear (mm)
Males (N=11)	Mean	34.4	166.8	57.7	19.4	13.9
	Range	30-37.5	153-182	52-65	18-21	13-16
Females (N=15)	Mean	35.5	165.0	57.2	19.2	13.5
	Range	27.5-43.1	150-181	52-64	17-21	10-15

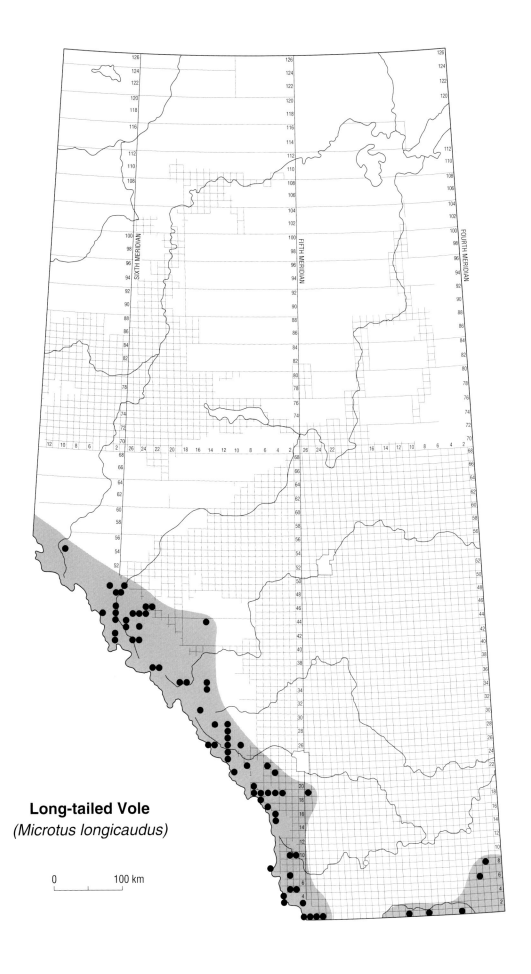

Long-tailed Vole
(Microtus longicaudus)

0   100 km

121

TAIGA VOLE
Microtus xanthognathus

Rodentia: Cricetidae

IDENTIFYING CHARACTERS

This large vole is distinguished by the rust-orange around the nose. The pelage varies from reddish brown to orangish brown along the back. The sides are dark brown with a hint of yellow and the belly is dark gray. The forefeet may have a thin band of white at the wrists. The tail is bicolored, dark on top, light below and is well furred.

The skull is robust with a relatively long, narrow rostrum. The incisive foramen is long and narrow through its entire length. The auditory bullae are relatively small and do not extend past the occiput. The cheek teeth are large and the upper incisors do not project past the nasal bones. The dental formula is I 1/1, C 0/0, P 0/0, M 3/3 x 2 = 16.

DISTRIBUTION

The only Albertan specimens were collected along the Athabasca River. The first specimen was collected in 1897, the last in 1904 (Preble 1908). No other specimens are known.

HABITAT

Upland areas along rivers near stands of horsetails *(Equisetum).*

STATUS

Rare, possibly extirpated. As none have been collected in Alberta since 1904, any specimens taken should be deposited in a major museum.

SIMILAR SPECIES

Water Voles are larger and lack the rusty nose. The hindfeet are larger. The skull is larger. The upper incisors project beyond the nasal bones and the incisive foramen flares widely at the front.

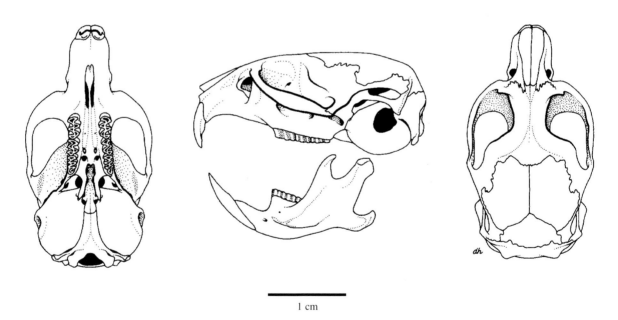

1 cm

Measurements

Sex		Weight (g)	Total Length (mm)	Tail (mm)	Hindfoot (mm)
Males (N=7)	Mean	98.4	193.4	38.7	25.0
	Range	87.9-112.6	178-208	33-46	24-26
Females (N=10)	Mean	98.9	196.0	40.5	25.3
	Range	82-112.7	185-207	38-43	24-26

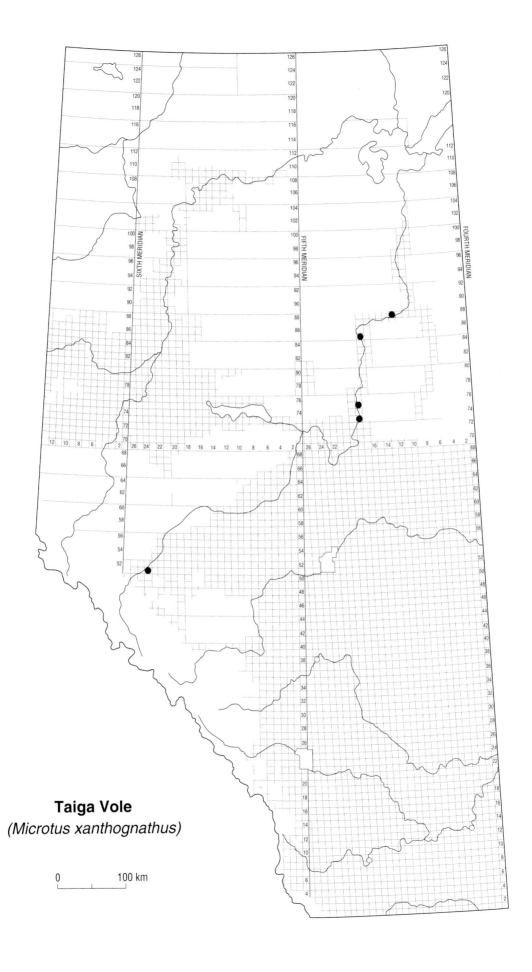

Taiga Vole

(Microtus xanthognathus)

0   100 km

PRAIRIE VOLE
Microtus ochrogaster

IDENTIFYING CHARACTERS

The pelage has a grizzled appearance because the dark brown and buffy hairs are intermixed. The back is darker than the sides and the belly is gray with an ochraceous wash. The tail is short, well furred, dark on top, gray on the underside. The feet are grayish.

The skull is narrow with a long rostrum and a relatively broad interorbital constriction. The upper M3 has two small closed triangles between the anterior and posterior loops. The dental formula is I 1/1, C 0/0, P 0/0, M 3/3 x 2 = 16.

DISTRIBUTION

The distribution is extremely patchy in the province. It is found mostly in the aspen parkland-aspen groveland areas of central Alberta. It has been collected as far west as the Red Deer area and as far north as St. Paul.

HABITAT

Upland prairie and grasslands enclosed by aspen.

STATUS

Sporadic. Most often this species occurs at very low densities and is seldom encountered in traplines. Occasionally the population will increase and large numbers of specimens may be collected.

SIMILAR SPECIES

Meadow Voles are larger, and lack the salt and pepper pelage. The most definitive character is the presence of a fifth loop on the upper M2.

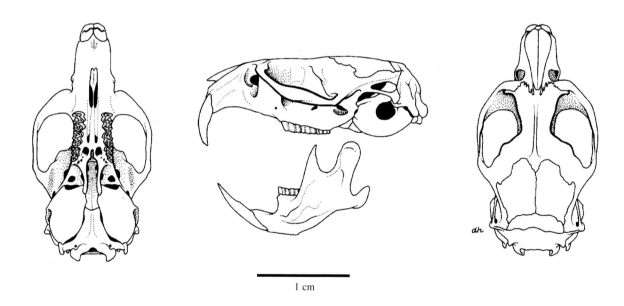

1 cm

Measurements

Sex	Weight (g)	Total Length (mm)	Tail (mm)	Hindfoot (mm)	Ear (mm)
Males (N=1)	26	138	30	15	11
Females (N=1)	--	130	25	17	--

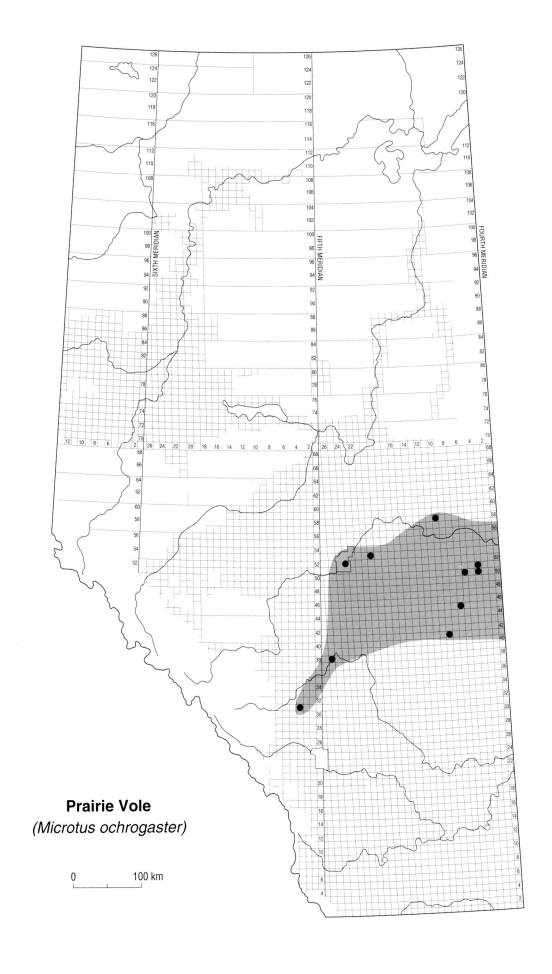

Prairie Vole
(Microtus ochrogaster)

0   100 km

WATER VOLE
Microtus richardsoni

IDENTIFYING CHARACTERS

This is the largest vole in Alberta (weighs up to 160 g). The hindfeet are also noticeably large. The pelage is reddish brown. It is darker along the back and gray on the belly. The tail is bicolored and is well furred.

The skull is robust and angular with a long, narrow rostrum. The incisive foramen is extremely constricted at the posterior end. The auditory bullae are relatively small. The cheek teeth are large and the upper incisors extend past the nasal bones. The dental formula is I 1/1, C 0/0, P 0/0, M 3/3 x 2 = 16.

DISTRIBUTION

Along the mountains in southwestern Alberta.

HABITAT

Alpine meadows in the vicinity of swift, clear streams.

STATUS

Uncommon. It may occur in fair numbers in certain areas but may be absent from other areas that appear to have similar habitat.

SIMILAR SPECIES

Taiga Voles are slightly smaller and have a patch of rust around the nose. The incisive foramen is long and narrow and does not flare at the front. These voles are not found in the mountains.

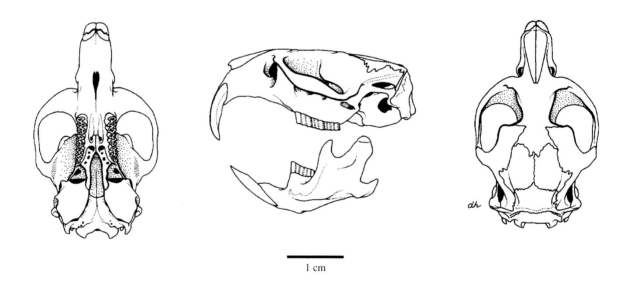

1 cm

Measurements

Sex		Weight (g)	Total Length (mm)	Tail (mm)	Hindfoot (mm)
Males (N=7)	Mean	149.0 (N=2)	245.4	72.6	27.9
	Range	137-161 (N=2)	228-259	64-80	27-30
Females (N=6)	Mean	--	234.2	67.6	27.8
	Range	--	229-240	62-78	27-29

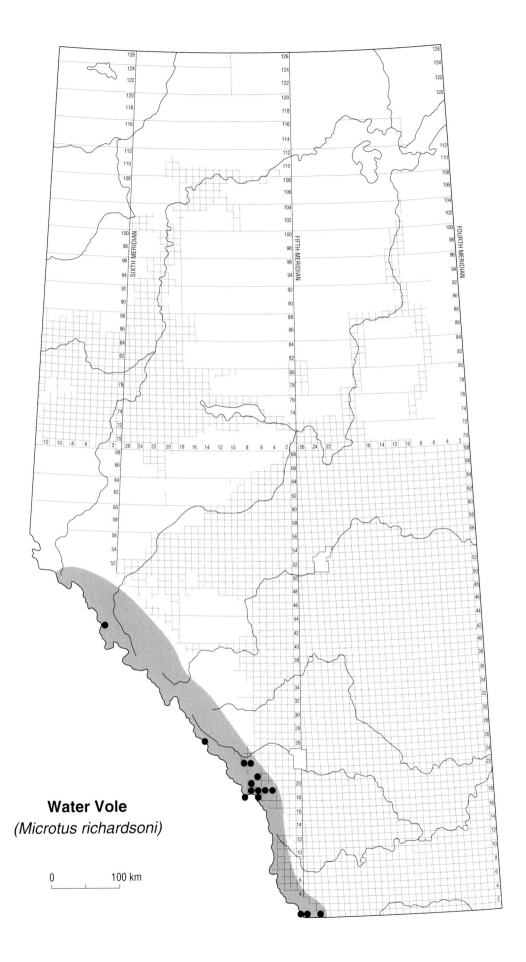

Water Vole
(Microtus richardsoni)

0   100 km

SAGEBRUSH VOLE
Lagurus curtatus

IDENTIFYING CHARACTERS

This the only sandy-colored vole found in Alberta. The pelage is long and lax. It is a pale sandy color that is darker on the back and lighter on the belly. The tail is very short.

The skull is angular with a short rostrum. In profile, the skull is flat and there may be a noticeable depression in the frontal region. The auditory bullae extend past the occiput. The re-entrant angles of the cheek teeth are nearly equal in depth but they are more widely spaced than in other small Alberta voles.

DISTRIBUTION

The Sagebrush Vole is found in the grassland areas of southern Alberta. It occurs as far north as Compeer in the east and Cochrane and the Porcupine Hills in the west.

HABITAT

Confined to those areas of the grassland where sagebrush is common.

STATUS

Uncommon. There may be localities where this species is common but overall it is not.

SIMILAR SPECIES

Meadow Voles and *Long-tailed Voles* are the only voles that occur within the range and habitat of this species. Both are much larger with longer tails, and are considerably darker.

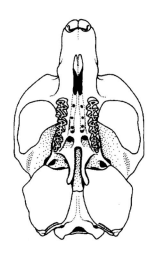 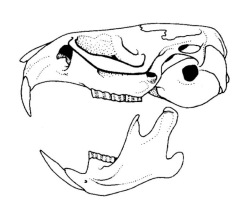 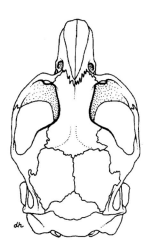

1 cm

Measurements

Sex		Weight (g)	Total Length (mm)	Tail (mm)	Hindfoot (mm)	Ear (mm)
Females (N=7)	Mean	29.8 *(N=3)*	126.4	18.6	17.4	10.3 *(N=3)*
	Range	29.0-30.5 *(N=3)*	116-134	16-20	16-18	9-11 *(N=3)*

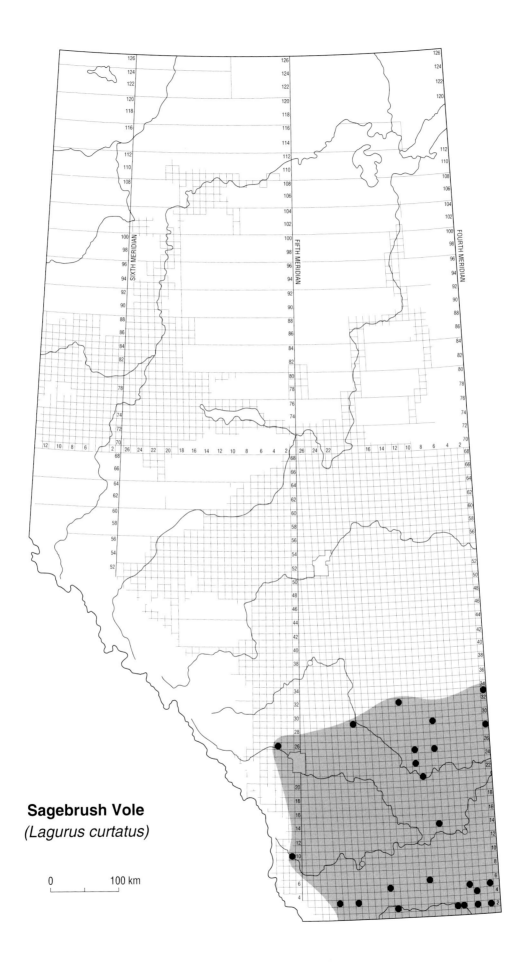

Sagebrush Vole
(Lagurus curtatus)

0   100 km

MUSKRAT
Ondatra zibethicus

Rodentia: Cricetidae

(plate 8)

IDENTIFYING CHARACTERS
This chunky vole is the largest one in Alberta. The pelage has long, lustrous guard hairs and a dense underfur. The underfur is lead-gray and the guard hairs vary from reddish brown to almost black. The tail is long, laterally compressed, and sparsely haired. The hindfeet are large with webbing between the toes. The frontfeet are smaller. The ears and eyes are small.

The skull is large and robust with a long rostrum. The cheek teeth are large with deep re-entrant angles. The upper incisors have an orange pigmentation and project slightly beyond the nasal bones. The dental formula is I 1/1, C 0/0, P 0/0, M 3/3 x 2 = 16.

DISTRIBUTION
Muskrats are found throughout the province wherever there is long-standing or permanent water.

HABITAT
Sloughs, lakes, marshes, streams.

STATUS
Common.

SIMILAR SPECIES
No other species should be confused with the Muskrat.

Beavers are much larger and have large, flattened tails.

Norway Rats are smaller, more slender-bodied, and have a thin, round tail.

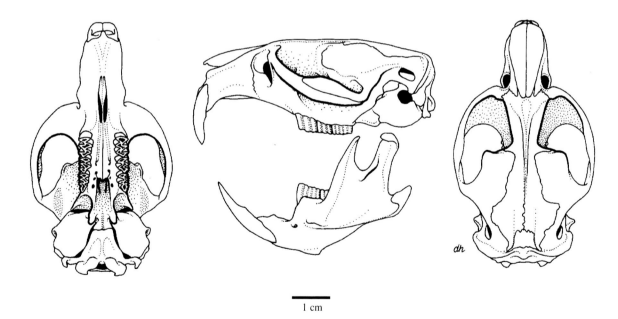

1 cm

Measurements

Sex		Weight (g)	Total Length (mm)	Tail (mm)	Hindfoot (mm)	Ear (mm)
Males (N=5)	Mean	1110.2	550.2	231.0	73.2	22.8
	Range	912-1438	520-585	210-250	68-77	19-25
Females (N=6)	Mean	1040.3	554.2	240.7	75.0	21.5
	Range	992-1120	533-585	217-268	72-80	17-24

130

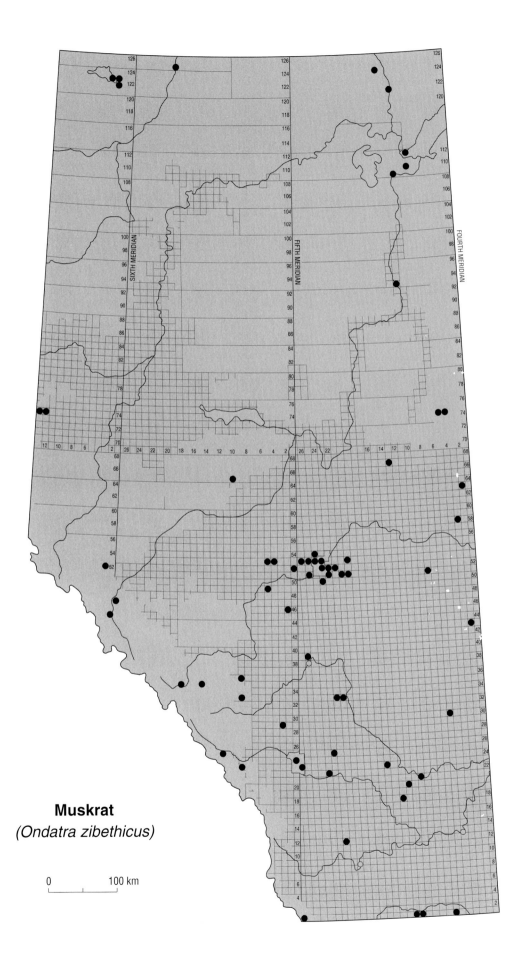

Muskrat

(Ondatra zibethicus)

0   100 km

131

BROWN LEMMING
Lemmus sibiricus

IDENTIFYING CHARACTERS

This chunky, short-tailed mouse is the most brightly colored mouse in Alberta. The base color of the pelage is reddish brown with shades of light orange or tawny on the hindquarters. The belly is dark gray tinged with buff. The tail is extremely short and well furred. The ears are short and hidden in the long fur.

The skull is rugose and angular. The zygomatic arches are sturdy and flare widely. The rostrum is short, the interorbital region is constricted, and the braincase is broad. The upper tooth rows diverge posteriorly. The outer re-entrant angles of the upper cheek teeth and the inner re-entrant angles of the lower teeth are very deep. The dental formula is I 1/1, C 0/0, P 0/0, M 3/3 x 2 = 16.

DISTRIBUTION

The only two museum specimens from Alberta (Smith and Edmonds 1985) were collected in the northern portion of the Rocky Mountains of Alberta.

HABITAT

The most recent specimen was obtained in hummocky, dwarf shrub-sedge meadow habitat in a subalpine forest at an elevation of 1500 metres (Smith and Edmonds 1985).

STATUS

Uncommon. The most recent museum specimen was picked up beside a lake where it had presumably drowned. Twenty-one carcasses were counted on the shore at that time. If the species occurs on a regular basis, it is extremely limited in distribution and probably not common.

SIMILAR SPECIES

None. It is the most brightly colored mouse in Alberta, with relatively short legs, rotund body, ears hidden in the long fur, and an extremely short tail.

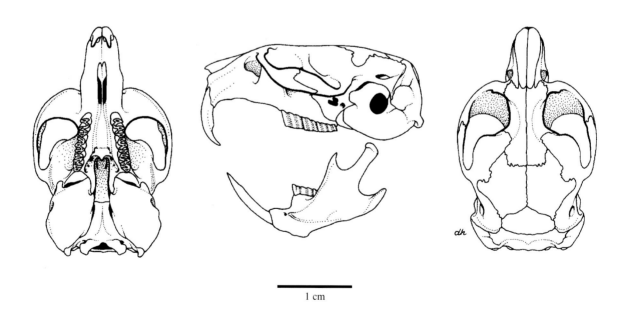

1 cm

Measurements

Sex	Weight (g)	Total Length (mm)	Tail (mm)	Hindfoot (mm)	Ear (mm)
Male (N=1)	37.6	122	15	20	12

132

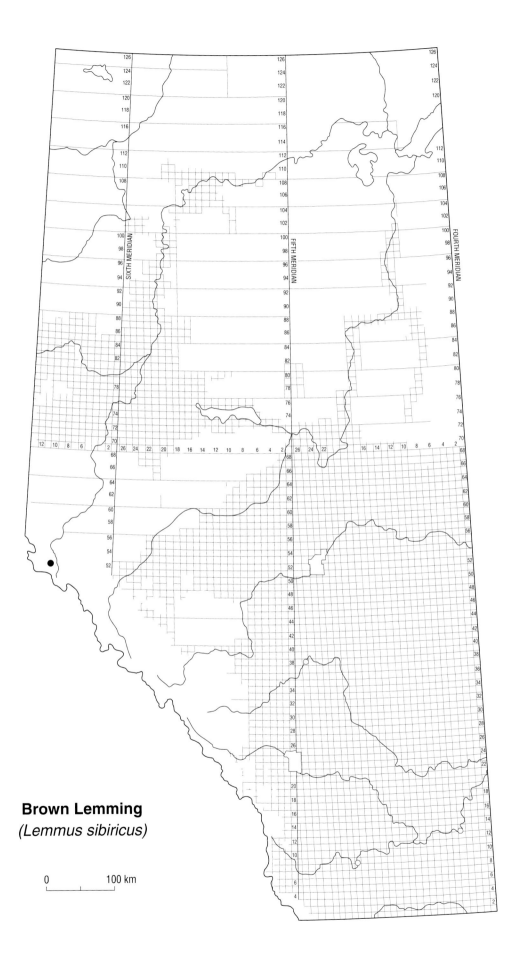

Brown Lemming
(Lemmus sibiricus)

0   100 km

NORTHERN BOG LEMMING
Synaptomys borealis

Rodentia: Cricetidae

IDENTIFYING CHARACTERS

The Northern Bog Lemming has an extremely short tail, grooved upper incisors, and molars with extremely deep re-entrant angles. The pelage is a grizzled, reddish brown on the back and gray on the belly. The hair is relatively long and loose. The very short tail is bicolored. The ears are concealed in the long pelage.

The skull is robust and angular with a short rostrum and a narrow interorbital region. The upper incisors are grooved with the groove near the outer edge. The re-entrant angles of the cheek teeth are very deep. The dental formula is I 1/1, C 0/0, P 0/0, M 3/3 x 2 = 16.

DISTRIBUTION

The Northern Bog Lemming is found throughout the northern forests south to the Cold Lake area in the east, Ministik Lake and Battle Lake in the central portion of the province,

and through the foothills and mountains to the Kananaskis area.

HABITAT

Moist meadows and bogs in the northern forest and subalpine areas.

STATUS

Uncommon. Although widely distributed, most records are of single specimens captured during general surveys.

SIMILAR SPECIES

Meadow Voles are much larger with a longer tail. The upper incisors are without longitudinal grooves. The cheek teeth have re-entrant angles of equal depth.

Heather Voles have upper incisors lacking longitudinal grooves. Cheek teeth are rooted. The tail is longer.

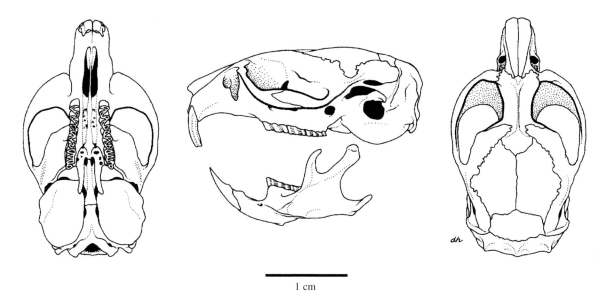

1 cm

Measurements

Sex		Weight (g)	Total Length (mm)	Tail (mm)	Hindfoot (mm)	Ear (mm)
Males (N=15)	Mean	31.5 (N=5)	126.5	19.9	19.0	13.8 (N=6)
	Range	27.9-36.8 (N=5)	120-138	15-24	18-20	13-16 (N=6)
Females (N=4)	Mean	--	127.8	20.5	17.7	--
	Range	--	124-133	18-24	17-19	--

134

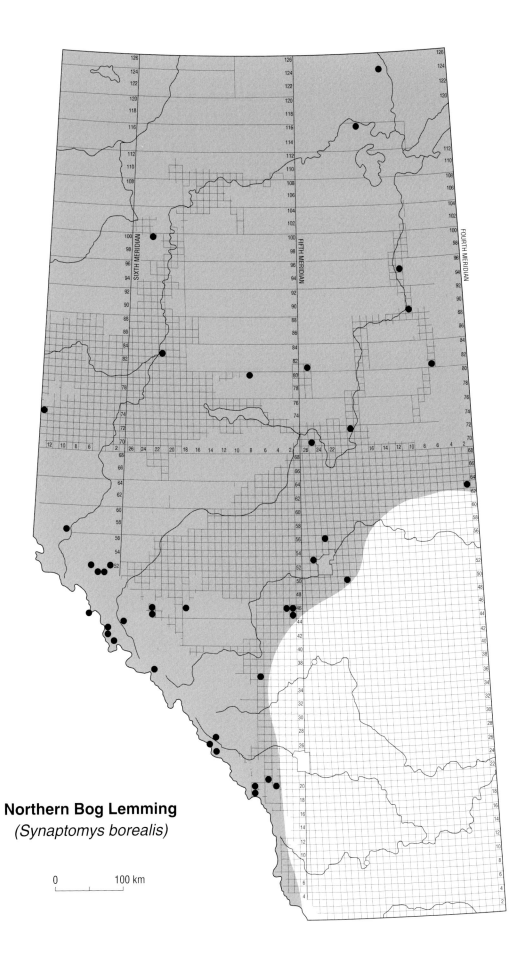

Northern Bog Lemming
(Synaptomys borealis)

0   100 km

BLACK RAT
Rattus rattus

IDENTIFYING CHARACTERS

The Black Rat is a medium-sized, long-tailed rodent with a pelage that is long and coarse. The pelage is dark gray or brown on the back and smoky gray on the belly. The tail is long and slender. It is longer than the head-body length and is sparsely haired and scaly. The ears are large (greater than 20 mm from the notch) and hairless.

The skull is long and narrow. The prominent temporal ridges bow outward in the middle. The cheek teeth are large, but are smaller than in the Norway Rat. The cusps are arranged in rows of three. The dental formula is I 1/1, C 0/0, P 0/0, M 3/3 x 2 = 16.

DISTRIBUTION

Small numbers of Black Rats have been captured in both Edmonton and Calgary. However, Soper (1964) does not mention this species in his account.

HABITAT

Human habitations.

STATUS

Rare in Alberta. The Black Rat, like the Norway Rat is subject to severe control measures.

SIMILAR SPECIES

Norway Rats are the more common of the two. They are stouter-bodied and have larger teeth. The length of the tail is less than the head-body length, and the shorter ears (less than 20 mm) have a covering of fine hairs. Temporal ridges on the skull are parallel.

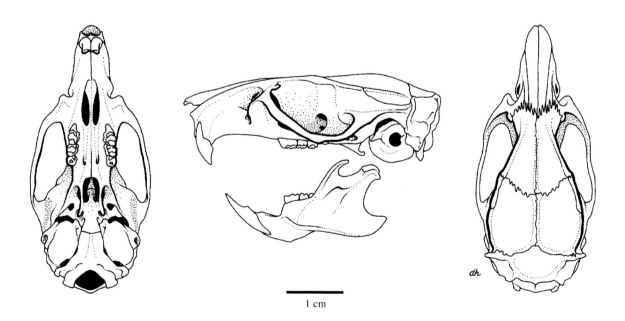

1 cm

Measurements

Sex	Weight (g)	Total Length (mm)	Tail (mm)	Hindfoot (mm)	Ear (mm)
Male (N=1)	206.5	416	238	38	29

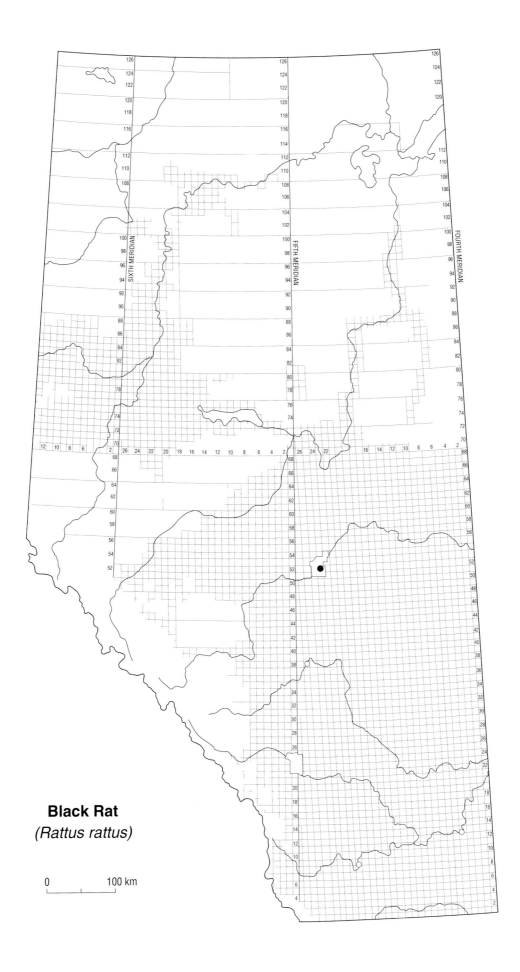

Black Rat

(Rattus rattus)

0   100 km

NORWAY RAT
Rattus norvegicus

IDENTIFYING CHARACTERS

This rodent has a large head, a plump body, and a long scaly tail. The pelage is long and coarse and is reddish brown on the back and gray on the belly. The tail is stout and shorter than the head-body length. The ears are large but less than 20 mm long and are covered with fine hairs.

The skull is long and relatively narrow with parallel temporal ridges. The cheek teeth are large, and upper molars have cusps in three longitudinal rows. The dental formula is I 1/1, C 0/0, P 0/0, M 3/3 x 2 = 16.

DISTRIBUTION

The Norway Rat is strictly controlled by provincial pest control officers. It has not been able to establish itself in Alberta. These rats accompany human enterprises and disperse using various modes of human transportation. Most records are from along the Alberta-Saskatchewan border.

HABITAT

Houses, warehouses, granaries, garbage dumps, and farmsteads.

STATUS

Uncommon to rare.

SIMILAR SPECIES

Black Rats are slimmer and darker with a longer, thinner tail. The large ears are hairless. Ears are greater than 20 mm. Temporal ridges are not parallel.

Muskrats have a plumper body, larger hind feet, a glossier pelage, and a longer, laterally compressed tail.

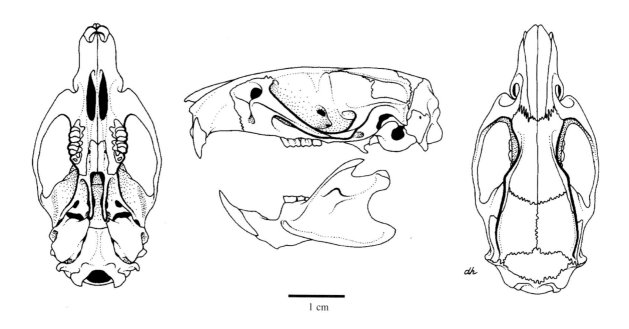

1 cm

Measurements

Sex	Total Length (mm)	Tail (mm)	Hindfoot (mm)	Ear (mm)
Male (N=1)	407	185	43	17
Female (N=1)	375	167	41	20

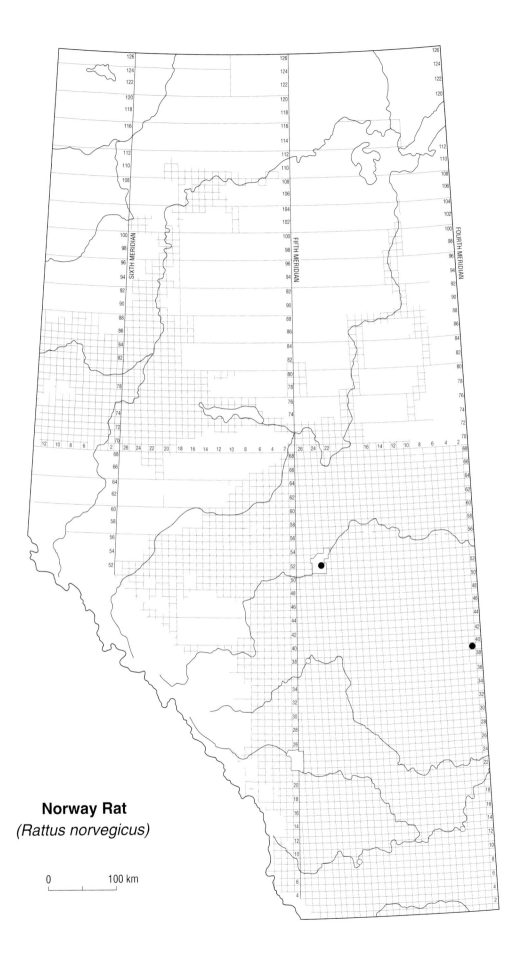

Norway Rat
(Rattus norvegicus)

0   100 km

HOUSE MOUSE
Mus musculus

Rodentia: Muridae

IDENTIFYING CHARACTERS

The House Mouse is a small, uniformly gray mouse with a long, sparsely haired, scaly tail, and large, almost hairless, ears. The pelage is darker on the back and lighter gray on the sides. The sides may have a slight yellow wash. The belly is smoky gray.

The skull is delicate and relatively flat. The cheek teeth are small and upper molars have cusps in three longitudinal rows. The palate extends past the last molars. The dental formula is I 1/1, C 0/0, P 0/0, M 3/3 x 2 = 16.

DISTRIBUTION

House Mice can occur wherever there is human habitation. There have, however, been no records from the extreme northern parts of the province or from the mountain parks. Holroyd and Van Tighem (1983) reported a specimen collected from Canmore. "Wild" House Mice have been collected at several places on the grasslands.

HABITAT

The usual habitat for this mouse is human habitations. In southeastern Alberta they have been collected around granaries and shrubby areas on the open grasslands.

STATUS

Common.

SIMILAR SPECIES

Deer Mice are larger with a bicolored pelage. The upper cheek teeth have cusps in two longitudinal rows.

Western Harvest Mice have grooved upper incisors.

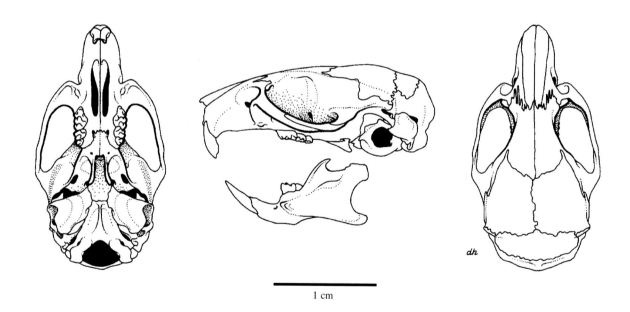

1 cm

Measurements

Sex		Weight (g)	Total Length (mm)	Tail (mm)	Hindfoot (mm)	Ear (mm)
Males (N=14)	Mean	21.7	165.6	79.8	18.6	14.1
	Range	16.4-26.9	147-181	71-88	17-20	11-16
Females (N=6)	Mean	26.1	174	85.5	19.0	15.3
	Range	16.9-43.1	161-193	78-90	18-21	13-16

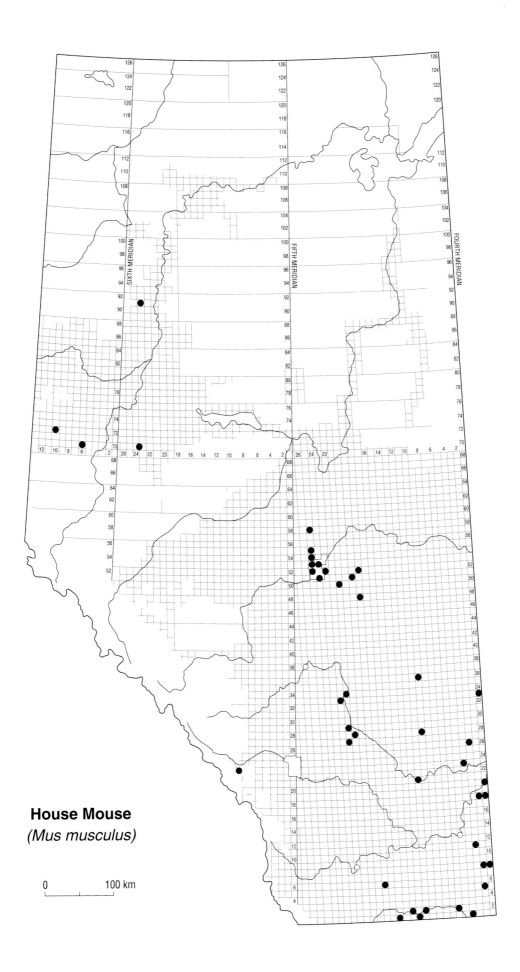

House Mouse
(Mus musculus)

0   100 km

MEADOW JUMPING MOUSE
Zapus hudsonius

Rodentia: Zapodidae

IDENTIFYING CHARACTERS

Jumping mice have remarkably long tails, large hind feet, and long, coarse hair. The Meadow Jumping Mouse is generally small and the pelage is light. There is a broad, dark stripe along the back; the sides are lighter with a faint, thin orange-yellow line separating the sides from the white belly. Occasionally the belly is washed with pale orange. The eyes are large and the ears are small.

The skull is short and narrow (skull length mean 23.25 mm, range 22.42-23.96 mm, and zygomatic width mean 11.32 mm, range 10.76-11.87 mm) with large, oval infra-orbital foramina. The incisive foramina are short (mean 4.46 mm, range 4.29-4.60 mm) and the sides bow outward. The posterior portion of the septum that separates the incisive foramina is broad. The upper incisors are deeply grooved and heavily pigmented. There are four teeth in the upper cheek tooth row. The premolar is small and peglike. The length of the upper tooth row averages 3.61 mm (range 3.34-3.74 mm). The dental formula is I 1/1, C 0/0, P 1/0, M 3/3 x 2 = 18.

DISTRIBUTION

The northern three-quarters of the province. It has not been recorded from the grasslands or the mountains and foothills.

HABITAT

Moist meadows especially areas along streams and bogs.

STATUS

Common.

SIMILAR SPECIES

Western Jumping Mice are generally larger and more robust. The skull is longer and wider, the upper tooth row is longer, and the pelage of the belly has a stronger orange tinge. The septum that divides the incisive foramen is very thin. The sides of the incisive foramen are parallel and the foramen is longer.

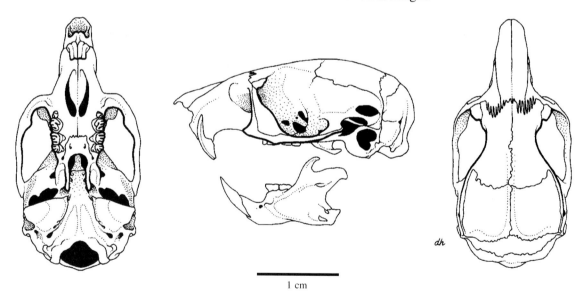

1 cm

Measurements

Sex		Weight (g)	Total Length (mm)	Tail (mm)	Hindfoot (mm)	Ear (mm)
Males (N=25)	Mean	17.5	209.6	129.7	30.6	15.5
	Range	14.0-22.2	180-225	106-138	27-36	13-19
Females (N=15)	Mean	18.6	214.1	130.7	30.9	14.7
	Range	13.1-24.8	200-233	120-144	29-32	12-16

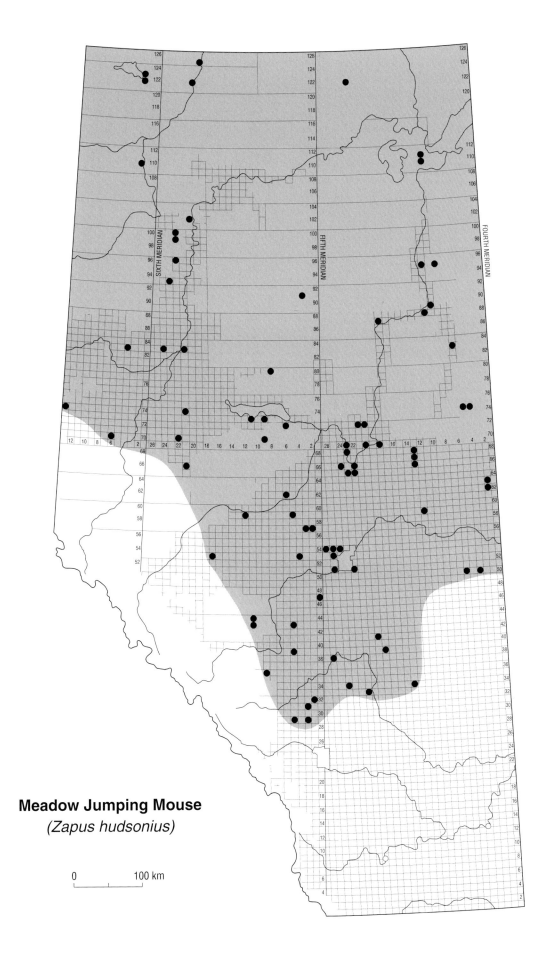

Meadow Jumping Mouse
(Zapus hudsonius)

0   100 km

WESTERN JUMPING MOUSE
Zapus princeps

IDENTIFYING CHARACTERS

The pelage is relatively coarse. There is a broad, dark, olive-brown stripe along the back. The sides are lighter and are washed with a pale orange tinge. A thin, pale creamy-orange line separates the sides from the belly. The belly is whitish and may have a faint orange wash. The extremely long and tapered tail appears scaly and hairless. It is, however, bicolored, dark on top, light on the underside. The hindlegs are much larger than the frontlegs.

The skull is delicate with large, oval infraorbital foramina. The posterior portion of the septum separating the two incisive foramina is extremely thin. The sides of the incisive foramina are parallel and average 2.56 mm apart (range 2.25-2.97 mm). The foramen length averages 5.44 mm (range 4.80-5.81 mm). The nasal bones extend past the upper incisors which are heavily pigmented and grooved. The upper tooth row consists of four teeth. The premolar is small and peg-like. The length of the upper tooth row averages 4.20 mm (range 3.89-4.46 mm). The dental formula is I 1/1, C 0/0, P 1/0, M 3/3 x 2 = 18.

DISTRIBUTION

Throughout the southern half of the province. The northern border trends in a northwest-southeast direction from Ray Lake in the west, south of Lesser Slave Lake in the centre, to just south of Cold Lake in the east.

HABITAT

Moist meadows bordered by brush or along streams.

STATUS

Common.

SIMILAR SPECIES

Meadow Jumping Mice are smaller with a shorter, narrower skull. The posterior portion of the septum that separates the incisive foramina is wide. The foramina are short and the sides bow outward.

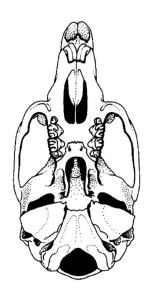 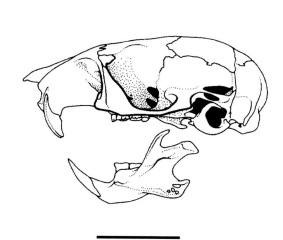 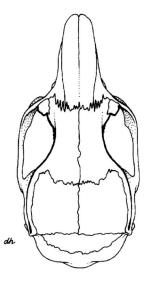

1 cm

Measurements

Sex		Weight (g)	Total Length (mm)	Tail (mm)	Hindfoot (mm)	Ear (mm)
Males (N=25)	Mean	27.1	235.3	141.9	31.2	15.0
	Range	21.2-35.5	219-274	126-176	29-35	13-18
Females (N=15)	Mean	30.0	236.2	141.6	31.1	15.5
	Range	23.8-37.0	215-249	124-152	28-33	13-17

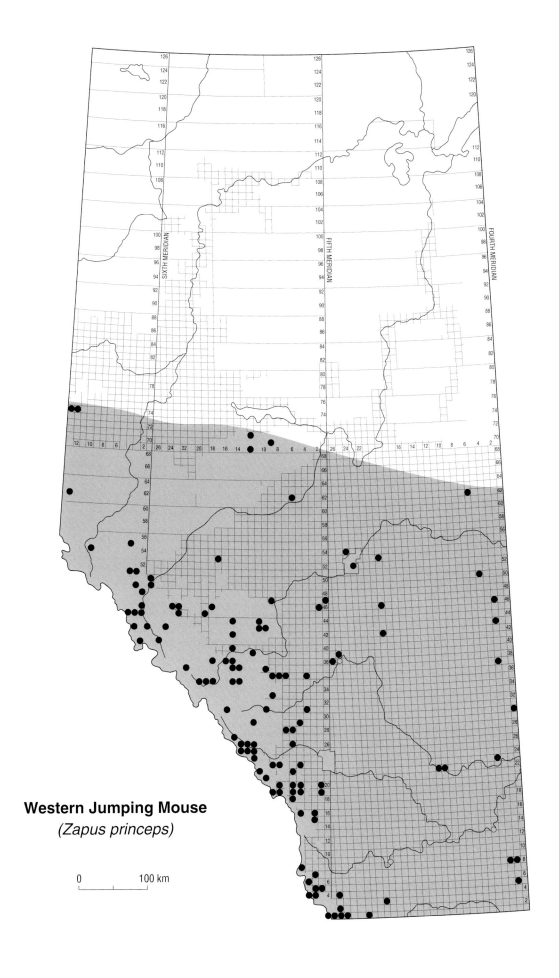

Western Jumping Mouse
(Zapus princeps)

0   100 km

PORCUPINE
Erethizon dorsatum

IDENTIFYING CHARACTERS

The Porcupine is a large (weighs up to 12 kg), cumbersome-looking, slow-moving rodent. The head, back, sides, and tail are covered with sharp, stiff quills. The pale yellow guard hairs are long and coarse. The underfur is dense and woolly, and is dark brown or black. The soles of the feet are naked and the toes have strong, sharp claws. The tail is stout and muscular with quills on the sides and top.

The massive skull features large infra-orbital foramina. The upper incisors are heavily pigmented and extend well past the nasal bones. The cheek teeth are large. The dental formula is I 1/1, C 0/0, P 1/1, M 3/3 x 2 = 20.

DISTRIBUTION

Found throughout the province.

HABITAT

Mixed forests in the north and wooded riparian areas in the south.

STATUS

Common.

SIMILAR SPECIES

Beavers have skulls as large but they lack the large infra-orbital foramen.

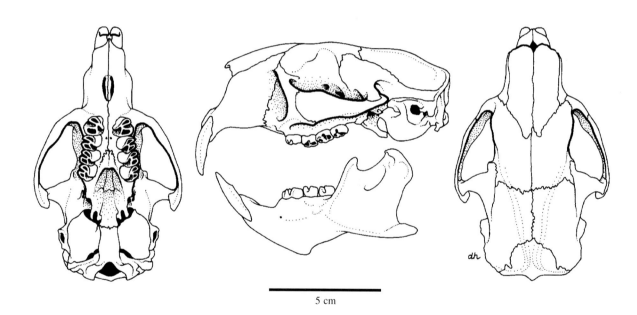

5 cm

Measurements

Sex		Weight (kg)	Total Length (mm)	Tail (mm)	Hindfoot (mm)
Males (N=7)	Mean	9.1	783.3	220.4	104.0
	Range	6.3-11.6	708-870	180-280	90-117
Females (N=4)	Mean	8.9	774.8	227.5	96.0
	Range	7.3-9.8	710-905	196-285	90-101

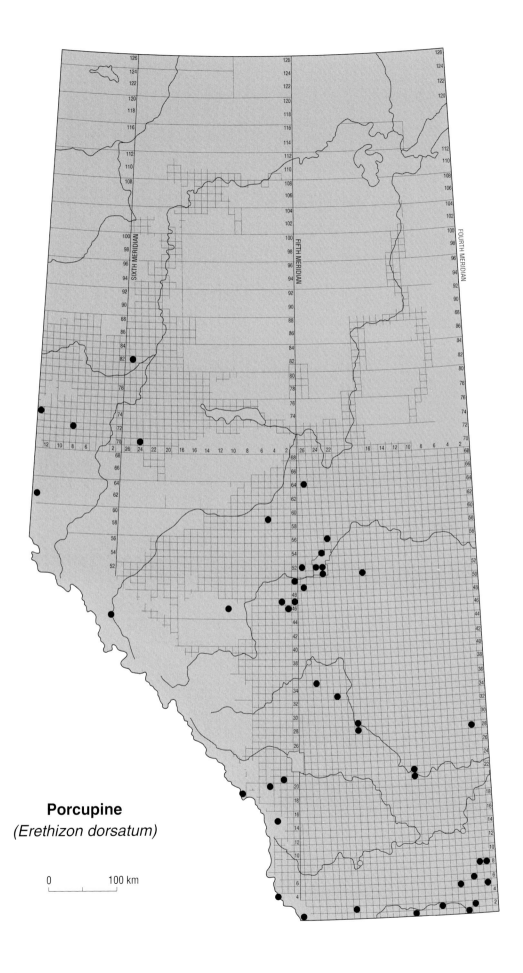

Porcupine

(Erethizon dorsatum)

0   100 km

Little Brown Bat   Text: p. 36
Myotis lucifugus

Northern Long-eared Bat   Text: p. 38
Myotis septentrionalis

Long-eared Bat   Text: p. 40
Myotis evotis

Western Small-footed Bat   Text: p. 44
Myotis ciliolabrum

Plate 1

Merlin D. Tuttle, Bat Conservation International

Silver-haired Bat   Text: p. 46
Lasionycteris noctivagans

Red Bat   Text: p. 50
Lasiurus borealis

Hoary Bat   Text: p. 52
Lasiurus cinereus

Pika   Text: p. 56
Ochotona princeps

Plate 2

Nuttall's Cottontail   Text: p. 58
Sylvilagus nuttallii

Snowshoe Hare   Text: p. 60
Lepus americanus

White-tailed Jack Rabbit   Text: p. 62
Lepus townsendii

Least Chipmunk   Text: p. 70
Tamias minimus

Plate 3

Woodchuck   Text: p. 76
Marmota monax

Yellow-bellied Marmot   Text: p. 78
Marmota flaviventris

Hoary Marmot   Text: p. 80
Marmota caligata

Richardson's Ground Squirrel   Text: p. 82
Spermophilus richardsonii

Plate 4

Columbian Ground Squirrel
Spermophilus columbianus

Text: p. 84

Thirteen-lined Ground Squirrel
Spermophilus tridecemlineatus

Text: p. 86

Franklin's Ground Squirrel
Spermophilus franklinii

Text: p. 88

Plate 5

Golden-mantled Ground Squirrel
Spermophilus lateralis

Text: p. 90

Gray Squirrel
Sciurus carolinensis

Text: p. 92

Red Squirrel
Tamiasciurus hudsonicus

Text: p. 94

Northern Flying Squirrel
Glaucomys sabrinus

Text: p. 96

Plate 6

Ord's Kangaroo Rat   Text: p. 102
Dipodomys ordii

Beaver   Text: p. 104
Castor canadensis

Bushy-tailed Woodrat   Text: p. 112
Neotoma cinerea

Plate 7

Southern Red-backed Vole — Text: p. 114
Clethrionomys gapperi

Meadow Vole — Text: p. 118
Microtus pennsylvanicus

Muskrat — Text: p. 130
Ondatra zibethicus

Brown Lemming — Text: p. 132
Lemmus sibiricus

Plate 8

Porcupine   Text: p. 146
Erethizon dorsatum

Coyote   Text: p. 152
Canis latrans

Gray Wolf   Text: p. 154
Canis lupus

Arctic Fox   Text: p. 156
Alopex lagopus

Plate 9

Red Fox   Text: p. 158
Vulpes vulpes

Swift Fox   Text: p. 160
Vulpes velox

Plate 10

Gray Fox   Text: p. 162
Urocyon cinereoargenteus

Black Bear   Text: p. 164
Ursus americanus

Grizzly Bear   Text: p. 166
Ursus arctos

Raccoon   Text: p. 168
Procyon lotor

Plate 11

Ermine					Text: p. 174
Mustela erminea

B. M. Wolitski; Photo courtesy Alberta Fish and Wildlife

Long-tailed Weasel				Text: p. 178
Mustela frenata

Mink					Text: p. 182
Mustela vison

B. M. Wolitski; Photo courtesy Alberta Fish and Wildlife

Wolverine				Text: p. 184
Gulo gulo

Plate 12

Badger   Text: p. 186
Taxidea taxus

Striped Skunk   Text: p. 188
Mephitis mephitis

B. M. Wolitski: Photo courtesy Alberta Fish and Wildlife

River Otter   Text: p. 190
Lutra canadensis

Cougar   Text: p. 192
Felis concolor

Plate 13

Canada Lynx   Text: p. 194
Felis canadensis

Wapiti   Text: p. 202
Cervus elaphus

Mule Deer   Text: p. 204
Odocoileus hemionus

White-tailed Deer   Text: p. 206
Odocoileus virginianus

Plate 14

Moose   Text: p. 208
Alces alces

Caribou   Text: p. 210
Rangifer tarandus

Pronghorn   Text: p. 212
Antilocapra americana

Plate 15

Bison   Text: p. 214
Bison bison

Mountain Goat   Text: p. 216
Oreamnos americanus

Bighorn Sheep   Text: p. 218
Ovis canadensis

Plate 16

Order: Carnivora

This is a widespread Order with terrestrial members occupying most land masses except for Australia, Antarctica, and the oceanic islands. They are characterized by large, conical canines present in all species. The fourth upper premolar (P4) and the first lower molar (M1) work together in a shearing fashion and are termed "carnassial teeth." The molars behind the carnassials are frequently reduced in number.

Throughout the world there are 10 families with approximately 270 species (Anderson and Jones 1984). There are 23 species in six families in Alberta. They range in size from the Least Weasel (21 g) to the Grizzly Bear (450 kg). Many species in this group are valuable fur bearers. Some are considered agricultural pests while others provide economic benefit by consuming rodents.

Key to the Carnivores (Carnivora)

1. Claws retractable; fewer than 30 teeth 2
   Claws always visible; more than 30 teeth 4

2. Tail over 700 mm; weight greater than 36 kg; 30 teeth . . . . *Felis concolor* (p. 192)
   Tail less than 200 mm; weight less than 20 kg; 28 teeth 3

3. Tip of tail black on both top and bottom, tail lacks barring; ear tufts
      long; feet large (hindfoot length greater than 220 mm) . . . . *Lynx canadensis* (p. 194)
   Tip of tail black on top only, bottom of tail white, faint barring
      on tail; ear tufts short; feet small (hindfoot length less than
      185 mm) . . . . *Lynx rufus* (p. 196)

4. Teeth 40 or more 5
   Fewer than 40 teeth 13

5. Tail bushy with black bands; black band across eyes; 40 teeth . . . . . *Procyon lotor* (p. 168)
   Tail length variable; 42 teeth 6

6. Weight 80 kg or greater; tail extremely short 7
   Weight less than 80 kg; tail long and bushy 8

7. Front claws longer than hind claws; hump on shoulders; facial
      profile 'dished' or concave; upper M2 longer than 31mm . . . . *Ursus arctos* (p. 166)
   Front claws approximately same length as hind claws; forehead
      gently sloped; upper M2 shorter than 31 mm . . . . *Ursus americanus* (p. 164)

Ursus arctos   *Ursus americanus*

concave facial profile

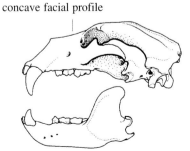
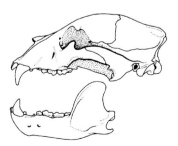

8.   Weight greater than 7 kg; hindfoot greater than 170 mm; condylobasal
     length greater than 160 mm 9
     Weight less than 7 kg; hindfoot less than 175 mm; condylobasal
     length less than 150 mm 10

9.   Hindfoot greater than 200 mm; nose pad greater than 25 mm wide;
     condylobasal length greater than 210 mm; lower M1 greater than
     25 mm . . . . *Canis lupus* (p. 154)
     Hindfoot less than 200 mm; nose pad less than 25 mm wide; condy-
     lobasal length less than 190 mm; lower M1 less than 25 mm . . . . . *Canis latrans* (p. 152)

10. Total length less than 760 mm; weight less than 2.5 kg . . . . *Vulpes velox* (p. 160)
     Total length greater than 800 mm; weight greater than 2.5 kg 11

11. Dark or black stripe along centre line of tail; prominent temporal
     ridges meet to form U-shape . . . . *Urocyon cinereoargenteus* (p. 162)
     Pelage white to red or brownish; temporal ridges not prominent . . . 12

Urocyon cinereoargenteus   *Vulpes vulpes*

temporal ridge —

12. Pelage red, orange-red, or black and silver, but not white; ear
     greater than 89 mm; weight greater than 3.6 kg; rostrum long and
     tapered . . . . *Vulpes vulpes* (p. 158)
     Pelage white or brownish; ear less than 75 mm; weight less than
     3.3 kg; rostrum short and broad . . . . *Alopex lagopus* (p. 156)

13. Weight 2-20 kg and/or pelage black with white stripes 14
     Weight less than 2 kg; pelage brown, tan, or white 18

14. Pelage solid color without stripes 15
     Pelage with one or two stripes 16

15. Tail long, cylindrical, tapering from thick base; toes webbed; head
     flat and broad . . . . *Lutra canadensis* (p. 190)
     Tail long, bushy; toes not webbed . . . . *Martes pennanti* (p. 172)

16. Pelage black with sharply contrasting broad white stripes; tail
     bushy . . . . *Mephitis mephitis* (p. 188)
     Pelage reddish brown or grizzled brown; stripes paler, not sharply
     contrasting, or a short single central stripe 17

17. Legs long; body erect; front claws same length as hind claws;
     pelage reddish brown with two pale flank stripes . . . . *Gulo gulo* (p. 184)

     Legs short; body squat; front claws significantly longer than hind
     claws; pelage grizzled gray, single white stripe from centre of
     head may extend to shoulders, cheeks white, dark patches around
     eyes . . . . *Taxidea taxus* (p. 186)

18. Pelage long, lustrous, reddish brown to dark brown; tail long and
     bushy 19

     Pelage relatively short, brownish to tan or white; tail length
     variable, either short without a black tip or long and black-
     tipped 20

19. Pelage solid color (dark to reddish brown), except for white patch
     on throat; ear less than 28 mm; hindfoot less than 76 mm . . . . *Mustela vison* (p. 182)

     Pelage reddish brown, head grayish, throat patch orange or creamy,
     feet and tail darker; ear greater than 42 mm; hindfoot greater than
     84 mm . . . . *Martes americana* (p. 170)

20. Weight less than 50 g; tail short without black tip . . . . *Mustela nivalis* (p. 176)

     Weight greater than 50 g; tail long and black-tipped 21

21. Feet black, black band across muzzle through eyes . . . . *Mustela nigripes* (p. 180)

     Face lacks black band across muzzle through eyes 22

22. Total length greater than 350 mm; tail length greater than 120 mm;
     summer pelage reddish brown on the back with an orange belly . . *Mustela frenata* (p. 178)

     Total length less than 350 mm; tail length less than 110 mm;
     summer pelage light brown with a white belly washed with
     sulphur-yellow . . . . *Mustela erminea* (p. 174)

COYOTE
Canis latrans

IDENTIFYING CHARACTERS

The Coyote is a medium-sized canid (weighs up to 18 kg). The pelage varies from light yellowish brown to dark sandy brown and is suffused with buff or cinnamon. The back is darker than the sides and there is occasionally a darker band across the shoulders. The tail is long and bushy. The legs are slender and the feet small. A Coyote runs with its tail held low.

The skull is medium-sized. The rostrum is long and narrow and slopes gently to the forehead. The nasal bones are long and narrow and flare at the distal end. The braincase is slightly inflated and in older animals a sagittal crest is evident. The canine teeth are long and slender. The dental formula is I 3/3, C 1/1, P 4/4, M 2/3 x 2 = 42.

DISTRIBUTION

Found throughout the province.

HABITAT

Coyotes have broad habitat tolerances, from open grasslands, to parklands, to dense northern forests.

STATUS

Variable in numbers, Coyotes are common throughout the province.

SIMILAR SPECIES

Gray Wolves are much larger than coyotes, with a larger head, bigger feet, and longer legs. The nose pad of the wolf is larger than that of the Coyote. When running, the wolf holds its tail high.

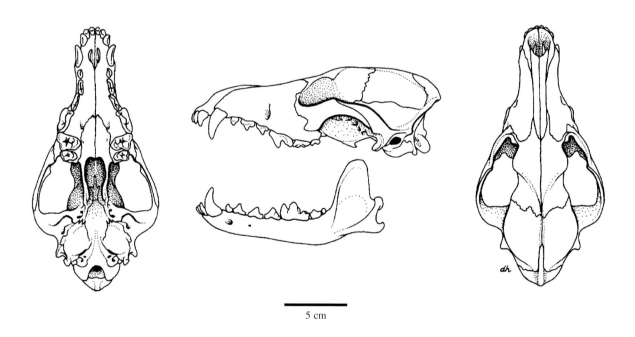

5 cm

Measurements

Sex		Weight (kg)	Total Length (mm)	Tail (mm)	Hindfoot (mm)
Males (N=20)	Mean	13.7 *(N=12)*	1241	368.8	194.7
	Range	11.3-18.1 *(N=12)*	1130-1370	295-460	180-214
Females (N=17)	Mean	11.9 *(N=6)*	1172.2	362.6	182.9
	Range	11.3-13.2 *(N=6)*	1093-1250	290-430	169-203

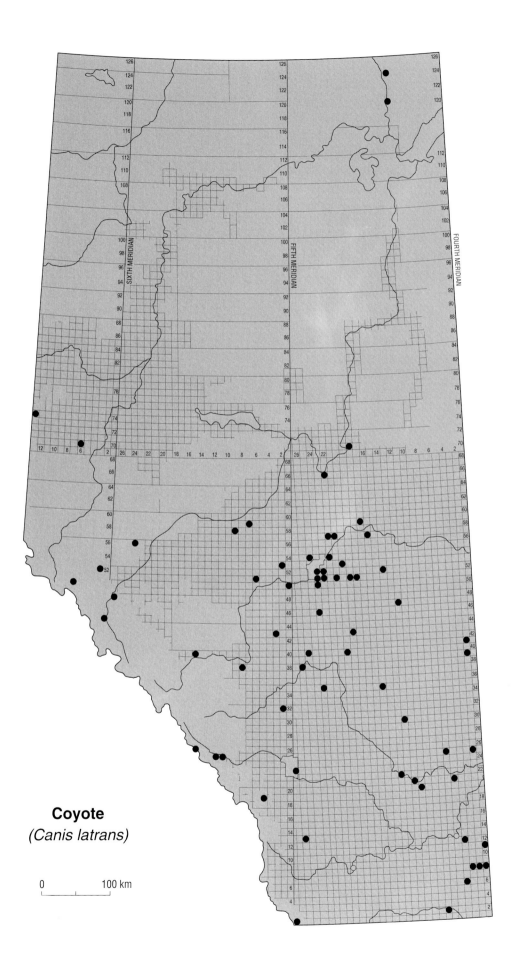

Coyote

(Canis latrans)

0   100 km

GRAY WOLF
Canis lupus

IDENTIFYING CHARACTERS

The Gray Wolf is the largest wild canid in Alberta. It can weigh up to 70 kg (Carbyn 1987). The pelage is extremely variable, ranging from almost pure white to black. The usual color is dark gray with dark hairs sprinkled throughout. The legs are long and the feet are large. A wolf runs with its tail held up.

The skull is large and rugose, the rostrum is long, the canines are large with a broad base, and the carnassial teeth are massive. The dental formula is I 3/3, C 1/1, P 4/4, M 2/3 x 2 = 42.

DISTRIBUTION

The wolf is widely distributed throughout northern Alberta. It occurs south to the Cold Lake area, west to the Swan Hills, then south to Rocky Mountain House, and throughout the western parklands, foothills, and mountains to Waterton Lakes National Park. Extralimital sightings and specimens have been recorded from grassland and grovelands: Elk Island National Park (Burns and Cool 1984), Fenn (PMA specimen), southeastern Alberta (Smith 1986), and Waterton (Nielsen 1973). Nielsen considered the Waterton animals to be wanderers.

HABITAT

The wolf is adaptable to a variety of habitats, from dense forests to open areas.

STATUS

Common. Gunson (1983) estimated the provincial population at approximately 5000 wolves. Carbyn (1987) estimated a population of 4500 and considered the population to be stable.

SIMILAR SPECIES

Coyotes are smaller: smaller head, shorter legs, and smaller feet. When running, the Coyote holds its tail low.

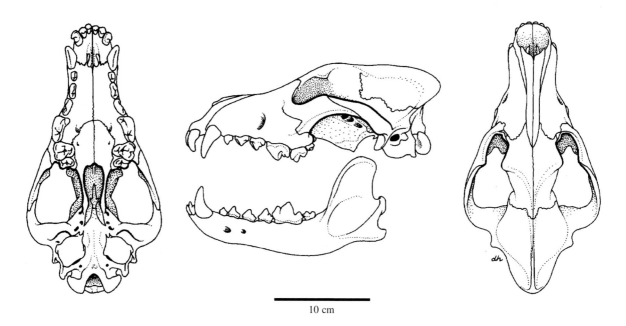

10 cm

Measurements

Sex		Weight (kg)	Total Length (mm)	Tail (mm)	Hindfoot (mm)
Males (N=20)	Mean	45.5	1763.5	472.2	296.9
	Range	26.8-57.6	1655-1870	405-540	280-310
Females (N=20)	Mean	40.9	1662.0	444.8	281.0
	Range	33.6-53.1	1500-1870	400-490	240-300

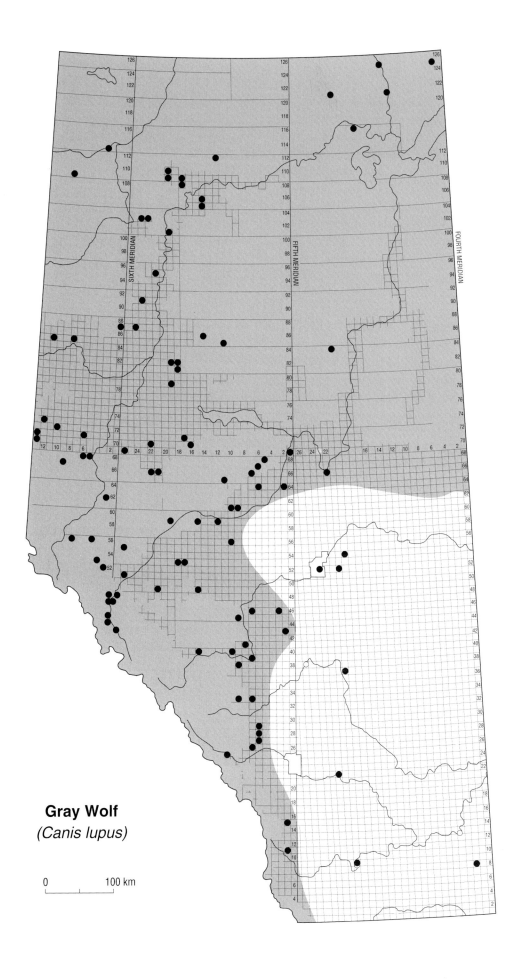

Gray Wolf
(Canis lupus)

0   100 km

ARCTIC FOX
Alopex lagopus

IDENTIFYING CHARACTERS

This small fox is the only Alberta fox that has seasonally distinct pelages. The winter pelage is entirely white and the summer pelage is brownish. The small size, short ears, and long, bushy tail should be sufficient to identify this animal. The soles of the feet are well furred. The winter pelage is dense with long hair.

The skull is small with a short, broad rostrum. The braincase is shorter and broader than other Alberta foxes. The teeth are crowded. The dental formula is I 3/3, C 1/1, P 4/4, M 2/3 x 2 = 42.

DISTRIBUTION

Soper (1942) reported that several of these foxes had been trapped north of Lake Athabasca and east of the Slave River. He also reported that single animals had been trapped 140 miles west of Lake Athabasca and 60 miles north of Fort McMurray (Soper 1964). Boyd (1977), referring to affidavits from trappers, showed a much wider distribution with some reports as far south as 55° N and as far west as 118° W. He did caution, however, that this information may be flawed and that verification by specimen collection had not been made. To date there is only one museum specimen record for this species from Alberta.

HABITAT

Open forested areas in the north.

STATUS

Unknown. Probably a scarce, winter wanderer.

SIMILAR SPECIES

Red Foxes are much larger and have a red, silver, or black pelage.

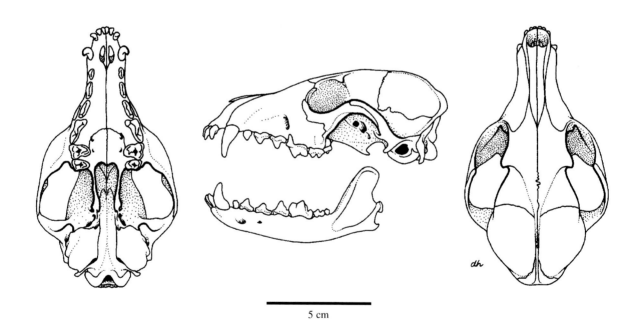

5 cm

Measurements

Sex	Total Length (mm)	Tail (mm)
Male (N=1)	840	293

Note: measurements are from a skinned carcass.

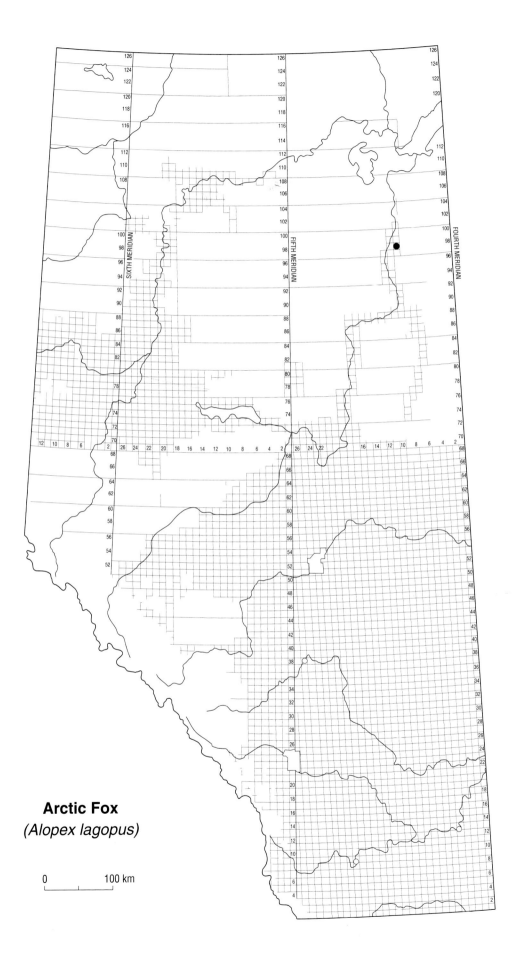

Arctic Fox

(Alopex lagopus)

0   100 km

RED FOX
Vulpes vulpes

IDENTIFYING CHARACTERS

The pelage is rusty or orange-red but occasional black or silver individuals occur. The tail tip is white as is the throat. The back of the ears, the lower legs, and feet are black. The feet are small.

The skull is triangular from above with a long tapered rostrum The cranium is pear-shaped. A sagittal crest occurs in older animals. The dental formula is I 3/3, C 1/1, P 4/4, M 2/3 x 2 = 42.

DISTRIBUTION

Found throughout the province.

HABITAT

Adaptable to a variety of habitats, from open grasslands to dense forests.

STATUS

Until recently the Red Fox could have been considered scarce or uncommon. However, the population has increased considerably in the past few years and it is now common in southern Alberta. In the northern parts of the province it may still be uncommon but indications are that the population is increasing.

SIMILAR SPECIES

Swift Foxes are much smaller and sandy-brown in color with black-tipped tail.

Coyotes are much larger and lighter in color.

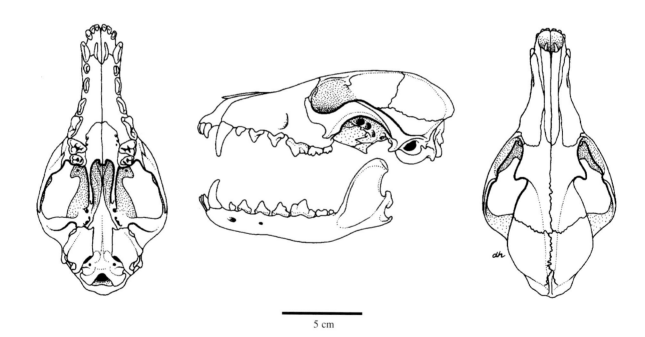

5 cm

Measurements

Sex		Weight (kg)	Total Length (mm)	Tail (mm)	Hindfoot (mm)	Ear (mm)
Males	Mean	4.27 *(N=3)*	1025.5 *(N=4)*	403.0 *(N=4)*	167.8 *(N=4)*	98.3 *(N=3)*
	Range	3.8-4.6 *(N=3)*	942-1110 *(N=4)*	350-443 *(N=4)*	156-174 *(N=4)*	95-102 *(N=3)*
Females	Mean	3.98 *(N=5)*	995.3 *(N=6)*	370.5 *(N=6)*	163.8 *(N=6)*	91.8 *(N=5)*
	Range	3.6-4.3 *(N=5)*	935-1035 *(N=6)*	365-380 *(N=6)*	155-168 *(N=6)*	89-95 *(N=5)*

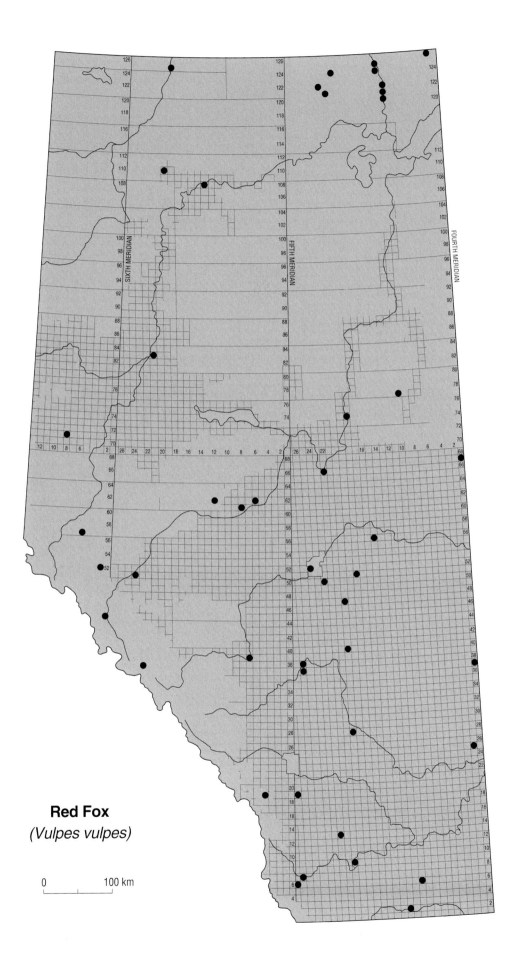

Red Fox

(Vulpes vulpes)

0   100 km

SWIFT FOX
Vulpes velox

IDENTIFYING CHARACTERS

This is the smallest wild canid in Alberta. It weighs less than 3.0 kg and measures about 30 cm high at the shoulder. The pelage is brownish gray with pale orange sides. The throat and belly are white. Dark patches occur on either side of the muzzle and the tip of the tail is black.

The skull is typically canid with a long, narrow rostrum and wide zygomatic arches. The braincase is inflated and relatively smooth. Faint temporal ridges extend from the postorbital processes rearward and meet to form a lyre-shape. The dental formula is I 3/3, C 1/1, P 4/4, M 2/3 x 2 = 42.

DISTRIBUTION

Formerly distributed throughout much of southern Alberta. Any sightings will be of captive-bred animals released to the wild in southeastern Alberta.

HABITAT

Open grasslands.

STATUS

Probably extirpated. Although attempts to release animals into suitable habitat have been made, it is too early at this time to judge if this has been successful.

SIMILAR SPECIES

Red Foxes are much larger and have a rusty-red pelage and white-tipped tail.

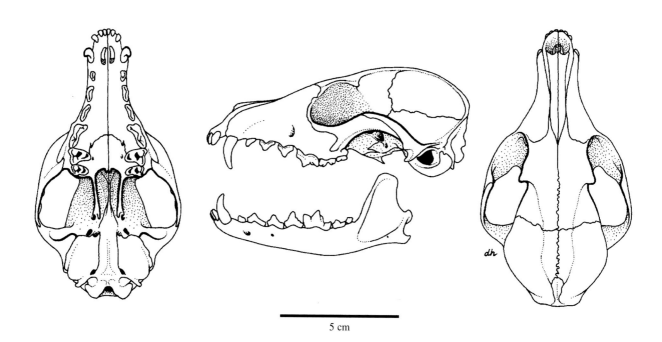

5 cm

Measurements

Sex		Weight (kg)	Total Length (mm)	Tail (mm)	Hindfoot (mm)	Ear (mm)
Females (N=4)	Mean	1.8	734.3	267.8	118.8	66.5
	Range	1.5-2.0	680-757	225-296	110-123	62-70

Note: measurements are from museum specimens that were obtained from animals raised on game farms. None are from wild or native foxes.

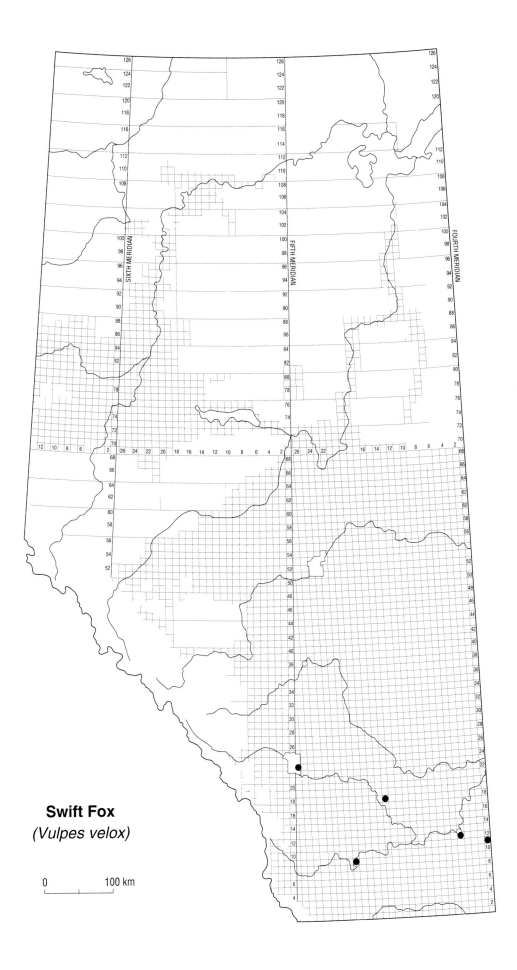

Swift Fox

(Vulpes velox)

0   100 km

161

GRAY FOX
Urocyon cinereoargenteus

IDENTIFYING CHARACTERS

The Gray Fox is a medium-sized canid with a slim body and a long, black-tipped, bushy tail. The pelage is grayish sprinkled with black hairs to give a grizzled appearance. The neck and legs are buffy and the belly and throat are white. There is a dark or black stripe along the centre line of the tail.

The skull has a relatively short, narrow rostrum and a narrow braincase. The temporal ridges are prominent and meet to form a lyre-shape. The mandible has a 'step' at the posterior end of the lower edge. The lyre-shaped temporal ridge and the stepped mandible are distinctive features of the Gray Fox skull.

DISTRIBUTION

Moore (1952b) reported the only provincial record of Gray Fox, a specimen from near Lake Athabasca. Soper (1964) mentioned a gray-colored fox sighted along the Milk River, but its identity is uncertain. The range of the Gray Fox covers much of the United States, exclusive of the Great Basin and Great Plains, south through Mexico to South America. It has been found in Ontario in this century.

HABITAT

Deciduous woodlands.

STATUS

Accidental. Only one Albertan specimen record exists for this animal. There are no records from Montana (Hoffmann and Pattie 1968) or Saskatchewan (Beck 1958). Jones et al. (1983) indicated that it may be extending its range westward, as a specimen was obtained in western South Dakota.

SIMILAR SPECIES

Red Foxes have a reddish pelage, black legs, and white-tipped tail.

Swift Foxes are smaller and have a pale pelage.

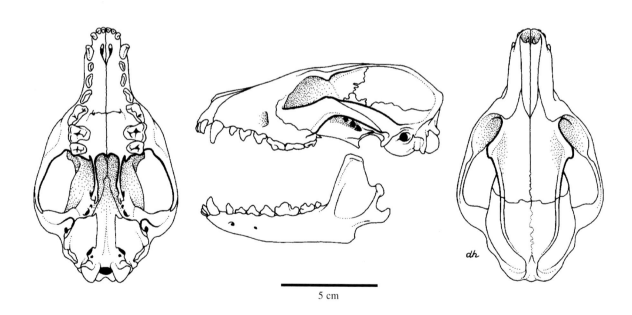

5 cm

There are no measurements available for Alberta specimens

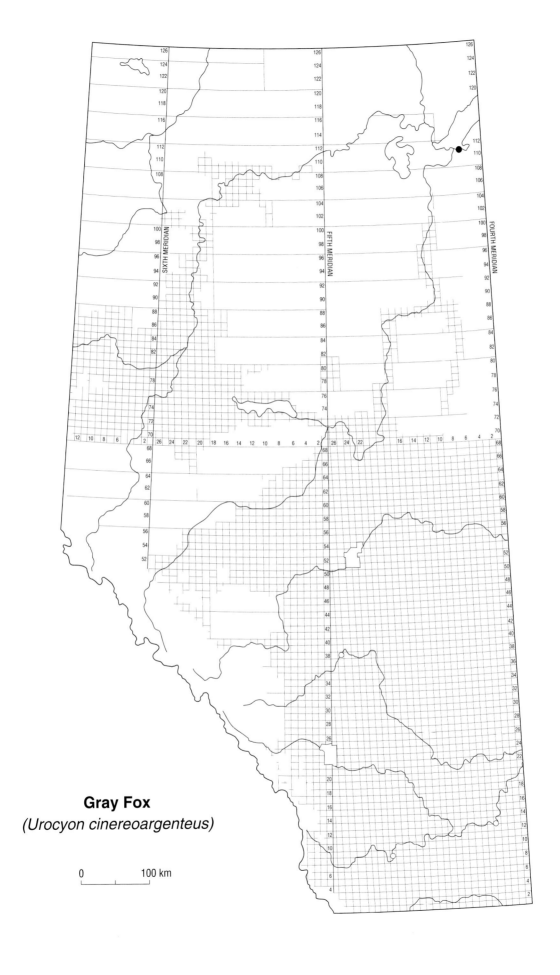

Gray Fox

(Urocyon cinereoargenteus)

0   100 km

BLACK BEAR
Ursus americanus

Carnivora: Ursidae

(plate 11)

IDENTIFYING CHARACTERS

The Black Bear is a small-to-medium sized bear with short claws on the front feet, and no shoulder hump. The gently sloped forehead makes the tawny muzzle and the nose appear longer. The pelage is generally black with a white blaze across the chest. However, the pelage is extremely variable in color and may range from black to reddish brown, light tan to white. The ears are prominent, the eyes small, and the tail is extremely short. These characters must be used in combination to identify a Black Bear.

The skull is large with a broad rostrum and a domed cranium; a sagittal crest may occur in older animals. The upper M2 is usually less than 31 mm long. Although variable, the number of teeth in adults conforms to the dental formula of I 3/3, C 1/1, P 4/4, M 2/3 x 2 = 42.

DISTRIBUTION

Black Bears are found throughout the forested areas of northern Alberta and south through the foothills and mountains in the southwest. Extra-limital sight and specimen records exist for Elk Island National Park (Burns and Cool 1984), Ellerslie and Devon (Smith 1979), Edmonton and Calgary (local press), and Strathmore (Pat Dunford, personal communication).

HABITAT

Coniferous and mixed forests.

STATUS

Common. In some areas of the province it is sufficiently common to be considered an agricultural pest.

SIMILAR SPECIES

Grizzly Bears are larger; they have longer front claws, a dish-shaped face, and a shoulder hump. The upper M2 is greater than 31 mm long and the lower M1 is greater than 20.4 mm long.

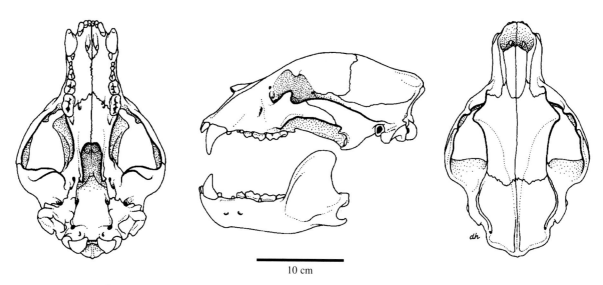

10 cm

Measurements[1]

Sex		Weight (kg)	Total Length (mm)	Tail (mm)	Hindfoot (mm)	Ear (mm)
Males (N=7)	Mean	89.7	1617	122 *(N=5)*	259.3	132
	Range	79.0-102.3	1490-1740	100-175 *(N=5)*	240-280	125-140
Females	Mean	72.9 *(N=3)*	1415.8 *(N=6)*	99.8 *(N=4)*	227 *(N=6)*	125.3 *(N=6)*
	Range	63.0-90.8 *(N=3)*	1375-1455 *(N=6)*	80-115 *(N=4)*	220-250 *(N=6)*	118-140 *(N=6)*

[1]Includes data from Russell et al. 1979.

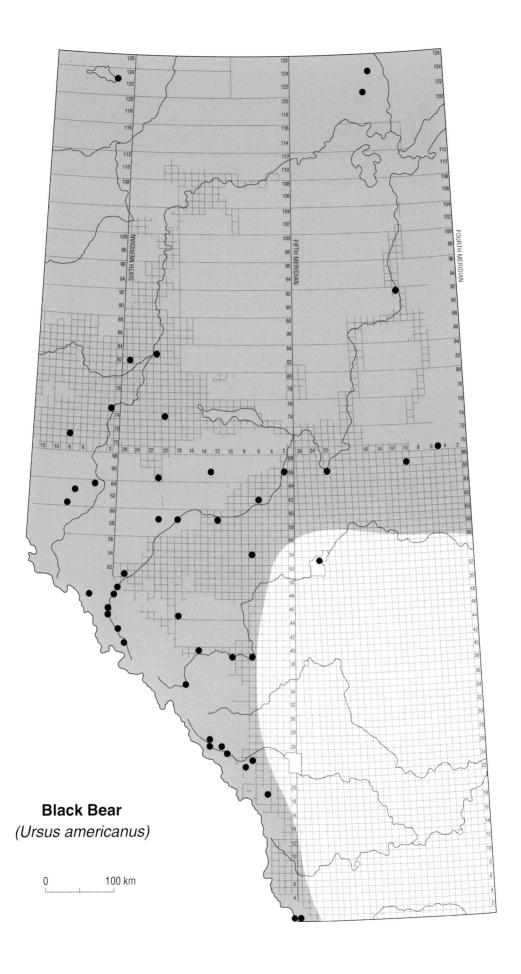

Black Bear

(Ursus americanus)

0   100 km

GRIZZLY BEAR
Ursus arctos

Carnivora: Ursidae

(plate 11)

IDENTIFYING CHARACTERS

In combination, large size, concave-shaped face, rounded ears, shoulder hump, and extremely long front claws identify the Grizzly Bear. Pelage coloration may vary from black to almost blond, but it is generally reddish brown.

The skull is massive. The rostrum is broad and relatively short. A sagittal crest is well developed in older individuals, and the zygomatic arches flare widely. The upper M2 is greater than 31 mm long and the lower M1 is greater than 20.4 mm long. The dental formula is I 3/3, C 1/1, P 4/4, M 2/3 x 2 = 42.

DISTRIBUTION

Grizzly Bears range throughout western Alberta from the mountains and foothills in the southwest, to the Swan Hills, east to Calling Lake, and northwest to Zama Lake. A gap exists in the Peace River-Grande Prairie area (Nielsen 1975).

HABITAT

Grizzly Bears occupy a variety of habitats but prefer open areas, river valleys, and brush lands. At certain times of the year they frequent alpine meadows.

STATUS

Unknown. It is difficult to assess accurately the size of the Alberta population because individual Grizzly Bears have large territories. In general, the Grizzly Bear population in Alberta is stable.

SIMILAR SPECIES

Black Bears are smaller, have shorter front claws, a longer, straighter nose, and lack the shoulder hump; the pelage is normally black. The molar teeth in the Black Bear are smaller.

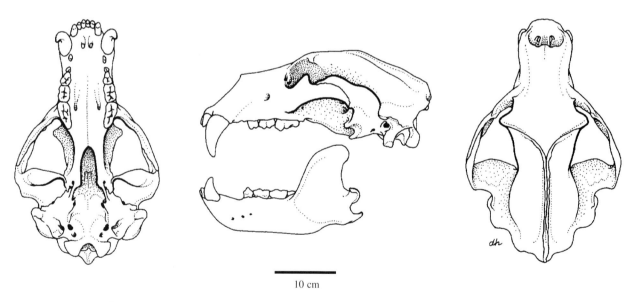

10 cm

Measurements[1]

Sex		Weight (kg)	Total Length (mm)	Tail (mm)	Hindfoot (mm)	Ear (mm)
Males	Mean	222.2 *(N=28)*	1959 *(N=29)*	104 *(N=24)*	331.5 *(N=20)*	121.2 *(N=25)*
	Range	110-400.8 *(N=28)*	1720-2260.6 *(N=29)*	70-145 *(N=24)*	247-395 *(N=20)*	110-135 *(N=25)*
Females (N=11)	Mean	121	1692	110	298 *(N=12)*	121
	Range	88.0-225.0	1490-2130	90-123	260-340 *(N=12)*	110-130

[1]Includes data from Russell et al. 1979.

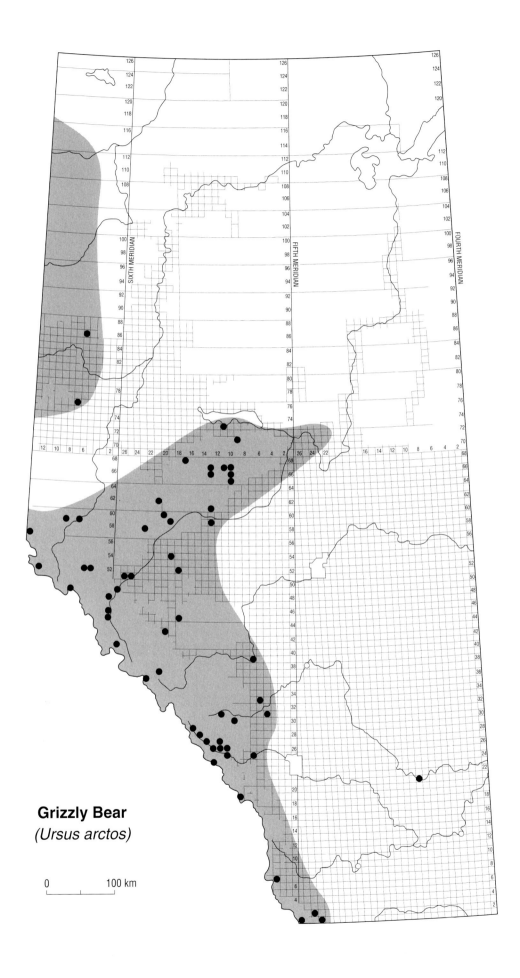

Grizzly Bear
(Ursus arctos)

0   100 km

167

RACCOON
Procyon lotor

Carnivora: Procyonidae

(plate 11)

IDENTIFYING CHARACTERS

The Raccoon features a dark mask across the eyes and a long, bushy, ringed tail. The pelage is long, thick, and grayish but, because of numerous dark hairs, it appears grizzled. The tail has alternating dark and light rings. The body is chunky and, with the hindlegs longer than the front, the rump is higher than the forequarters.

The skull is large with a short rostrum and a broad, rounded braincase. A sagittal crest may be present on older individuals. The teeth do not appear to be as robust as in other carnivores. The dental formula is I 3/3, C 1/1, P 4/4, M 2/2 x 2 = 40.

DISTRIBUTION

The Raccoon is found in Alberta south from a line between Cold Lake and Westlock and east of a line from Red Deer to Pincher Creek. There is a specimen record from Banff and Soper (1942) reported specimens taken in the Lake Claire area of Wood Buffalo National Park.

HABITAT

Open wooded areas that are associated with river valleys.

STATUS

Common in southern Alberta. In the north it is uncommon but the population may be increasing as there are more frequent reports of its occurrence there.

SIMILAR SPECIES

None.

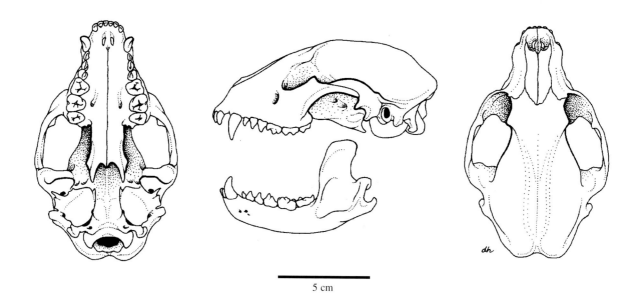

5 cm

Measurements

Sex		Weight (kg)	Total Length (mm)	Tail (mm)	Hindfoot (mm)	Ear (mm)
Males (N=4)	Mean	8.2	894.0	277.0	122.3	67.0
	Range	6.0-11.0	808-948	245-321	115-130	61-72
Females (N=1)		5.2	750	230	105	58

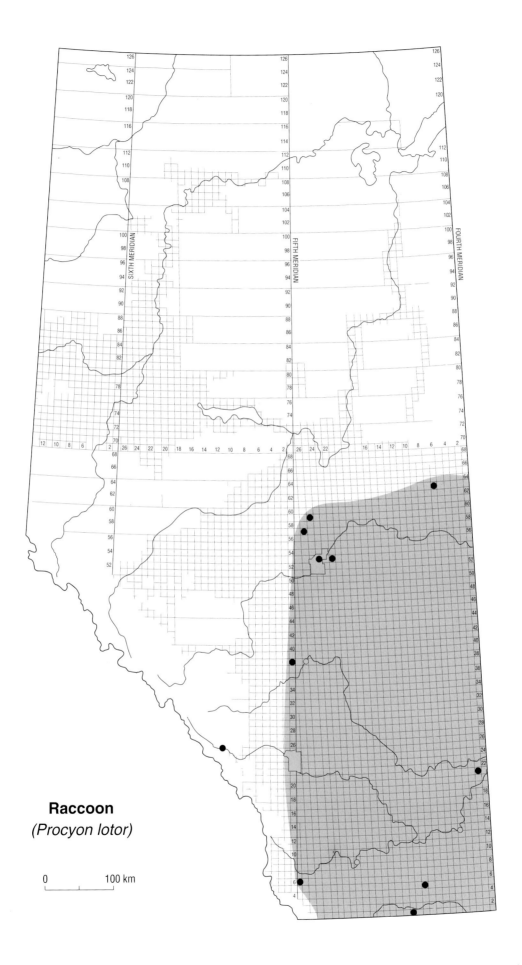

Raccoon
(Procyon lotor)

0   100 km

MARTEN
Martes americana

Carnivora: Mustelidae

IDENTIFYING CHARACTERS

The Marten is a medium-sized member of the weasel family. The face is triangular, the ears prominent, the body sinuous, and the legs short. The pelage is long, dense, soft, and lustrous. It is reddish brown except on the head which tends to be grayish. The tail and feet are darker. There is frequently an orange or cream-colored patch on the throat. The tail is long and well furred.

The skull is long and relatively narrow. The rostrum is short and the braincase is slightly inflated. The dental formula is I 3/3, C 1/1, P 4/4, M 1/2 x 2 = 38.

DISTRIBUTION

Throughout the forested regions of northern Alberta and south through the mountains to Waterton Lakes National Park.

HABITAT

Mature coniferous forest.

STATUS

Common.

SIMILAR SPECIES

Fishers are larger with a more grizzled appearance.

Mink are smaller with white throat patches; they are associated more with aquatic environments.

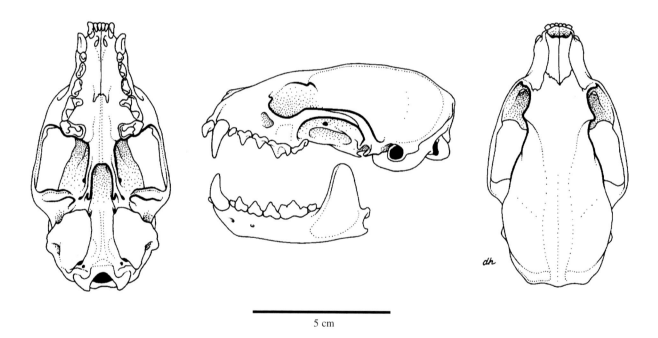

5 cm

Measurements

Sex		Weight (g)	Total Length (mm)	Tail (mm)	Hindfoot (mm)	Ear (mm)
Males (N=4)	Mean	895.6	612.3	185.0	90.0	48.3
	Range	775.3-989.3	583-642	165-200	84-96	42-51
Females (N=2)	Mean	672.4	574.0	164.0	88.5	42.5
	Range	652.0-692.8	570-578	161-167	88-89	42-43

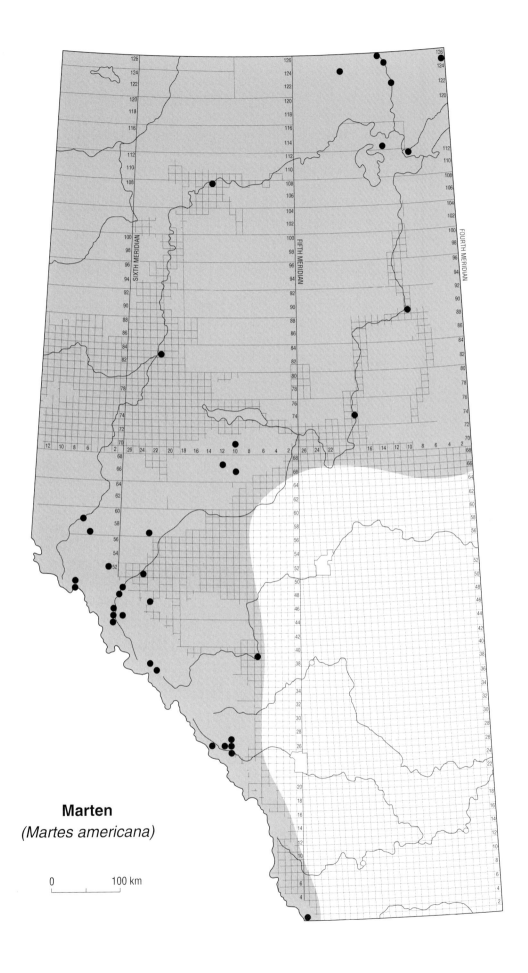

Marten
(Martes americana)

0   100 km

FISHER
Martes pennanti

Carnivora: Mustelidae

IDENTIFYING CHARACTERS

The Fisher is a large-sized member of the weasel family. The pelage is dark brown, but grayish on the head and shoulders, very dark on the rump, tail, and legs. The hair is thick and lustrous. The tail is long, well furred, and bushy.

The skull is large with a moderately long, broad rostrum. The braincase is narrow but, because the zygomatic arches flare widely posteriorly, the skull has a triangular appearance. In old males a large sagittal crest is present. The canines are large and robust. The dental formula is I 3/3, C 1/1, P 4/4, M 1/2 x 2 = 38.

DISTRIBUTION

The northern forest areas from about 56° N on the Saskatchewan border to south of Lesser Slave Lake. In the mountains the range includes Jasper and the northern part of Banff National Parks.

HABITAT

Dense coniferous forest.

STATUS

Uncommon to rare.

SIMILAR SPECIES

Marten are smaller and slimmer with an orange throat patch.

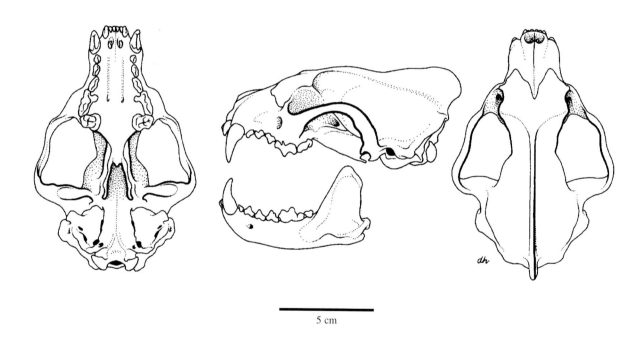

5 cm

Measurements

Sex		Total Length (mm)	Tail (mm)	Hindfoot (mm)
Males (N=1)		1067	415	135
Females (N=3)	Mean	905.7	370.7	117.7
	Range	897-910	354-380	113-120

172

Fisher
(Martes pennanti)

0   100 km

ERMINE
Mustela erminea

IDENTIFYING CHARACTERS

The Ermine is a medium-sized weasel. The pelage is light brown in summer and white in winter. The white hairs are suffused with a tinge of sulphur-yellow, especially on the belly, rump, and tail. The tip of the tail is black in all seasons. The tail length is approximately 28 percent of the total length. The body is slim; the legs are short; and the head, ears, and feet are small.

The skull is narrow with a short, broad rostrum. The braincase is long and flat. The mandible is short, the bottom margin is slightly curved, and the coronoid process is tall and triangular. The dental formula is I 3/3, C 1/1, P 3/3, M 1/2 x 2 = 34.

DISTRIBUTION

Ermine are found throughout the northern forests, the parklands, and grovelands south as far as Brooks and throughout the mountains.

HABITAT

Coniferous and mixed forests.

STATUS

Common in the north, less common or scarce through the parklands and groveland areas.

SIMILAR SPECIES

Least Weasels are smaller with a shorter tail that lacks a black tip.

Long-tailed Weasels are larger and have a longer tail. In summer the belly is orange rather than white.

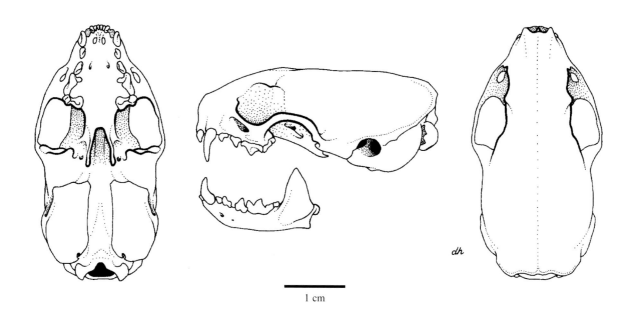

1 cm

Measurements

Sex		Weight (g)	Total Length (mm)	Tail (mm)	Hindfoot (mm)	Ear (mm)
Males (N=6)	Mean	152.4	320.8	91.0	43.8	19.8
	Range	135.1-170.8	300-340	81-98	38-47	17-22
Females (N=7)	Mean	70.2	243.0	60.6	32.1	14.1
	Range	54.8-90.2	218-265	45-70	30-37	12-17

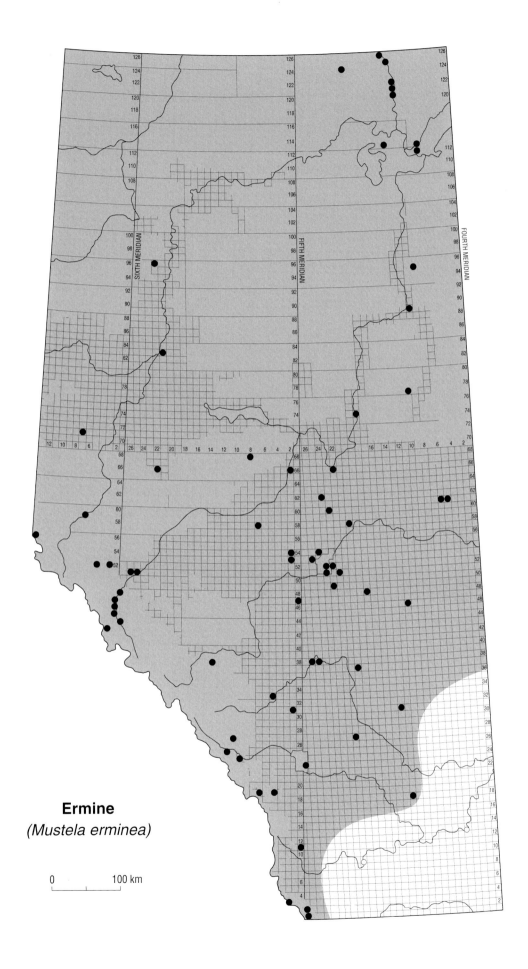

Ermine

(Mustela erminea)

0   100 km

LEAST WEASEL
Mustela nivalis

IDENTIFYING CHARACTERS

This is a small weasel with a short tail which lacks a black tip. It is the smallest carnivore in Alberta. The pelage changes seasonally; in summer it is light brown on the back and white on the belly. In winter the pelage is entirely white.

The skull is small, delicate, and narrow. The rostrum is short, the braincase is long, slightly domed, and smooth. The mandible is short, with a curved lower margin and a tall, triangular coronoid process. The teeth are small. The dental formula is I 3/3, C 1/1, P 3/3, M 1/2 x 2 = 34.

DISTRIBUTION

Found throughout the province.

HABITAT

It occurs in coniferous and mixedwood forests in the north, and southward through the aspen parkland and the arid grasslands.

STATUS

Common in most areas. Holroyd and Van Tighem (1983) reported that it is rare in Banff and Jasper National Parks.

SIMILAR SPECIES

Ermine are larger with longer, black-tipped tails.

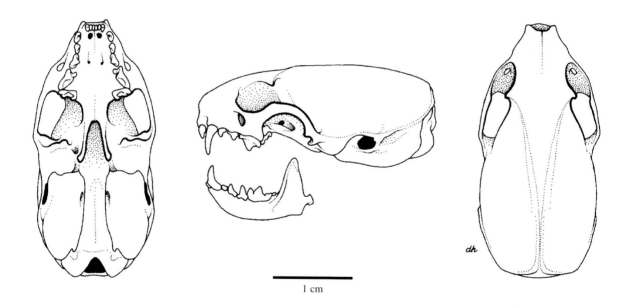

1 cm

Measurements

Sex		Weight (g)	Total Length (mm)	Tail (mm)	Hindfoot (mm)	Ear (mm)
Males (N=5)	Mean	34.4	176.6	33.6	22.0	11.8
	Range	28.2-43.5	165-181	29-39	21-23	10-14
Females (N=6)	Mean	29.5	162.7	27.7	22.3	11.8
	Range	21.5-38.8	153-171	27-29	20-29	11-14.5

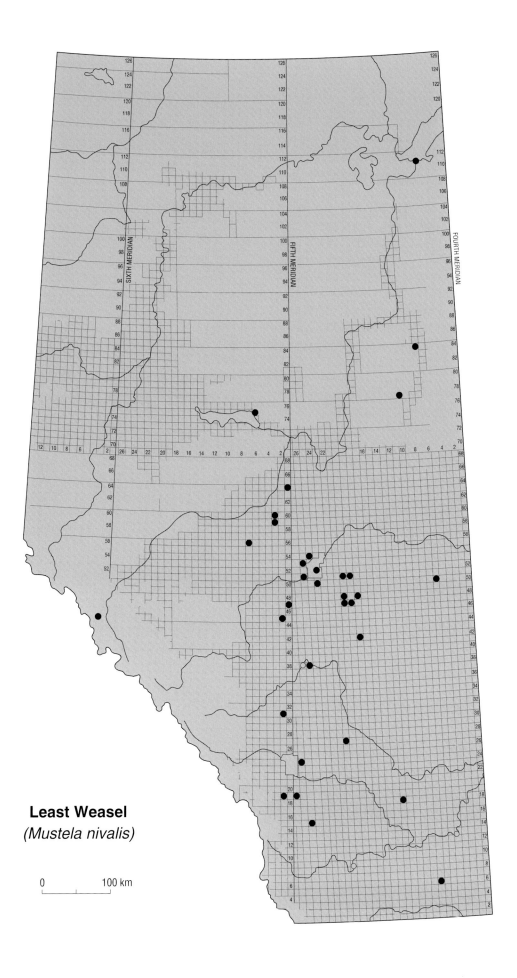

Least Weasel

(Mustela nivalis)

0　　　　　100 km

LONG-TAILED WEASEL
Mustela frenata

IDENTIFYING CHARACTERS
The pelage of this long, slim-bodied weasel is seasonally variable. In winter, it is entirely white except for the black tail-tip. Summer pelage is reddish brown on the back and dull orange on the underside; the chin is white and the tail is brown underneath. During the spring transition, the belly may be white. The head and feet are small, the ears large, the legs short.

The skull is long and narrow. The rostrum is short and relatively broad. The braincase is long, flat in profile, and slightly inflated. In mature animals a sagittal crest is present. The mandible is short with a curved lower edge and a tall, triangular coronoid process. The dental formula is I 3/3, C 1/1, P 3/3, M 1/2 x 2 = 34.

DISTRIBUTION
Two-thirds of the province south from Fairview in the northwest and approximately Cold Lake in the east. Soper (1964) regards records from the Grande Prairie area to be extralimital.

Long-tailed Weasels occur in the mountains from Rock Lake to Waterton.

HABITAT
Grasslands, parklands, and open coniferous forests.

STATUS
The grassland population may be in decline but there are no hard data to substantiate this. They are relatively common on the plains. Holroyd and Van Tighem (1983) considered this species uncommon in Banff and Jasper National Parks.

SIMILAR SPECIES
Ermine are smaller and have a shorter tail; the belly is white with a hint of sulphur-yellow.

Least Weasels are smaller; the very short tail lacks a black tip.

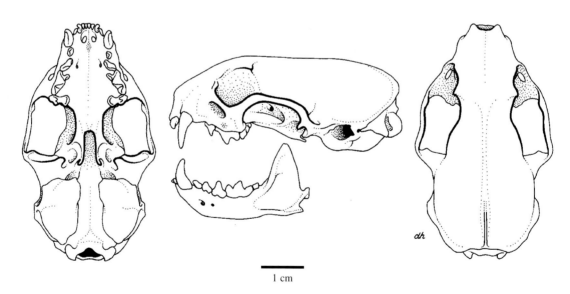

1 cm

Measurements

Sex		Weight (g)	Total Length (mm)	Tail (mm)	Hindfoot (mm)	Ear (mm)
Males (N=20)	Mean	341.2	438.1	161.6	49.5	25.0
	Range	242.3-423.7	416-469	141-178	46-55	21-31
Females (N=11)	Mean	210.8	378.8	139.1	42.5	22.3 *(N=10)*
	Range	154.3-242.6	363-408	125-166	35-49	21-25 *(N=10)*

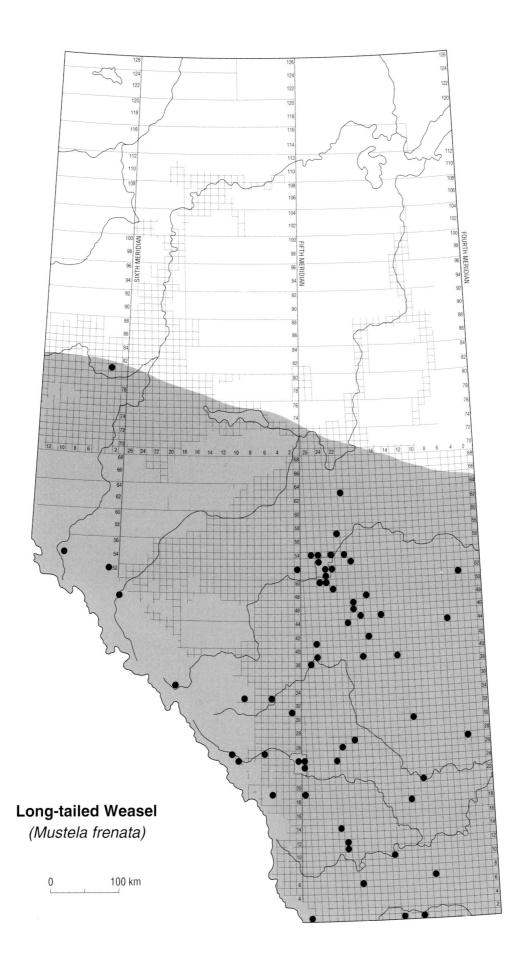

Long-tailed Weasel
(Mustela frenata)

0   100 km

179

BLACK-FOOTED FERRET
Mustela nigripes

Carnivora: Mustelidae

IDENTIFYING CHARACTERS

The Black-footed Ferret is a large-sized weasel. Its slim, muscular body, long, black-tipped tail, short, black legs and feet, and black mask across the eyes are distinctive. The buffy tan pelage is short. The head is relatively large and the ears are prominent.

The skull is robust with a short, broad rostrum. The braincase is relatively flat. The lower jaw is mink-like but larger. The canines are large. The dental formula is I 3/3, C 1/1, P 3/3, M 1/2 x 2 = 34.

DISTRIBUTION

The grasslands of southeastern Alberta. The only specimen record from Alberta was obtained at Gleichen and is housed in the Field Museum of Natural History in Chicago. Anderson (1946) cites a record from Rosebud but no specimen is known.

HABITAT

Open grasslands.

STATUS

Extirpated. If it occurs it should be considered accidental.

SIMILAR SPECIES

Long-tailed Weasels are smaller and lack the black feet and band across eyes.

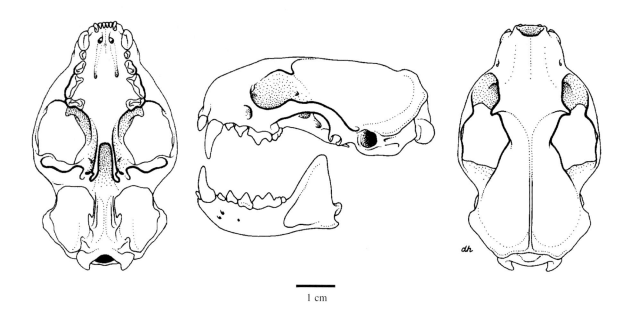

1 cm

There are no measurements available for Alberta specimens

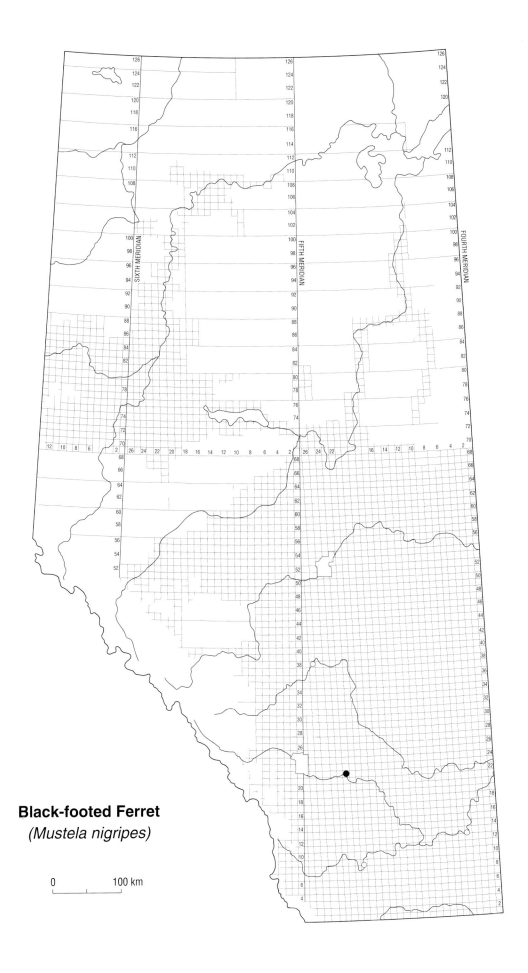

Black-footed Ferret

(Mustela nigripes)

0   100 km

181

MINK
Mustela vison

Carnivora: Mustelidae

(plate 12)

IDENTIFYING CHARACTERS

The lustrous pelage of the Mink is dark, reddish brown. The hair is relatively long and dense. It appears coarse but is soft to the touch; hence, the pelt of a prime mink is a luxurious fur that is highly prized. The legs are short, the body is long and slim, and the tail is long and bushy. A white patch is frequently present on the throat and chin.

The skull is low-crowned, the rostrum is short, and the braincase is long and triangular. A sagittal crest is present in older individuals. The lower jaw is short, the lower edge is curved, and the coronoid process is tall. The dental formula is I 3/3, C 1/1, P 3/3, M 1/2 x 2 = 34.

DISTRIBUTION

Mink are found throughout the province.

HABITAT

Around the margins of lakes, sloughs, creeks, rivers, and marshes.

STATUS

Common.

SIMILAR SPECIES

Marten are larger, occur in upland forests, and have an orange or yellow throat patch.

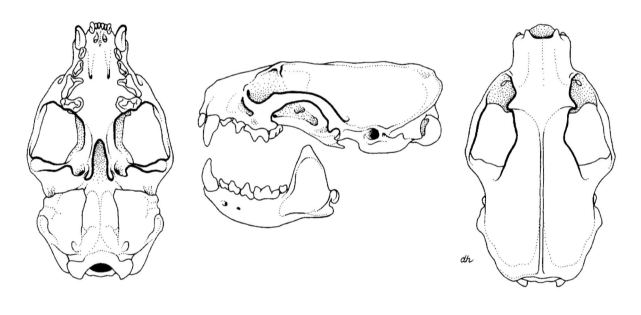

1 cm

Measurements

Sex		Weight (g)	Total Length (mm)	Tail (mm)	Hindfoot (mm)	Ear (mm)
Males (N=10)	Mean	1312.3	614.0	197.6	71.0	25.4
	Range	1007-1741	570-647	145-225	65-76	22-28
Females (N=7)	Mean	629.8	512.7	161.3	57.3	21.4
	Range	424.7-856.8	460-550	134-179	50-61	19-24

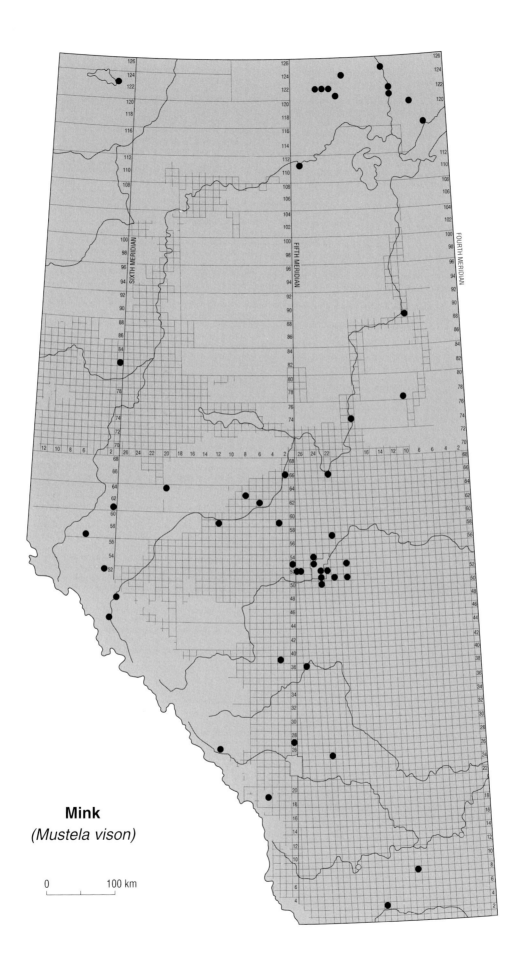

Mink
(Mustela vison)

0   100 km

WOLVERINE
Gulo gulo

Carnivora: Mustelidae

(plate 12)

IDENTIFYING CHARACTERS

The long pelage makes individuals appear shaggy. The basic color is reddish brown but this may vary from almost black through dark brown to a light brown. Two pale-colored stripes extend along the sides from the head and converge across the rump. The chest frequently bears a white blaze. The head and shoulders are frequently grizzled in appearance. The back is arched and the head and tail are carried low. The ears are short and the feet are relatively large.

The large, massive skull has a short, broad rostrum and a long, relatively narrow braincase. A sagittal crest is present and, in males, it extends past the occiput. The canines are robust and the carnassials large. The dental formula is I 3/3, C 1/1, P 4/4, M 1/2 x 2 = 38.

DISTRIBUTION

The Wolverine is found throughout the northern forests from Fort McMurray in the east to Rock Lake in the west, then south through the mountains and foothills to Waterton Lakes National Park.

HABITAT

Dense forests. Occasionally an individual will venture into open areas both above and below the tree line in the mountains.

STATUS

Rare in the mountains and scarce in other areas. Population is sufficiently stable to sustain an annual harvest.

SIMILAR SPECIES

This largest member of the weasel family, with its hunched back and loping gait, is unmistakable.

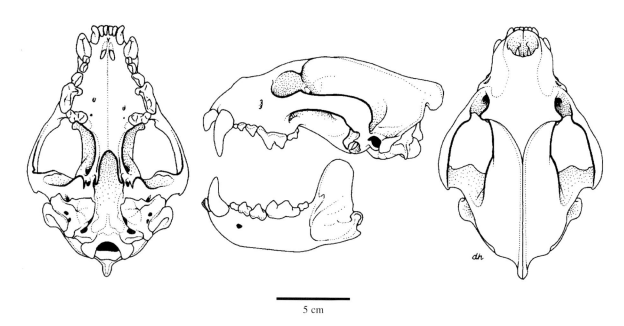

5 cm

Measurements

Sex		Weight (kg)	Total Length (mm)	Tail (mm)	Hindfoot (mm)	Ear (mm)
Males (N=3)	Mean	13.1	969.3	199	177	56.3
	Range	11.5-14.1	938-990	176-224	174-180	51-60
Females (N=1)		8.7	882	161	160	43

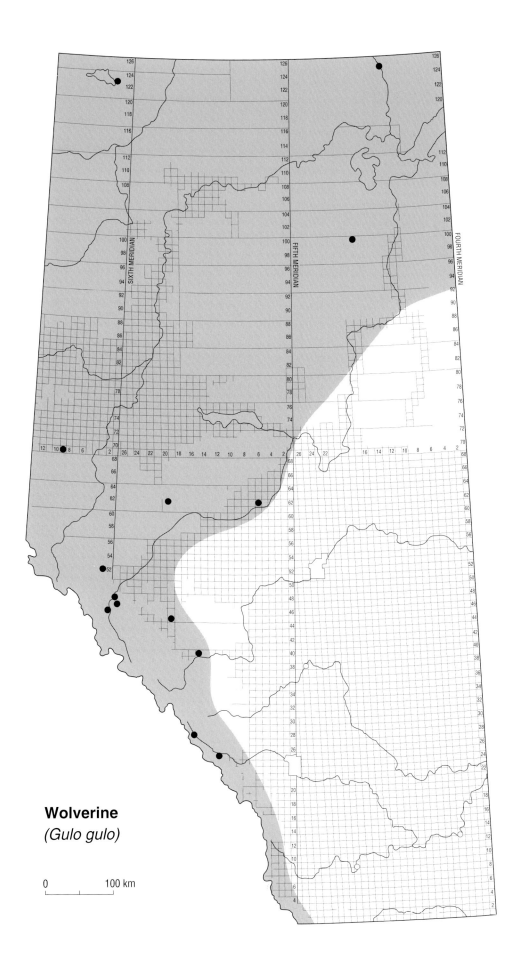

Wolverine
(Gulo gulo)

0   100 km

BADGER
Taxidea taxus

Carnivora: Mustelidae

(plate 13)

IDENTIFYING CHARACTERS

The Badger is squat-bodied and short-legged. The pelage is long and coarse. It is grizzled gray on the back, ochraceous white on the belly, and white on the throat and chin. A prominent white stripe extends from the nose to the back of the head and occasionally onto the shoulder area. Dark patches on the face extend from the eyes to the muzzle. The cheeks are white. The head is large and triangular. The feet and legs are dark. The front feet have long, curved claws. The tail is short, stout, and well furred.

The skull is massive. In profile view it is slightly domed and in dorsal view it is triangular. The rostrum is short and broad. A low sagittal crest may occur in some individuals. The upper and lower canines are sturdy with pointed tips. The dental formula is I 3/3, C 1/1, P 3/3, M 1/2 x 2 = 34.

DISTRIBUTION

Badgers occur from the southern grassland north to approximately the North Saskatchewan River and from the Saskatchewan border westward to Waterton Lakes and Banff National Parks. They do not occur in the heavily forested areas. They are closely associated with ground squirrels and pocket gophers upon which they prey.

HABITAT

Open grasslands and aspen parklands.

STATUS

Relatively common. Much maligned by ranchers and farmers, they may not occur in areas where they were once found.

SIMILAR SPECIES

None.

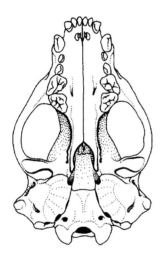 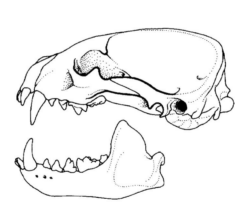 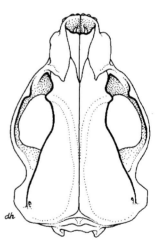

5 cm

Measurements

Sex		Total Length (mm)	Tail (mm)	Hindfoot (mm)	Ear (mm)
Males (N=3)	Mean	814.3	157.7	119.7	50.0
	Range	780-840	130-195	115-124	45-55
Females (N=3)	Mean	747.7	128.7	110.0	53.3
	Range	738-765	118-150	107-115	51-55

186

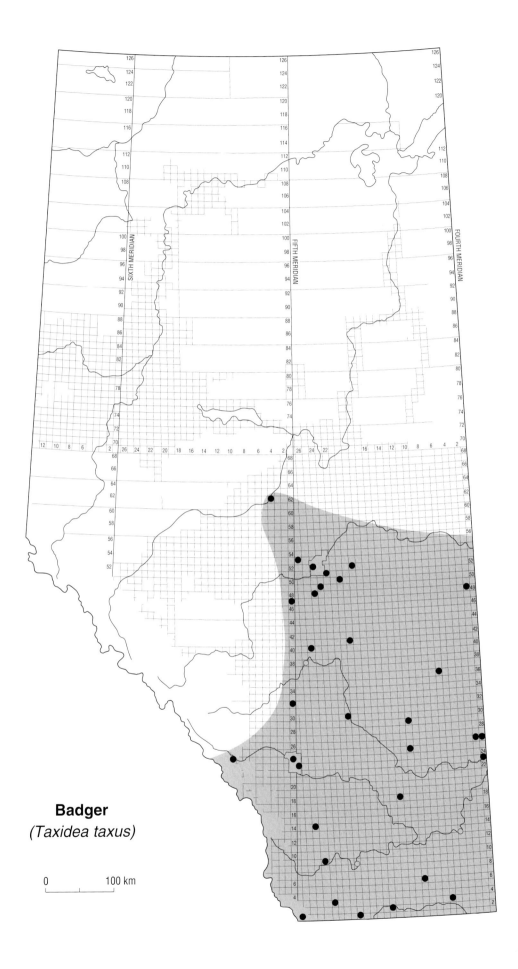

Badger
(Taxidea taxus)

0   100 km

STRIPED SKUNK
Mephitis mephitis

Carnivora: Mustelidae

(plate 13)

IDENTIFYING CHARACTERS

The Striped Skunk is one of those unique mammals that almost everyone knows either by reputation, because of its pungent odor, or because of the black and white pattern of the pelage. The skunk has a stout body, short legs, and a small head and ears. The tail is long and bushy. The pelage is long with a dull lustre; it is essentially black with a central white stripe on the head and two white stripes on the body. The amount of white varies from fairly prominent to almost absent.

The skull has a short rostrum, flared zygomatic arches, and in older individuals a sagittal crest. The auditory bullae are flat. The lower jaw is short and robust. The upper P4 and M1 are large, the other premolars and incisors are small. The crown of the lower canines hooks backward. The dental formula is I 3/3, C 1/1, P 3/3, M 1/2 x 2 = 34.

DISTRIBUTION

Found throughout the province.

HABITAT

Striped Skunks are found in a variety of situations, from open grasslands to northern uplands. They prefer uplands where their burrows cannot be flooded. Shelter belts around farms, old buildings, and rocky outcrops are suitable habitats.

STATUS

Common. In some areas of the province the Striped Skunk has been subject to extermination as a result of rabies control programs. In these areas the population may be small.

SIMILAR SPECIES

None with this distinctive color pattern.

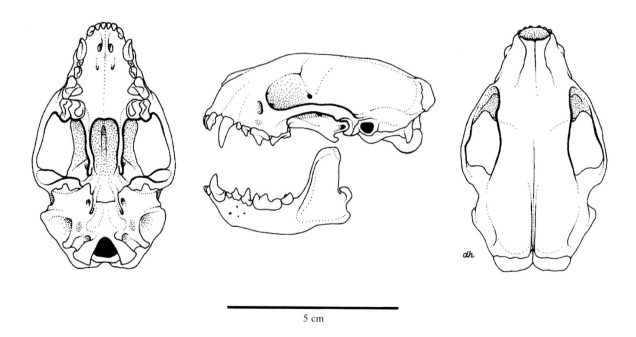

5 cm

Measurements

Sex		Weight (kg)	Total Length (mm)	Tail (mm)	Hindfoot (mm)
Females (N=4)	Mean	3.6	677.5	214.5	78.5
	Range	2.8-4.4	655-700	190-232	75-83

188

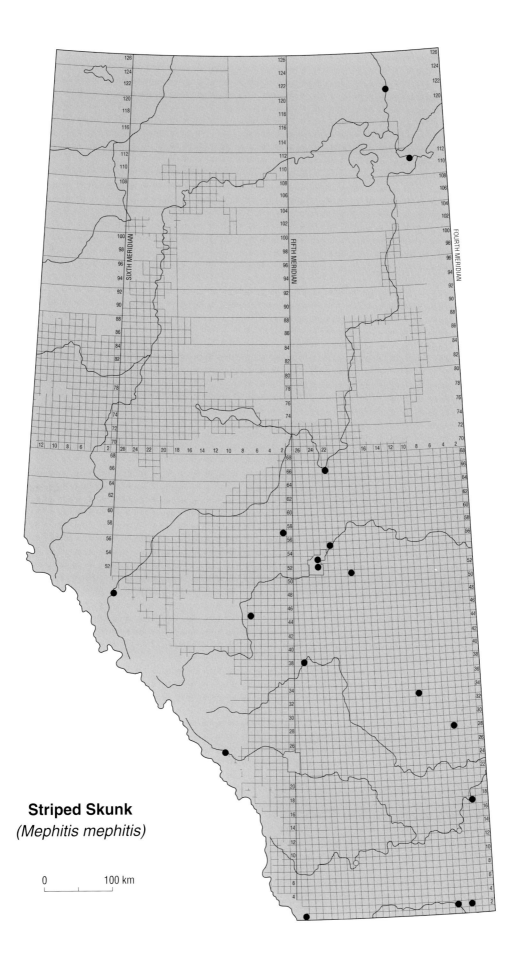

Striped Skunk

(Mephitis mephitis)

0   100 km

RIVER OTTER
Lutra canadensis

Carnivora: Mustelidae
(plate 13)

IDENTIFYING CHARACTERS

The River Otter has short legs, a long, tapering tail, and a long, sinuous body. The head is flat with a broad muzzle. The ears are short and inconspicuous. The rich reddish brown pelage is short and dense and has a high lustre. The throat is grayer than the rest of the body. The feet are webbed.

The skull is relatively flat with a short, broad rostrum, and a long, broad braincase. The interorbital area is narrow. The lower jaw is robust, slightly curved with a high, triangular coronoid process. The cheek teeth are large. The lower canines are short and the crown is bent slightly backward. The upper canines are long and cylindrical. The dental formula is I 3/3, C 1/1, P 4/3, M 1/2 x 2 = 36.

DISTRIBUTION

The River Otter is found throughout northern Alberta, south to the St. Paul area in the east and Rock Lake in the west. It has been reported from Jasper, Banff, and Waterton Lakes National Parks but it is believed that no otters occur in these areas now (Holroyd and Van Tighem 1983; Nielsen 1973). However, Dekker (1989) reported that otter sign was seen at several locations in Jasper National Park and that otters had been seen at Jasper Lake.

HABITAT

Rivers, creeks, lakes, and ponds in the northern forest.

STATUS

Uncommon. It is, however, frequently encountered in the northeast and east-central areas of Alberta. Its status in the mountains is not known.

SIMILAR SPECIES

This large and highly aquatic weasel with its long tapering tail, and a large, roundish, flat head is unmistakable.

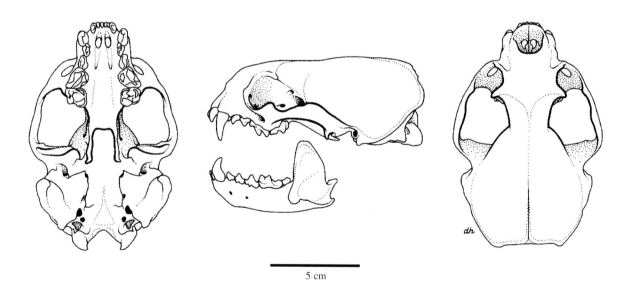

5 cm

Measurements

Sex		Weight (kg)	Total Length (mm)	Tail (mm)	Hindfoot (mm)
Males (N=20)	Mean	7.7	1151.0	433.0	119.9
	Range	6.1-9.3	1050-1220	370-480	110-130
Females (N=20)	Mean	7.3	1162.0	441.5	119.5
	Range	6.1-10	1060-1280	370-485	110-130

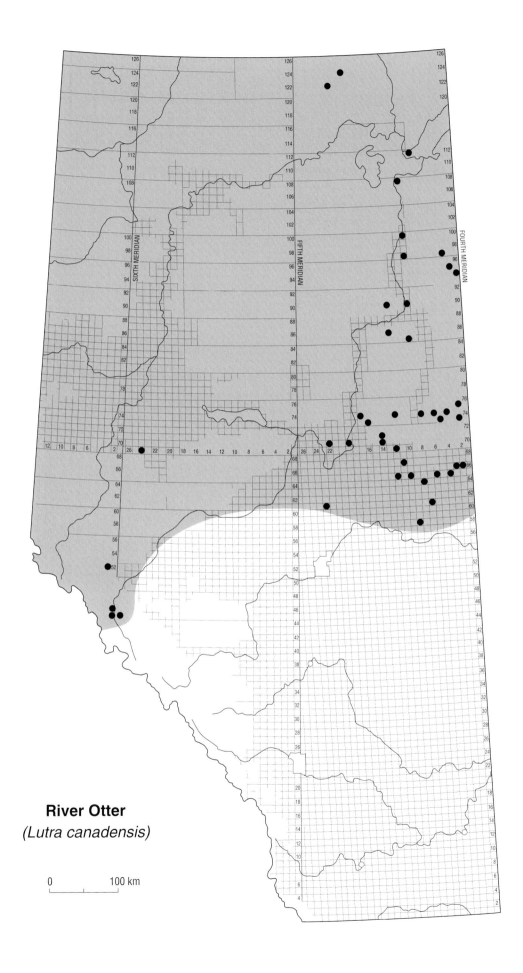

River Otter

(Lutra canadensis)

0   100 km

COUGAR
Felis concolor

Carnivora: Felidae

(plate 13)

IDENTIFYING CHARACTERS

This is the largest member of the cat family in Alberta. The roundish head, prominent, round ears, long, well furred tail, and lithe, muscular body should be sufficient clues to identify this animal for anyone fortunate enough to see a cougar in the wild. The tawny or reddish brown pelage is short and thick. The feet are large.

The skull is large and robust with a short rostrum. In older individuals a sagittal crest is present. The canines are robust. The dental formula is I 3/3, C 1/1, P 3/2, M 1/1 x 2 = 30.

DISTRIBUTION

Cougars may be found in any area of the province. However, the principal range is the Rocky Mountains and foothills of western Alberta. There are sight reports of Cougars in the Medicine Hat area and the Cypress Hills (Brown 1947), and also specimens from Whitecourt and Athabasca.

HABITAT

Mixed forest in the mountains and foothills.

STATUS

Uncommon. The population of Cougars is relatively stable. Pall (1986) estimated the provincial population to be between 600 and 1200 individuals. Alberta Fish and Wildlife Division estimated the 1988 population as approximately 500 (Anonymous 1989).

SIMILAR SPECIES

The Cougar's large size, long tail, roundish head, and short, round ears are like no other native mammal.

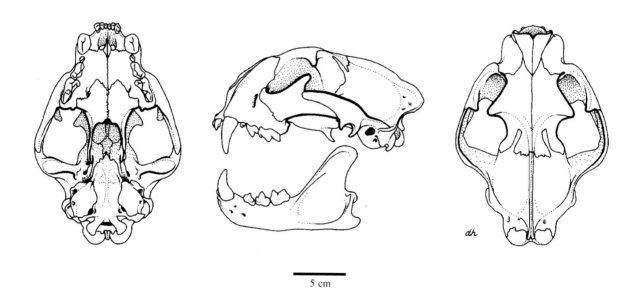

5 cm

Measurements

Sex		Weight[1] (kg)	Total Length[1] (mm)	Tail[1] (mm)	Hindfoot (mm)
Males	Mean	71 *(N=11)*	2170 *(N=12)*	790 *(N=12)*	276.3 *(N=4)*
	Range	60-82 *(N=11)*	2010-2330 *(N=12)*	730-850 *(N=12)*	254-290 *(N=4)*
Females	Mean	44 *(N=34)*	1940 *(N=36)*	710 *(N=36)*	--
	Range	36-52 *(N=34)*	1820-2060 *(N=36)*	600-820 *(N=36)*	--

[1] Data from Ross and Jalkotzy 1989.

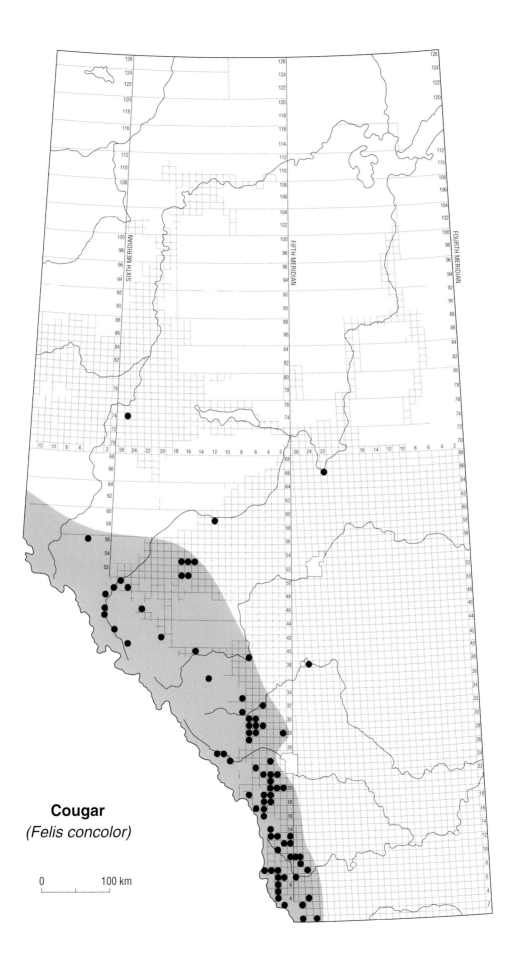

Cougar
(Felis concolor)

0 _____ 100 km

CANADA LYNX
Lynx canadensis

IDENTIFYING CHARACTERS

The Canada Lynx is a long-legged, short-tailed cat. The hindlegs are noticeably longer than the forelegs. The feet are large. The black-tipped ears have long, conspicuous tufts. The pelage is soft and dappled gray. The face is surrounded by a pronounced ruff. The tail is short and lacks barring; the tip is black above and below.

The skull has a short rostrum, extremely short nasal bones, and a domed cranium. The canines are long and sharp with shallow longitudinal grooves. The premolars and molars are reduced. The skulls of the Canada Lynx and Bobcat are very similar and can be differentiated only by direct comparison and detailed examination. Generally, the Canada Lynx skull is larger. The dental formula is I 3/3, C 1/1, P 2/2, M 1/1 x 2 = 28.

DISTRIBUTION

Lynx are residents of the forested regions of the north, the mountains, and the foothills. There are reports in the past of lynx occurring in the Cypress Hills, and lynx have been taken at Edmonton, Cochrane, and Calgary.

HABITAT

Coniferous and mixed forests.

STATUS

Common. The number of Canada Lynx is closely allied to the size of the prey base (e.g., Snowshoe Hares). As the number of prey increases the number of lynx increases. As the prey base declines the lynx population declines.

SIMILAR SPECIES

Bobcats are generally smaller, lack the long ear tufts, have smaller feet and a barred tail. The tip of the tail is black above and white below.

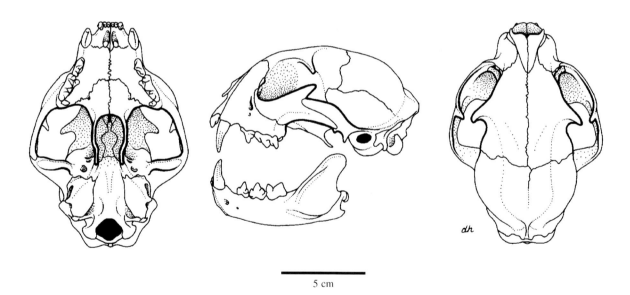

5 cm

Measurements

Sex		Total Length (mm)	Tail (mm)	Hindfoot (mm)	Ear (mm)
Males (N=4)	Mean	946.0	115.3	234.8	78.5
	Range	840-1000	100-130	220-250	77-80
Females	Mean	858 *(N=5)*	109.5 *(N=4)*	222.8 *(N=5)*	70 *(N=2)*
	Range	789-920 *(N=5)*	100-123 *(N=4)*	211-245 *(N=5)*	63-77 *(N=2)*

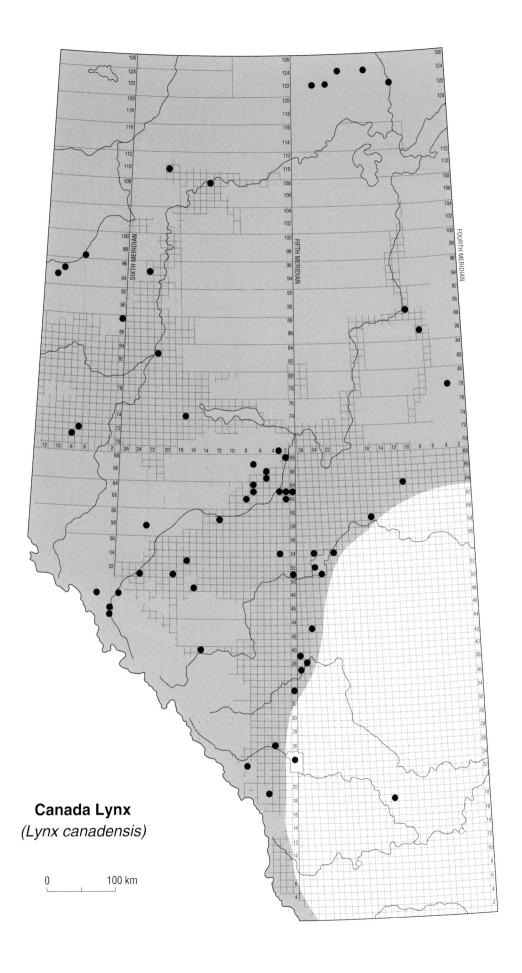

Canada Lynx
(Lynx canadensis)

0   100 km

BOBCAT
Lynx rufus

Carnivora: Felidae

IDENTIFYING CHARACTERS

The Bobcat is a short-tailed cat with short ear tufts and small feet. The tail has barring forward from the tip and the tip is black on the upper side only. The underside of the tail is white. The pelage is soft and is grayish brown flecked with black. The sides shade toward buff and the belly is white with black spots. The hind legs are longer than the front legs.

The skull has a short rostrum, a domed braincase, and reduced dentition. The canines are long and sharp with shallow, longitudinal grooves. The dental formula is I 3/3, C 1/1, P 2/2, M 1/1 x 2 = 28.

DISTRIBUTION

Bobcats are found in the grasslands of southern Alberta and along the foothills and front ranges of the Rocky Mountains north to Ram Mountain.

HABITAT

Found in southern Alberta along river valleys and coulees. It does not like dense forests.

STATUS

Uncommon. Records (both sightings and specimens) are sparse so it is difficult to assess the status of this animal. It is extremely secretive and few people encounter it.

SIMILAR SPECIES

Canada Lynx are the only animals that can be confused with the Bobcat. The lynx is slightly larger. It has much larger feet, longer ear tufts, no barring on the tail; the tip of the tail is black top and bottom.

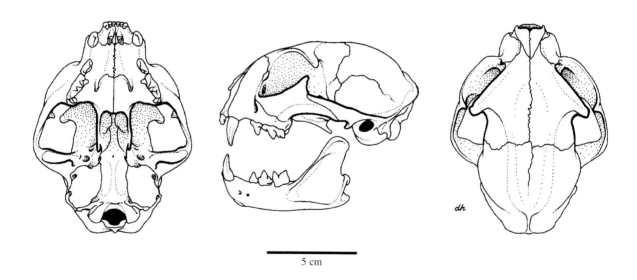

5 cm

Measurements

Weight (kg)	Total Length (mm)	Tail (mm)	Hindfoot (mm)
10	875	160	175

Note: measurements modified from Soper 1964.

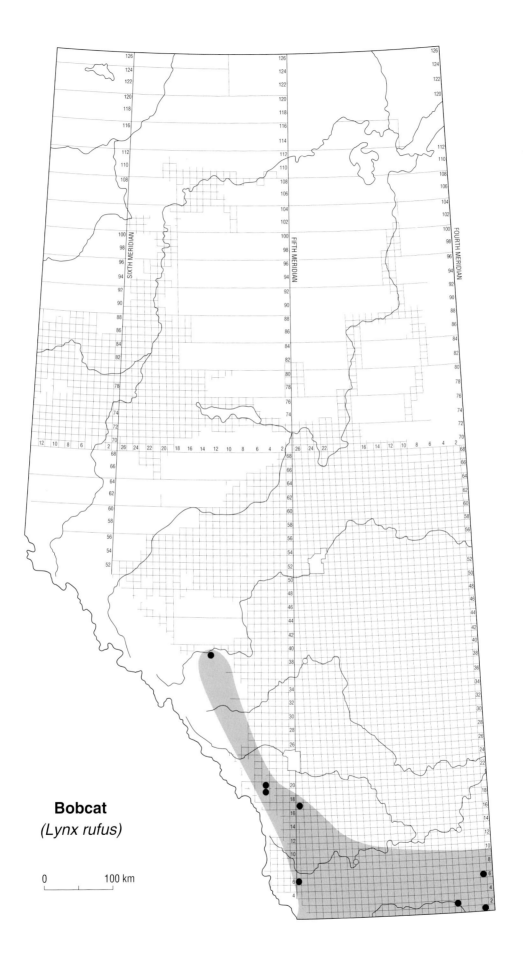

Bobcat

(Lynx rufus)

0   100 km

197

Order: Artiodactyla

Members of this Order have had a considerable impact on human affairs. Several species have been domesticated and provide humans with "beasts of burden," clothing, and food. With the exception of Antarctica, Australia, and New Zealand, the Order is worldwide in distribution. There are approximately 180 species grouped into nine families (Anderson and Jones 1984). In Alberta there are nine species representing three families.

The Order is characterized by having an even number of digits on each foot. Each metapodial is capped by a hoof. Upper incisors are absent. The upper canine is most frequently absent and the lower canine is incisiform. Horns or antlers are present on males and occasionally on females.

Key to the Ungulates (Artiodactyla)

1. Horns or horn cores present on both male and female. 2
   Deciduous, branched antlers present on males of all species and females of *Rangifer*; females of other species with smooth frontal bones. 5

2. Weight 350 kg or greater; condylobasal length of skull greater than 400 mm; horns relatively short and conical; head massive, hump on shoulders; pelage long and shaggy especially on forequarters . . *Bison bison* (p. 214)
   Weight less than 350 kg; condylobasal length of skull less than 400 mm; horns ringed or pronged 3

Oreamnos americanus

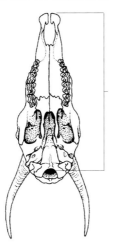

condylobasal length

3. Horn sheaths deciduous, pronged, tips bent inward; pelage sandy brown, large white rump patch, two wide white bands on throat. . . *Antilocapra americana* (p. 212)
   Horn sheaths permanent, ringed not pronged. 4

4. Horns brown, massive, and curled in males, considerably smaller and less curled in females, blunt tips; pelage brown to dark brown, white rump patch. . . . . *Ovis canadensis* (p. 218)
   Horns small, black, tips pointed in both sexes; pelage long, white or dirty white. . . . . *Oreamnos americanus* (p. 216)

5. Weight greater than 300 kg; nasal bones relatively short — less than premaxilla length; pelage dark brown to black; dewlap present; nose bulbous . . . . *Alces alces* (p. 208)

    Weight less than 300 kg; nasal bones relatively long — greater than premaxilla length; pelage variable; no dewlap 6

Cervus elaphus   **Alces alces**

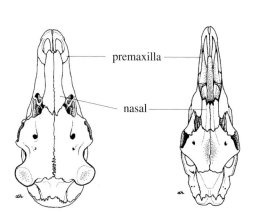

premaxilla

nasal

6. Posterior nares not divided by vomer; hindfoot greater than 640 mm; antlers massive, round in cross-section; pelage darker on the neck than on the body; large creamy rump patch . . . . *Cervus elaphus*   (p. 202)

    Posterior nares divided by vomer (vomer contacts posterior margin of palatines); hindfoot less than 625 mm; antlers variable; pelage variable 7

Cervus elaphus   **Rangifer tarandus**

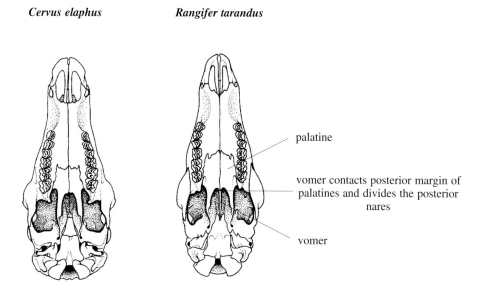

palatine

vomer contacts posterior margin of palatines and divides the posterior nares

vomer

7. Antlers palmate; pedicle in both sexes; neck light-colored with mane; hindfoot broad, toes splayed; ears less than 150 mm; upper canines present. . . . . *Rangifer tarandus* (p. 210)

    Antlers round in cross-section; pedicle absent in females; pelage uniform, gray to reddish brown on back; ear greater than 140 mm; upper canines absent. 8

8.	Tail relatively short, less than 210 mm, black-tipped; antler tines branch in pairs; ears relatively large; forehead dark; when animal runs tail is not raised; pre-orbital pit deep; metatarsal glands greater than 100 mm long . . . . *Odocoileus hemionus* (p. 204)

Tail large, underside white; when animal runs tail is raised and waved from side to side; single tines on antlers; ears relatively small; pre-orbital pit shallow; metatarsal glands less than 50 mm long . . . . *Odocoileus virginianus* (p. 206)

Odocoileus hemionus   **Odocoileus virginianus**

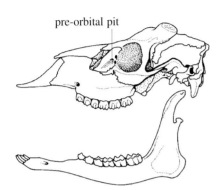
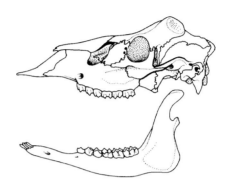

pre-orbital pit

WAPITI
Cervus elaphus

Artiodactyla: Cervidae

(plate 14)

IDENTIFYING CHARACTERS

The pelage on the head and neck is dark brown. In males, the hair in the neck region is long and forms a ventral mane. The body is reddish brown, the large rump patch is cream or tan-colored, and the legs and belly are dark brown. The legs and ears are long and the tail is short. The bulls have massive, branched antlers that project upward and backward from the skull. Those of the cows are small and simpler.

The skull is large, the nasal bones long, and the premaxilla relatively short. Wapiti lack upper incisors but do have a modified upper canine ("Elk tusk"). The lower canine tooth is incisiform. The dental formula is I 0/3, C 1/1, P 3/3, M 3/3 x 2 = 34.

DISTRIBUTION

Wapiti are found throughout the Rocky Mountains from Waterton Lakes to Jasper National parks and in the adjacent foothills. Transplants and introductions have occurred in several localities in northern Alberta and the Cypress Hills. Elk Island National Park is one of the few areas where the herd has been allowed to grow without introductions. At one time the range extended north to Fort Vermilion and Fort McMurray but only scattered bands of introduced animals occur in this area now.

HABITAT

Mixed wood forests.

STATUS

In the mountains and foothills and the Cypress Hills the Wapiti is common. In other areas it is sporadic.

SIMILAR SPECIES

Mule Deer and **White-tailed Deer** are both considerably smaller.

Caribou are smaller with more gracile, forward-curving antlers.

Moose are larger and blacker with large, palmate antlers.

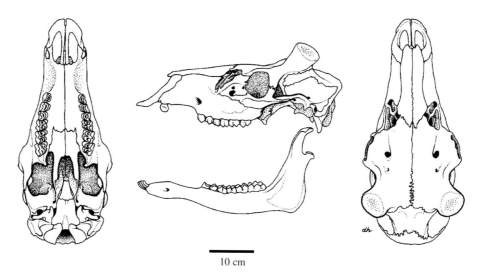

10 cm

Measurements

Sex		Total Length (mm)	Tail (mm)	Hindfoot (mm)	Ear (mm)
Males (N=4)	Mean	2432.5	168.8	680.0	199
	Range	2290-2640	160-175	645-710	197-200
Females (N=3)	Mean	2468.3	148.3	648.3	208.3
	Range	2420-2500	140-155	640-660	200-215

202

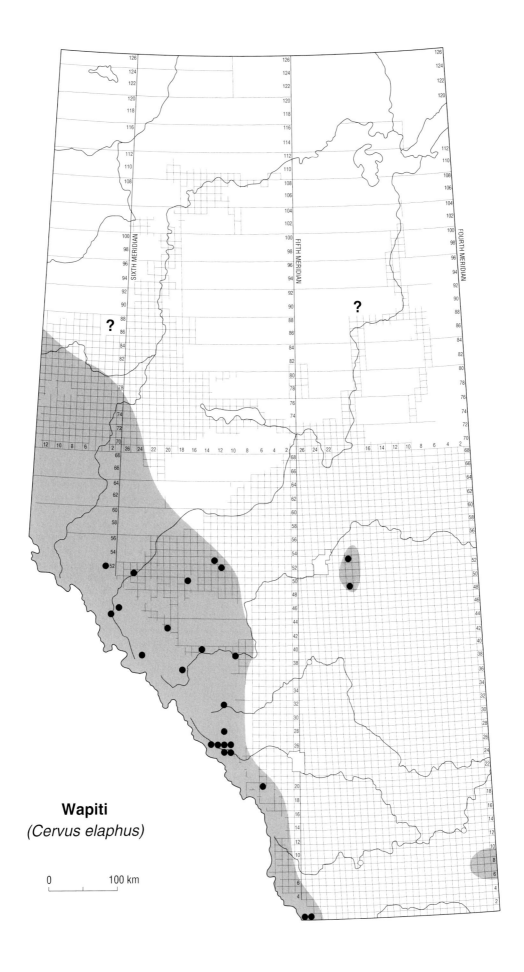

Wapiti

(Cervus elaphus)

0   100 km

MULE DEER
Odocoileus hemionus

Artiodactyla: Cervidae

(plate 14)

IDENTIFYING CHARACTERS

The Mule Deer is a relatively large animal [weighs up to 131 kg (Wishart 1986a)] that has a seasonally variable pelage. In summer the pelage is reddish brown and in winter it is bluish gray. The large rump patch is white. Males have a dark patch on the forehead. The tail is short and round, all white except for a prominent black tip; it is not raised when the animal is alarmed. The metatarsal glands, found on the lower outside of each hind leg, are long (125 mm) and covered with brown hairs (Wishart 1986a). Antlers are found on males only.

The skull is relatively wide between the orbits and the pre-orbital pit is deep. The incisors are wide and the canines incisiform. The dental formula is I 0/3, C 0/1, P 3/3, M 3/3 x 2 = 32.

DISTRIBUTION

Throughout most of southern Alberta north to approximately 57° N in the western part of the province, and 58° N in the east (Wallmo 1981).

HABITAT

River valleys, coulees, and sandhills in the south and mixedwood forests in the north and mountains.

STATUS

Common throughout most of its Alberta range, with the exception of the extreme north.

SIMILAR SPECIES

White-tailed Deer have a larger, bushier tail, brownish on top, white on the underside. The tail is held erect when the animal is alarmed. The metatarsal gland is small, about 25 mm long, and surrounded by white hairs. The skull is relatively narrow between the orbits and the pre-orbital pit is shallow.

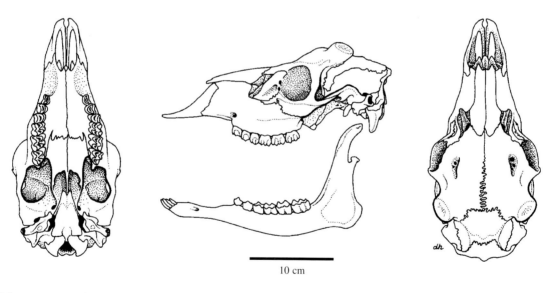

10 cm

Measurements

Sex	Weight[1] (kg)	Total Length[2] (mm)	Tail[2] (mm)	Hindfoot[2] (mm)	Ear[2] (mm)
Males	up to 131	1775 *(N=89)*	192 *(N=90)*	508 *(N=94)*	211 *(N=38)*
		1575-1981 *(N=89)*	127-254 *(N=90)*	460-559 (N=94)	190-230 *(N=38)*
Females	up to 80.3	1629 *(N=32)*	171 *(N=32)*	480 *(N=34)*	197 *(N=6)*
		1473-1753 *(N=32)*	121-216 *(N=32)*	457-500 *(N=34)*	184-220 *(N=6)*

[1]From Wishart 1986a. No sample size given.

[2]From Wishart 1986b.

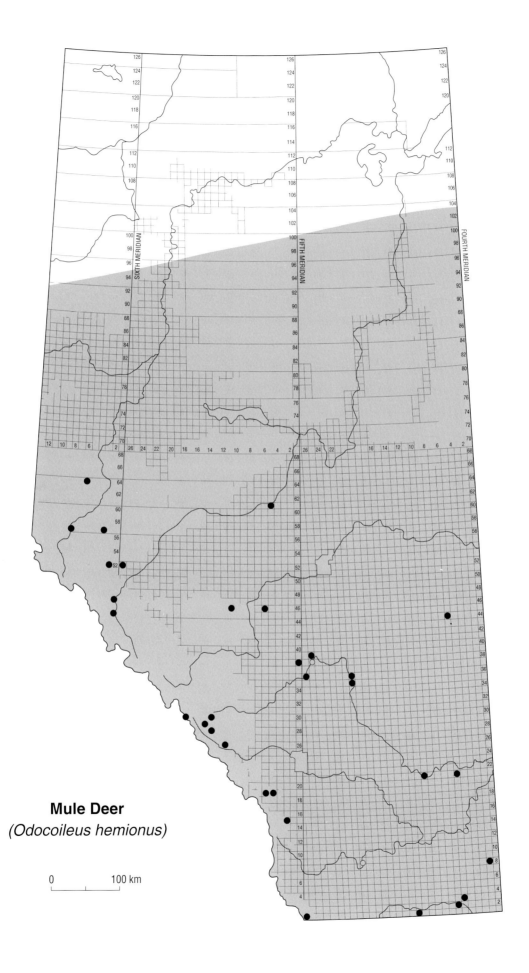

Mule Deer
(Odocoileus hemionus)

0   100 km

WHITE-TAILED DEER
Odocoileus virginianus

IDENTIFYING CHARACTERS

The pelage is seasonally variable. In summer it is reddish brown and in winter grayish brown. The belly and rump patch are white. The tail is long, bushy, brownish on top and white underneath. When alarmed, the tail is raised and 'flagged' from side to side. The metatarsal gland, located on the outside of the lower portion of each hind leg, is small (25 mm long) and is surrounded with white hairs (Wishart 1986a).

The skull is relatively narrow between the orbits and the pre-orbital pit is shallow. The incisors are narrow and the canine is incisiform. The dental formula is I 0/3, C 0/1, P 3/3, M 3/3 x 2 = 32.

DISTRIBUTION

Found throughout southern Alberta, north to the Calling Lake area, northwest to Grande Prairie and Peace River, and north along the Peace River to Fort Vermilion. They are found in the mountains from Waterton to Jasper. Occasional sightings have been reported along the Athabasca River almost to Lake Athabasca (Wishart 1984).

HABITAT

Deciduous forests with open glades, farm shelter belts in the south, and riparian forests in the north.

STATUS

Common in the south and central areas of the province; uncommon in the northern mountains and foothills.

SIMILAR SPECIES

Mule Deer have a narrow, round, black-tipped tail. The metatarsal gland is long (125 mm) and surrounded with brown hairs. The skull is broad across the orbits and the pre-orbital pit is deep.

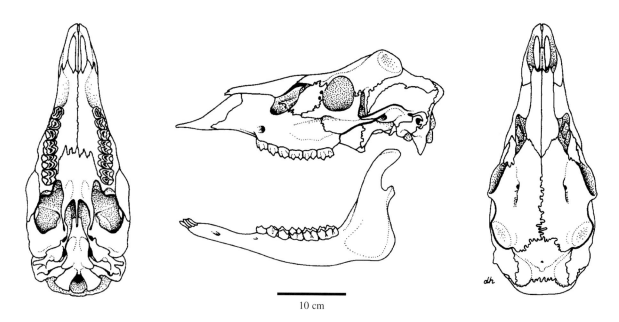

10 cm

Measurements

Sex		Weight[1] (kg)	Total Length[2] (mm)	Tail[2] (mm)	Hindfoot[2] (mm)	Ear[2] (mm)
Males	Mean	up to 130	1869 (N=442)	287(N=449)	498 (N=444)	160 (N=168)
	Range		1580-2134 (N=442)	180-406 (N=449)	440-565 (N=444)	140-190 (N=168)
Females	Mean	up to 80	1698(N=457)	251 (N=462)	467(N=464)	151(N=209)
	Range		1510-1980 (N=457)	170-356 (N=462)	410-521 (N=464)	130-170 (N=209)

[1]From Wishart 1986a. No sample size given.

[2]From Wishart 1986b.

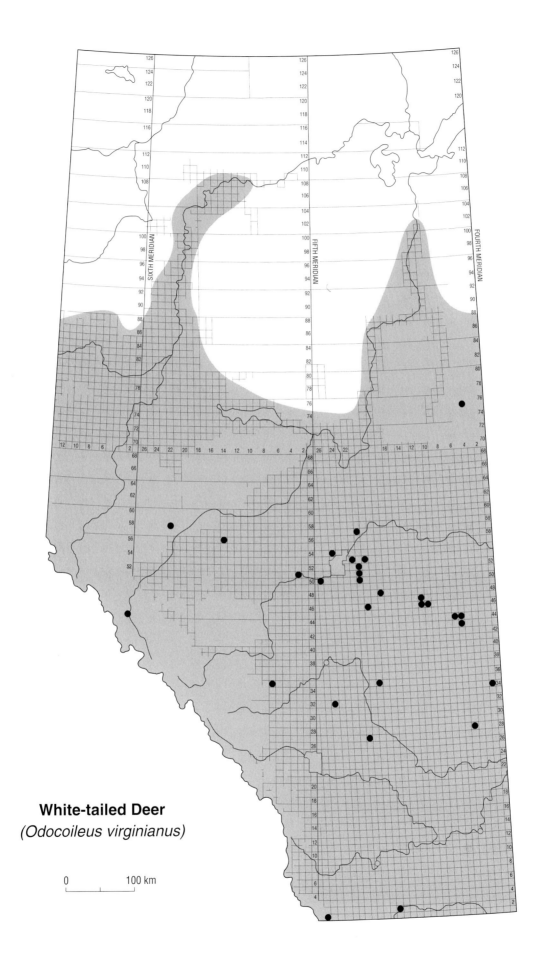

White-tailed Deer

(Odocoileus virginianus)

0   100 km

MOOSE
Alces alces

Artiodactyla: Cervidae

(plate 15)

IDENTIFYING CHARACTERS

The Moose is the largest deer in Alberta. The pelage varies from grayish brown to almost black. The legs are long and the lower portions are lighter colored. The ears are large and grayish. The tail is extremely short. There is a prominent hump at the shoulders. The nose is large and bulbous. A dewlap is present in all adults and in some individuals a 'bell' or a tassle hangs from the dewlap. Bulls possess large, palmate antlers that project laterally from the skull.

The skull is large. The nasal bones are small, the premaxillary bones long, hence the large nasal opening. The mandible is long and relatively shallow. The diastema is large. The incisors are large and spatulate. The canine is incisiform and is smaller than the incisors. The dental formula is I 0/3, C 0/1, P 3/3, M 3/3 x 2 = 32.

DISTRIBUTION

Found throughout the forested regions of the province, throughout the Rocky Mountains and foothills, and has been successfully introduced into the Cypress Hills.

HABITAT

Mixed woods. The Moose is frequently seen around the edges of lakes, bogs, and streams.

STATUS

Common.

SIMILAR SPECIES

The large, black body, long legs, bulbous nose, dewlap, and large, palmate antlers (in males) readily distinguish the Moose.

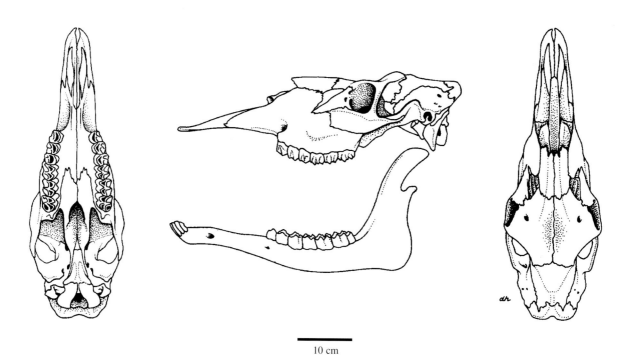

10 cm

Measurements

Sex		Weight (kg)	Total Length (mm)	Hindfoot (mm)
Males (N=10)	Mean	384.2	2548.5	803.5
	Range	281-499	2265-2890	780-850
Females (N=10)	Mean	377.5	2491.0	802.0
	Range	272-436	2280-2710	760-835

208

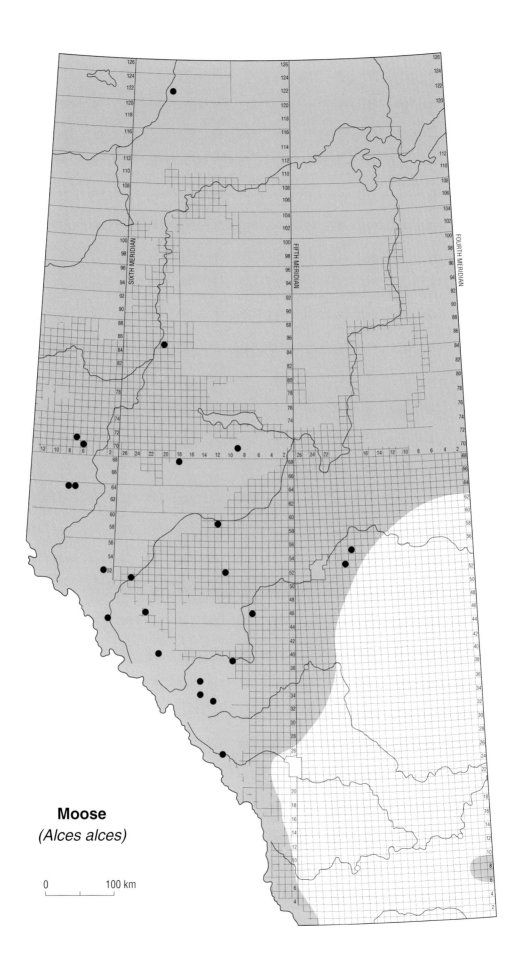

Moose

(Alces alces)

0 _____ 100 km

CARIBOU
Rangifer tarandus

IDENTIFYING CHARACTERS

The striking features of Caribou are the large, forward-curving antlers of mature males, the dark brown pelage, the cream-colored neck and mane, and the large hooves. The muzzle is broad and the head is the same color as the body. A fringe of white hairs circles each hoof. The ears and tail are short and well furred.

The nasal bones of the skull are much wider at the posterior end. Caribou are the only members of the deer family in which females regularly have antlers, albeit much smaller than those of the males. Upper canines may be present. Lower canines are incisiform. The dental formula is I 0/3, C 1/1, P 3/3, M 3/3 x 2 = 34.

DISTRIBUTION

Caribou have a disjunct distribution. They occur in the mountains south to the northern part of Banff National Park (Holroyd and Van Tighem 1983), in the northeast corner of the province, south to Winefred Lake and in the Lesser Slave Lake area (Edmonds 1986).

HABITAT

Mature coniferous and mixed wood forests.

STATUS

Considered a threatened species in Alberta. Estimated numbers in 1986 were 2000 (Edmonds 1986).

SIMILAR SPECIES

Wapiti are larger, tan colored, and have large backward-directed antlers.

Moose are larger, darker colored, and have large palmate antlers.

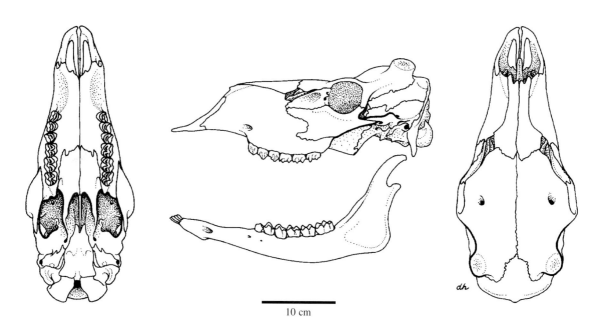

10 cm

Measurements

Sex		Weight[1] (kg)	Total Length[2] (mm)	Tail[2] (mm)	Hindfoot (mm)	Ear (mm)
Males (N=3)	Mean	190 *(N=17)*	2220 *(N=4)*	187 (N=4)	636.6 *(N=3)*	147.7 *(N=3)*
	Range	--	1970-2590 *(N=4)*	170-203 *(N=4)*	630-650 *(N=3)*	140-153 *(N=3)*
Females (N=1)	Mean	136 *(N=7)*	2189 *(N=27)*	168 *(N=27)*	597.5 *(N=2)*	142 *(N=1)*
	Range	--	1930-2340 *(N=27)*	130-230 *(N=27)*	585-610 *(N=2)*	

[1]From Fuller and Keith 1980.

[2]Includes data provided by J. Edmonds, Alberta Fish and Wildlife Division.

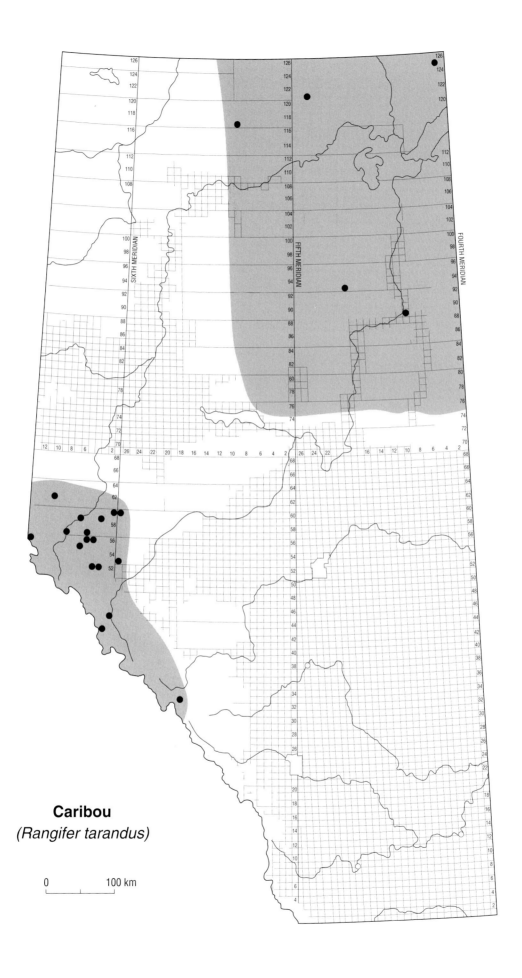

Caribou
(Rangifer tarandus)

0   100 km

PRONGHORN
Antilocapra americana

Artiodactyla: Antilocapridae

(plate 15)

IDENTIFYING CHARACTERS

The pelage is short, dense, and coarse, varying from dark tan to pale sandy-brown. The rump and belly are white. The throat area has alternating broad bands of brown and white. The top of the muzzle is black and in males there is a conspicuous dark patch below the ears. Horns occur on both sexes but on females they may be nothing more than slight bumps on the head and may not be noticeable. The horns on males are long, oval at the base and circular at the tips. The tips normally bend inward toward each other. The horns bifurcate at approximately the mid-point to form a prominent "prong", hence the name Pronghorn. The horn sheaths are unique in that they are shed annually.

The skull has a long, narrow rostrum. The horn cores are unbranched and are laterally compressed. They arise from directly above the orbits. The first two incisors are broad, the others are narrow. The canine is incisiform and narrow. The dental formula is I 0/3, C 0/1, P 3/3, M 3/3 X 2 = 32.

DISTRIBUTION

Pronghorn are found in much of southeastern Alberta. Recently, Pronghorn were seen overwintering near Millet (G. Kemp, personal communication).

HABITAT

Open grasslands.

STATUS

Common in southern Alberta. Population numbers fluctuate in response to severity of winter conditions.

SIMILAR SPECIES

None

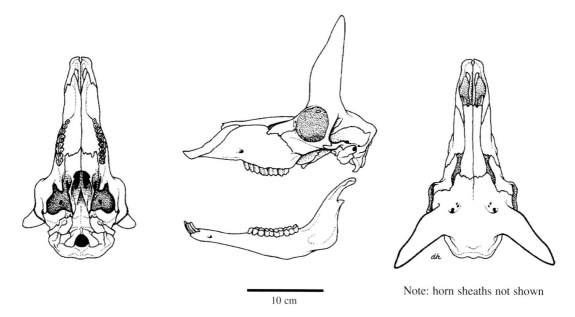

10 cm

Note: horn sheaths not shown

Measurements

Sex		Weight[1] (kg)	Total Length (mm)	Tail (mm)	Hindfoot (mm)	Ear (mm)
Males (N=9)	Mean	56.5 (N=16)	1421.0	116.4	411.3	134.9
	Range	46.6-70.5 (N=16)	1380-1490	85-144	392-430	120-145
Females (N=6)	Mean	50.6 (N=7)	1428.4	95.2	412.5	135.0
	Range	47.0-56.4 (N=7)	1385-1529	77-110	390-440	130-142

[1]Modified from Mitchell 1971.

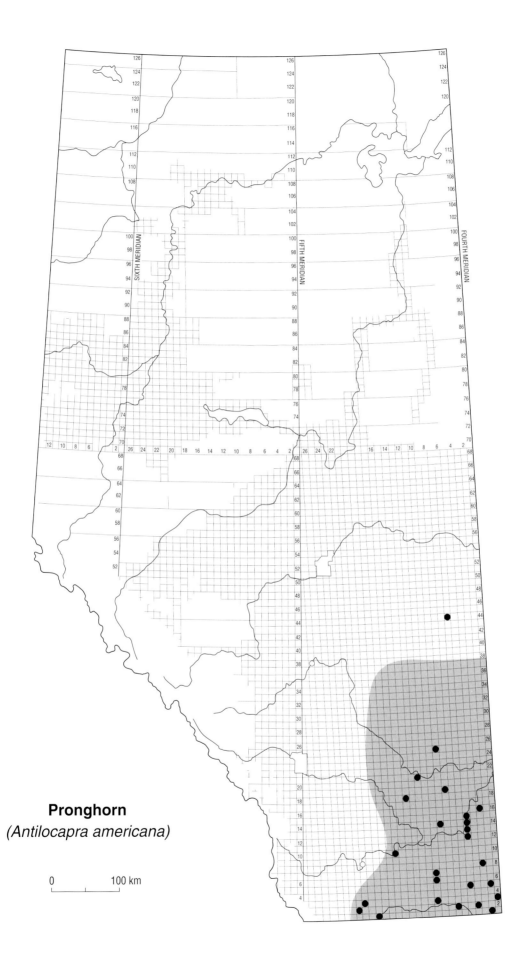

Pronghorn
(Antilocapra americana)

0   100 km

BISON
Bison bison

Artiodactyla: **Bovidae**

(plate 16)

IDENTIFYING CHARACTERS

The Bison is a massive, reddish brown to dark brown animal. The head and forequarters are covered with long, shaggy hair while the hindquarters are less so. There is a prominent shoulder hump and the head is carried low. The short, curved horns are black with a smooth surface. Horns occur on both sexes but those on the cows are smaller. The long tail has a long terminal tuft. The dental formula is I 0/3, C 0/1, P 3/3, M 3/3 x 2 = 32.

Two subspecies of *Bison bison* were found in Alberta: Wood Bison (*B. b. athabascae*) and Plains Bison (*B. b. bison*). According to van Zyll de Jong (1986), the Wood Bison is larger and darker; it has a more anteriorly placed shoulder hump, less hair on the head, and a thinner, more pointed beard. The Plains Bison has distinct "chaps" on the front legs.

DISTRIBUTION

Today substantial Bison herds are confined to Elk Island and Wood Buffalo National Parks. Smaller herds are located in Banff and Waterton Lakes National Parks. Some farmers and ranchers throughout the province are raising Bison commercially. Gainer (1985) reported free-ranging Bison outside Wood Buffalo National Park, in herds of up to 40 animals, between the west Park boundary and Fox Lake and as many as 250 in the "Lower Peace region." He also reported Bison from west of High Level, and one shot in the Buffalo Head Prairie area.

HABITAT

Historically, Bison preferred the grasslands of southern Alberta and the open meadows in the northern forests.

STATUS

In Alberta, wild bison are extremely rare. Protected in our National Parks, bison are common. Wood Bison is on the Canadian Endangered Species list although pure *B. b. athabascae* may no longer exist (van Zyll de Jong 1986). The Wood Buffalo National Park bison are considered hybrids (Reynolds and Hawley 1987) of the plains and wood forms. Most bison outside the park are Plains Bison.

SIMILAR SPECIES

None.

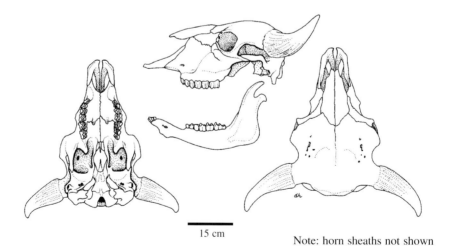

15 cm

Note: horn sheaths not shown

Measurements

Sex		Weight (kg)	Head/Body (mm)	Tail (mm)	Hindfoot (mm)
Males (N=28)	Mean	859.0	2790	470	639
	Range	680-1179	2250-3350	360-540	580-710
Females (N=22)	Mean	498.3	2387	394	588
	Range	390-640	2180-2850	280-480	560-660

Note: measurements are modified from van Zyll de Jong 1986.

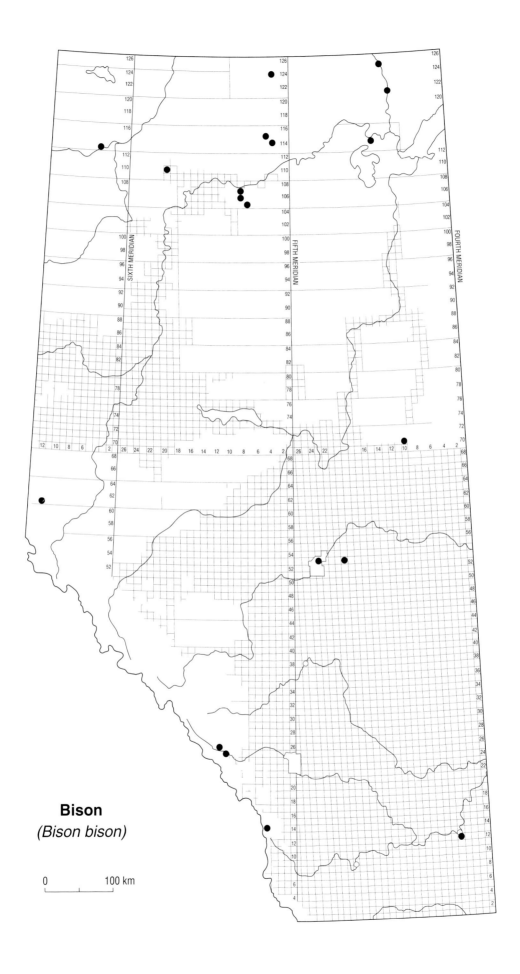

Bison

(Bison bison)

0   100 km

215

MOUNTAIN GOAT
Oreamnos americanus

Artiodactyla: Bovidae

(plate 16)

IDENTIFYING CHARACTERS

The long, dense, white pelage and the un-branched, sharp-tipped, black horns identify the Mountain Goat. In spring, an individual may appear ragged and unkempt as it sheds its winter coat. The pelage consists of long guard hairs and a dense, woolly undercoat. Adults have a beard.

The skull is delicate with a long, narrow rostrum and short nasal bones. Both sexes have horns; the cores rise posterior to the orbits. The dental formula is I 0/3, C 0/1, P 3/3, M 3/3 x 2 = 32.

DISTRIBUTION

The Mountain Goat is unevenly distributed throughout the Rocky Mountains of Alberta from Waterton Lakes National Park north to Torrens River (Soper 1947).

HABITAT

Rocky terrain in the alpine and subalpine zones. Some come to lower elevations to visit mineral licks.

STATUS

Sporadic. In some areas the species may be encountered frequently and be absent in others.

SIMILAR SPECIES

Bighorn Sheep are brown with much larger, curled, blunt-tipped horns.

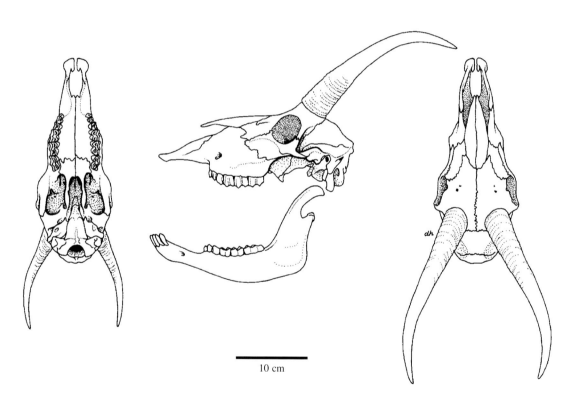

10 cm

Measurements[1]

Sex		Weight (kg)	Total Length (mm)	Tail (mm)	Hindfoot (mm)	Ear (mm)
Males	Mean	88.8 (N=5)	1599 (N=7)	134 (N=8)	362 (N=8)	132.5 (N=5)
	Range	64.9-114.3 (N=5)	1290-1830 (N=7)	90-160 (N=8)	336-389 (N=8)	115-149 (N=5)
Females	Mean	71.5 (N=29)	1571 (N=36)	101.7 (N=36)	344 (N=36)	120 (N=36)
	Range	62.1-84.1 (N=29)	1350-1940 (N=36)	73-140 (N=36)	305-375 (N=36)	95-145 (N=36)

[1]Includes data provided by K. Smith and M. Festa-Bianchette, Alberta Fish and Wildlife Division.

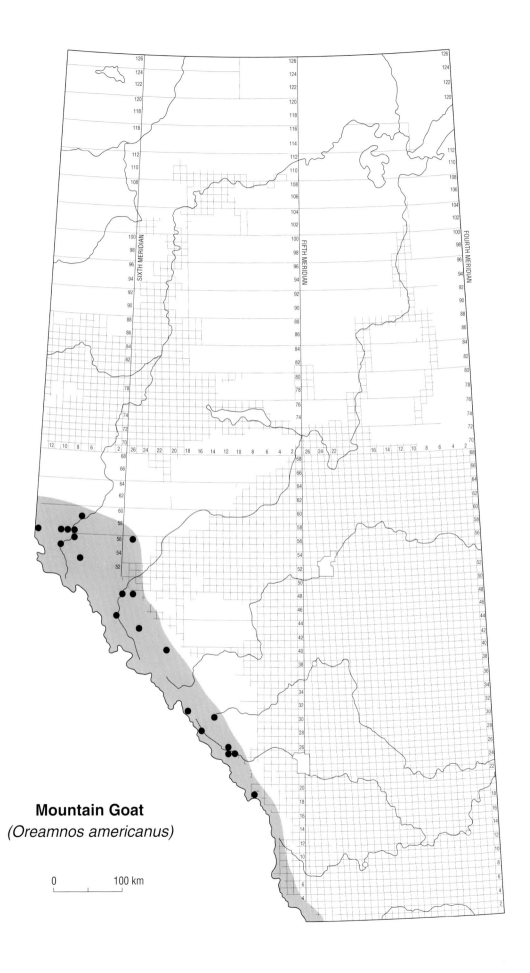

Mountain Goat

(Oreamnos americanus)

0   100 km

BIGHORN SHEEP
Ovis canadensis

IDENTIFYING CHARACTERS

The horns are massive; they curve backward and outward and, in adult rams, the tips curve forward. The horns of females and immature males are much smaller. The pelage is dense and varies from light to dark brown. The rump patch is large and white. The white extends down the inside and back of the hind legs. The muzzle is white. The tail is brownish black and is relatively short.

The skull is triangular in shape. It is broad across the orbits with a tapered rostrum. In mature rams, the horn cores have an extremely broad base. They curve backward and outward and terminate in a broad, blunt end. In females, the horn cores are shorter, with a narrow base, and a rounded, blunt tip. The cranium is deep. The dental formula is I 0/3, C 0/1, P 3/3, M 3/3 x 2 = 32.

DISTRIBUTION

Found throughout the Rocky Mountains of Alberta. Soper (1947) reported them north from Waterton Lakes National Park to the headwaters of the Kakwa, Sheep, Smoky, and Wildhay rivers.

HABITAT

Seasonally variable. Summer ranges are at higher elevations than the winter ranges. Open grassy meadows are preferred in summer and snow-free areas are favored during the winter. They select areas near rocky ledges and cliffs.

STATUS

Relatively common in some areas but may be absent in others. Populations tend to fluctuate and individuals are susceptible to pneumonia. If winter conditions are severe, die-offs can occur.

SIMILAR SPECIES

None.

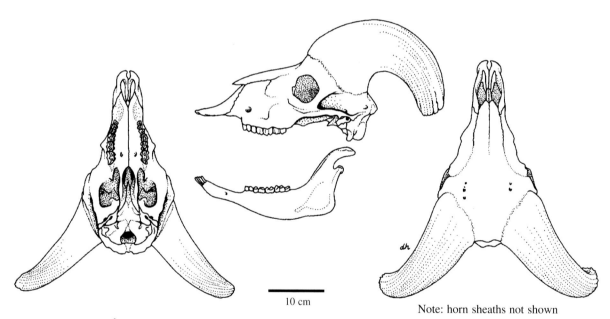

10 cm

Note: horn sheaths not shown

Measurements[1]

Sex		Weight (kg)	Total Length (mm)	Tail (mm)	Hindfoot (mm)	Ear (mm)
Males (N=21)	Mean	94.5	1695	110	446.8	110 *(N=1)*
	Range	73.0-118.0	1555-1797	83-146	425-465	
Females (N=21)	Mean	66.6	1535	101.3	418.8	--
	Range	49.0-82.5	1465-1639	75-136	400-433	--

[1]Includes data provided by J. Jorgenson, Alberta Fish and Wildlife Division.

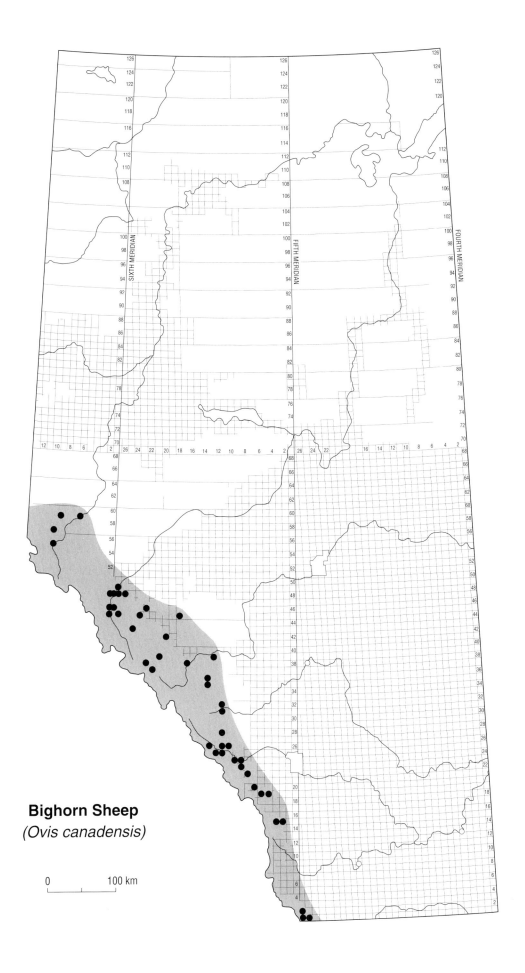

Bighorn Sheep
(Ovis canadensis)

0   100 km

SIXTH MERIDIAN

FIFTH MERIDIAN

FOURTH MERIDIAN

219

Domestic Mammals

In addition to the 86 indigenous mammals in Alberta, there are two of accidental occurrence (Gray Fox, Black-footed Ferret) and four introduced "wild" species. However, the users of this guide may also encounter several species of domesticated animals. On the assumption that whole individuals of these latter species will be easily recognized, the following section will assist in identifying isolated skulls. Common domestic animals include cats, dogs, horses, cattle (oxen), sheep, goats, and pigs. These seven species are arranged in scientific fashion as follows.

Order Carnivora - Carnivores
    Family Canidae - Wolves, Foxes, Dogs, etc.
        Dog (*Canis familiaris*)
    Family Felidae - All Cats
        Cat (*Felis catus*)
Order Perissodactyla - Horses, Rhinos, Tapirs
    Family Equidae - Horses
        Horse (*Equus caballus*)
Order Artiodactyla - Deer, Bison, Sheep, etc.
    Family Bovidae - Bison, Domestic Ox, etc.
        Ox (*Bos taurus*)
        Sheep (*Ovis aries*)
        Goat (*Capra hircus*)
    Family Suidae - Swine
        Pig (*Sus scrofa*)

The carnivores will be recognizable for the prominent, pointed canine teeth and the shearing capability of the cheek teeth. The horse can be recognized as a large herbivore with upper incisors, a large diastema, and a battery of exclusively grinding cheek teeth. The artiodactyls (except the pig) are medium to large herbivores that have no upper incisors (e.g., bison and deer); they do have a diastema followed by grinding cheek teeth. These cheek teeth have a W-shaped (uppers) or M-shaped (lowers) profile as well as a roughly W-shaped enamel pattern on the chewing surfaces. Pig skulls are much smaller than horses but share with horses the possession of upper incisors and canine teeth. The cheek teeth are bunodont; that is, they possess low crowns with many small cusps and cusplets.

Difficulties in identification of these domesticated species arise from the fact that each species (except pigs) must be distinguished from closely related wild species in Alberta. Selective breeding and, in some cases, hybridization with wild species renders some identifications exceedingly difficult.

Descriptions

Domestic Dog (*Canis familiaris*)
    Using the key to the Carnivora, domestic dogs can be identified to *Canis*, as they are decidedly different from the foxes. Dogs possess no skull characters that are unique for the species; the size, shape, number of teeth, and other characters are highly variable. However, it is generally true that the forehead region in dogs, when viewed in profile, has a "stepped" appearance, due to the enlarged frontal sinuses. Wolves and Coyotes usually present a straighter line in profile (Fig. 11), as do some dog breeds with longer, narrower muzzles (e.g., collies). Clearly, some dog breeds will be distinctive. Statistical treatment may occasionally confirm the identity of canid skulls, and reference to the skulls of known breeds and/or hybrids in museum collections may

Canis familiaris

stepped forehead

5 cm

Canis lupus

10 cm

Figure 11. Comparison of Domestic Dog (*Canis familiaris*) and Wolf (*Canis lupus*) skulls.

also be informative. The dental formula is I 3/3 C 1/1 P 4/4 M 2/3 x 2 = 42.

Cats (*Felis catus*)

The cat skull, like those of other felids, is short and broad with a very short rostrum (see Fig. 12), but may possess 30 teeth. The dental formula is I 3/3 C 1/1 P 2/2 or P 3/2 M 1/1 x 2 = 28 or 30, variably with the addition of the extra upper premolars. Domestic cat skulls rarely exceed 100 mm long and 75 mm wide. Thus, a small felid with three upper premolars is unmistakable, even from the Canada Lynx and Bobcat.

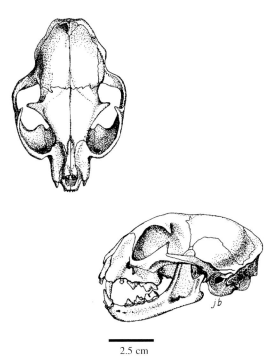

2.5 cm

Figure 12. Dorsal and profile views of a Cat (*Felis catus*) skull.

Horse (*Equus caballus*)

The horse skull is long and broad, with a rostrum narrowing toward the front; the brain case is small relative to the length of the skull. The anterior part of the upper jaw (composed of the two premaxillary bones) contains six incisors. These are followed in the maxilla by a pointed canine tooth on each side (in stallions only) and a diastema (Fig. 13). Cheek teeth, with flattish chewing surfaces, normally number six on each side of the skull and lower jaw, but a very small upper first premolar may persist in young animals.

The dental formula for a stallion is I 3/3 C 1/1 P 3/3 or P 4/3 M 3/3 x 2 = 40 or 42; the mare has no functional canines and, therefore, has 36 or 38 teeth. The lower jaw is very deep and the lower margin at the rear (the "angle") is robust and broadly curved.

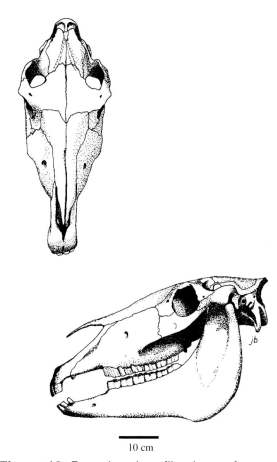

10 cm

Figure 13. Dorsal and profile views of a Horse (*Equus caballus*) skull.

Domestic Cattle or Oxen (*Bos taurus*)

Superficially, an ox resembles a Bison (see also *Bison* account). There are skull shape differences, and the character of the horns and horn cores is usually distinct in each species. Hybrids (e.g., "beefalo") may not be distinguishable. There are no upper incisors, in any case.

Bison skulls are more nearly "triangular" than those of cows in dorsal view: broad across the occiput (at rear) and narrowing consistently toward the front. The ox skull is narrower overall with a long, narrow rostrum exhibiting nearly parallel sides. The rearward extension of the premaxilla usually makes contact with the nasal bone in the ox, but does not do so in *Bison* (see Fig. 14).

Bison horn cores project to the side, then backward and upward; a line drawn between the horn core tips normally passes posterior to the occiput. On the other hand, ox horn cores usually project to the side, then forward; the tips may turn upward slightly, depending on the breed. The tip-to-tip line in the ox passes across the top of the skull.

In profile view, Bison skulls tend to present a rounded dorsal outline, whereas, those of oxen have a flat dorsal profile. Although horns are normally present in both sexes of cattle, some breeds include hornless females. Too, cattle farmers may remove horns to reduce the danger of injury to other herd members.

The dental formula is the same as for *Bison*: I 0/3 C 0/1 P 3/3 M 3/3 x 2 = 32.

Domestic Sheep (*Ovis aries*)

The skull of sheep is roughly hexagonal in dorsal view, with the widest part being across the posterior margins of the orbits (see Fig. 15). In profile, the dorsal outline drops quickly down over the braincase posterior to this point. Anteriorly, the dorsal line drops more gently to the tips of the premaxillae. The highest point coincides with the widest point. Skull length does not normally exceed about 250 mm; this separates sheep from oxen.

Many domestic sheep breeds do not bear horns. When they do, the curl can be great but, unlike the Rocky Mountain Bighorn Sheep, the horn tips may quickly spiral outward. The horn cores, with flattened anterior surfaces, are less massive in the domestic sheep and they project laterally, backward, and down. In bighorns, the massive horn cores also have flat anterior surfaces and are somewhat laterally compressed; projecting from the top of the skull, the cores arch upward, back, and then down.

Bos taurus   *Bison bison*

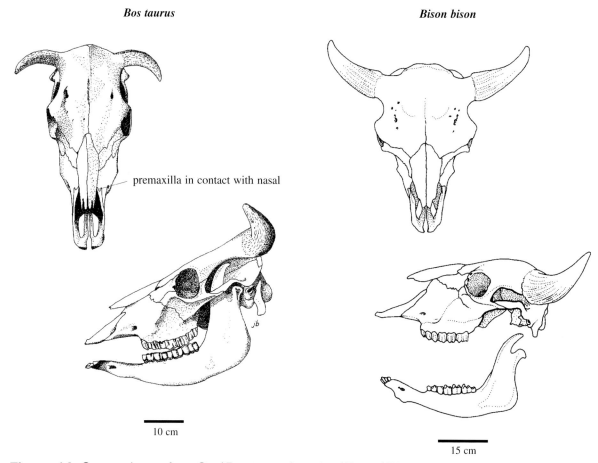

premaxilla in contact with nasal

10 cm

15 cm

Figure 14. Comparison of an Ox (*Bos taurus*) and a Bison (*Bison bison*) skull.

222

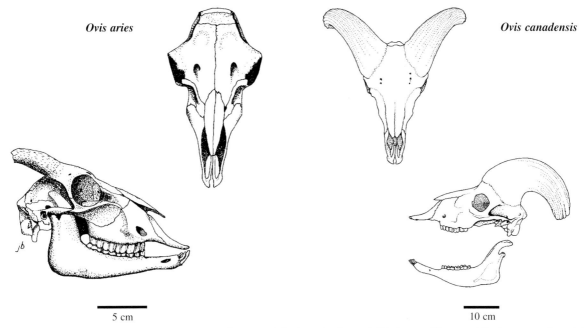

Ovis aries

Ovis canadensis

5 cm

10 cm

Figure 15. Comparison of Domestic Sheep (*Ovis aries*) and Bighorn Sheep (*Ovis canadensis*) skulls.

The rearward extension of the premaxilla does not make contact with the nasal bone. The domestic sheep also possesses a deep lachrymal, or pre-orbital, pit which is not present in domestic goats. The dental formula for both sheep is I 0/3 C 0/1 P 3/3 M 3/3 x 2 = 32.

Domestic Goats (*Capra hircus*)

Skulls of goats are similar to sheep in size, shape, and general proportions. Variation due to the effects of domestication may make it difficult to distinguish goat from sheep skulls. The dental formula for both is I 0/3 C 0/1 P 3/3 M 3/3 x 2 = 32.

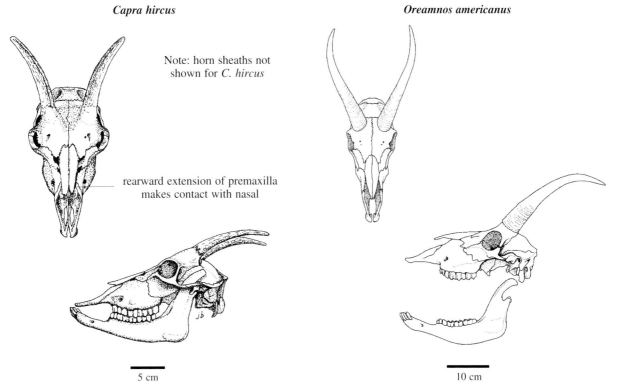

Capra hircus

Oreamnos americanus

Note: horn sheaths not shown for *C. hircus*

rearward extension of premaxilla makes contact with nasal

5 cm

10 cm

Figure 16. Comparison of the skulls of a domestic goat (*Capra hircus*) and a Mountain Goat (*Oreamnos americanus*).

Useful features of *Capra* skulls are (in combination) the absence of the lachrymal (pre-orbital) pit, and a premaxilla whose rearward extension contacts the nasal bone (see Fig. 16). The teeth are not readily distinguishable from those of sheep.

Horns are normally present in all breeds and in both sexes. The horn cores are slender, usually cylindrical, and pointed, arching upward and backward from the frontal bones. Mountain goats (genus *Oreamnos*) have longer, lower-crowned skulls than the domestic goat, with a relatively longer, narrower rostrum; the nasals are very long, narrow, and parallel-sided; the horn cores are not noticeably different from domestic goats. The lachrymal pit in *Oreamnos* is absent, and the premaxilla does not contact the nasal bone, as it does in *Capra*.

Pigs (*Sus scrofa*)

Pigs are classified as split-toed ungulates, but they differ from other artiodactyls like deer (Cervidae) and cattle (Bovidae) in having four separate (not fused) metacarpals and metatarsals in the feet, and in having upper incisors.

The skull is exceptional in having a short, high-crowned braincase and a flat, sloping or dished forehead (see Fig. 17). In dorsal view, the postorbital region of the skull features a short, deep fossa for the attachment of the relatively massive temporal muscles; the postorbital processes are robust.

Most distinctive is the array of numerous cusps and cusplets on the more posteriorly placed premolars and the molars, unlike the W-shaped pattern on the chewing surface of cervid and bovid teeth. As well, the upper cheek tooth rows

Sus scrofa

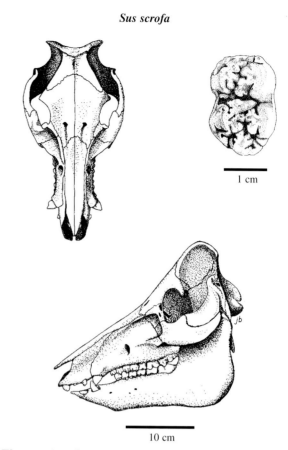

1 cm

10 cm

Figure 17. Skull of a Domestic Pig (*Sus scrofa*) and a generalized Pig tooth showing the distinctive cusp arrangement.

diverge towards the front, whereas, in the artiodactyls, the rows are parallel or they bow outwards. Canine teeth are often prominent both in the upper and lower dentitions, occurring as upper "tusks" in some older male individuals.

James A. Burns, Ph.D.
Curator, Quaternary Paleontology
Provincial Museum of Alberta

Glossary

Anterior
A position in front of, or toward the front; facing front.

Antlers
Paired, branched, bony outgrowths of the frontal bones, that are covered by a velvety skin during the growing period and shed annually.

Auditory Bulla
One of a pair of bony structures on the skull that house the bones of the inner ear.

Auditory Canal
A bony canal that leads from the outer to the inner ear.

Bilobed
Referring to an incisor tooth with two lobes.

Calcar
A spur of bone or cartilage extending from the ankle of many species of bats that helps to support the tail flight membrane.

Canine
One of four kinds of teeth found in mammals. It is a single-rooted, unicuspid tooth situated between the incisors and the premolars.

Carnassial Teeth
Shearing, blade-like teeth found in carnivores. Carnassial teeth include upper premolar 4 and lower molar 1.

Cervid
A collective term that refers to members of the deer family.

Cheek Teeth
A collective term referring to those teeth located behind the canines and including premolars, if present, and molars.

Condylobasal Length (basilar length)
The distance between the anteriormost point on the premaxilla and the anterior margin of the foramen magnum

Coronoid Process
A process, on the rising posterior portion of the mandible, upon which some chewing muscles insert.

Crown
Generally, that portion of a tooth visible above the gum line and covered with enamel.

Cusp
With reference to teeth, a point or bump on the crown of a tooth.

Cuspidate
Referring to teeth that have cusps.

Dental Formula
A method for identifying and numbering teeth.

Dentary
One of two bones that form the lower jaw.

Dewlap
A prominent ventral extension of the skin of the throat, covered with hair and hanging loosely; best exemplified in the Moose (*Alces*)

Diastema
A distinct space or gap between teeth, such as the gap between the incisors and cheek teeth in species that do not have canine teeth (e.g., rodents).

Disjunct
Divided or separated; split.

Dorsal
A position along or associated with the back of an animal; in quadrupeds, the top side. Also dorso-ventral: a direction from backside to belly, top to bottom.

Extirpated
Refers to the status of a species that once occurred in an area but is no longer found there. It is present elsewhere, by definition.

Fenestrate

Having lattice-like openings usually associated with the skulls of hares and rabbits.

Foramen

An opening or hole, in the skull and other bones, that allows passage of blood vessels and/or nerves. Plural: foramina.

Foramen Magnum

A large opening in the back or base of the skull through which the spinal cord passes.

Fossorial

Pertains to the habit of digging burrows and dens for life underground.

Frontal

One of a pair of skull bones that form the anterior dorsal portion of the braincase. The frontals form the base of antlers and horn cores.

Globose

Pertaining to the skull, having a round or globe-shaped outline.

Holarctic

A collective term that refers to the combined Palearctic and Nearctic zoogeographic regions.

Horn Core

A bony projection of the skull that arises from the rear of the frontal bone. Horns are usually found on males of members of the family Bovidae.

Horn Sheath

A hard, ever-growing material that covers the horn core. It is the same material as fingernails and hoof coverings.

Incisiform

With reference to the teeth, it is a tooth that is incisor-like in form.

Incisive Foramen

An opening at the anterior end of the hard palate just posterior to the incisors.

Incisor

One of the groups of teeth that make up mammalian dentition. Incisors are the most anterior teeth present, and generally have a nipping function.

Infra-orbital Canal or Foramen

An opening in the skull that extends anteriorly from the orbits to the face along the side of the rostrum.

Interorbital

The distance or area on the skull between the orbits.

Maxilla

A bone of the skull that forms part of the rostrum. It is the bone in which the upper canine, premolar, and molar teeth are located.

Medial Tine

A small projection on the incisors of some shrews, especially the Dusky Shrew.

Metapodial

A collective term referring to certain bones of the foot, i.e., the equivalents of slender bones of the palm of the hand and the sole of the foot. Includes metacarpals (front limbs) and metatarsals (hind limbs).

Metatarsal Gland

A gland situated low on the hind leg of mule and white-tailed deer; it is used in scent-marking.

Molar Teeth

The most posterior teeth in the tooth row. Located behind the premolars, they generally perform a grinding function.

Moult Lines

Lines marking the extent of seasonal loss and/or replacement of hair, usually noticed as a narrow band on the animal's back. Pocket gophers and marmots provide good examples.

Nares

Openings at both ends of the nasal passages; referred to as anterior (external) and posterior (internal) nares.

Nearctic

A biogeographic region defining North America excluding Mexico.

Occipital Bone

The bone at the back of the skull where the foramen magnum is located.

Occiput

A collective term for the posterior portion of the skull.

Occlusal Surface

Pertains to the chewing surface of a tooth. It is the contact surface between the upper and lower teeth.

Palearctic

A zoogeographic term for the northern portions of the Eurasian land mass.

Palmate

With reference to antlers on Moose and Caribou, a broad, flat-surfaced portion of the antler.

Patagium

The skin that forms the flight membranes in bats.

Pedicle (also pedicel)

The bony extension of the frontal bone of the skull from which an antler grows; the knob remaining after the antler is shed.

Pelage

A collective term for the hair or fur of mammals.

Posterior

Position behind, or towards the back; facing the rear.

Postorbital

Refers to that portion of the skull that is immediately behind the orbit.

Premaxilla

One of a pair of bones at the front of the skull. It forms the anterior portion of the rostrum. The upper incisor teeth, when present, are found in this bone.

Premolar

One of four kinds of teeth in mammals. Premolars are situated between the canines and the molars, and vary in function depending on the tooth form.

Pre-orbital Pit

A pit or depression on the side of the rostrum immediately in front of the orbit. The pit often contains a gland that secretes a scented fluid.

Prismatic

Pertains to the teeth of voles and lemmings. The occlusal surface of the teeth exhibits a series of prisms or triangles.

Quadruped

An animal that habitually walks on four feet. This assumes that all four appendages are used in locomotion. Humans are bipedal (two-footed).

Re-entrant Angle

With reference to the prismatic teeth of certain rodents, it is an infolding of the enamel on the sides of the cheek teeth.

Rooted Tooth

A tooth that stops growing when the root canal is closed off. Rooted teeth generally have well defined crowns and roots.

Rootless Tooth

A tooth that grows continuously because the root canals remain open; a common condition in rodents and several other groups. Crowns and roots are not well defined in these teeth.

Rostrum

That portion of the skull that is anterior to the orbits; the snout.

Rufous

Reddish or reddish-brown.

Rugose

Rugged, bumpy. With specific reference to antler bases, the rugose surface of the antler where sunken veinlets that supply the velvet alternate with elevated bony ridges that protect the vessels from injury.

Sagittal Crest

A ridge of bone extending along the dorsal mid-line of the skull.

Septum

A partition between two areas or spaces; with reference to the nasal passages, a bony partition (the vomer bone) that separates the rear end of the passage into two openings.

Suture

A line between two bones of the skull that forms an immovable joint.

Temporal Ridges

A pair of bony ridges, on the temporal bone of the skull of some mammals, which serve as attachments for jaw muscles.

Total Length

A measurement frequently taken on mammals during the preparation of a museum specimen. It is the length of the specimen, laid flat, from the tip of the nose to the last vertebra in the tail.

Tragus

A fleshy projection in front of the ear. It is most prominent in bats.

Trilobed

Referring to an incisor tooth with three lobes.

Unicuspid

Refers to a tooth with a single cusp. The term is frequently used to refer to a group of upper teeth in shrews.

Ventral

Literally, of the stomach or belly, the belly side; in quadrupeds, the underside.

Vibrissae

The longer, often bristly hairs located towards the front of the muzzle and associated with the sense of touch; whiskers.

Zygomatic Arch

A bridge of bone on the side of the skull; the cheek bone.

LITERATURE CITED

Anderson, E., S.C. Forrest, T.W. Clark, and L. Richardson. 1986. Paleobiology, biogeography, and systematics of the black-footed ferret, *Mustela nigripes* (Audubon and Bachman), 1851. Great Basin Naturalist Memoirs 8:11-62.

Anderson, R.M. 1946. Catalogue of Canadian Recent mammals. National Museum of Canada, Bulletin 103, Biological Series 31. 238 pp.

Anderson, S. and J.K. Jones, Jr. (eds.). 1984. Orders and Families of Recent Mammals of the World. John Wiley and Sons, New York. 686 pp.

Anonymous. 1989. Guide to big game hunting. Alberta Forestry, Lands and Wildlife. 39 pp.

Armstrong, D.M. 1972. Distribution of mammals in Colorado. Museum of Natural History, The University of Kansas, Lawrence. No. 3. 415 pp.

Bayer, S. 1975. Letter to editor. Calgary Field Naturalist 7 (3):78.

Beck, W.H. 1958. A guide to Saskatchewan mammals. Saskatchewan Natural History Society, Special Publication No. 1. 52 pp.

Boyd, M. 1977. Analysis of fur production records by individual fur-bearing species for registered trapping areas in Alberta 1970-75. Report prepared for Alberta Fish and Wildlife Division, Alberta Recreation, Parks and Wildlife. 72 pp.

Brown, A.W.A. 1947. Cougar seen near Medicine Hat, Alberta. Canadian Field-Naturalist 61:44.

Burns, G.R. and N.L. Cool. 1984. A biophysical inventory of the non-ungulate mammals of Elk Island National Park. A report prepared for Parks Canada, Calgary by the Canadian Wildlife Service. 195 pp.

Burns, J.A. 1980. The brown lemming, *Lemmus sibiricus* (Rodentia, Arvicolidae), in the late Pleistocene of Alberta and its postglacial dispersal. Canadian Journal of Zoology 58:1507-1511.

Carbyn, L. N. 1987. Gray wolf and red wolf. Pp. 358-376, *in* Wild furbearer management and conservation in North America (M. Novak, J.A. Baker, M.E. Obbard, B. Malloch, eds.). Ministry of Natural Resources, Whitney Block, Queen's Park, Toronto, Ontario.

Churcher, C.S., P.W. Parmalee, G.L. Bell, and J.P. Lamb. 1989. Caribou from the Late Pleistocene of northwestern Alabama. Canadian Journal of Zoology 67:1210-1216.

Clements, F.E. 1916. Plant succession: Analysis of the development of vegetation. Carnegie Institute of Washington, Publication 242: 1-512.

Clements, F.E. 1936. Nature and structure of the climax. Journal of Ecology 24: 252-284.

Dekker, D. 1989. Otters return to Jasper National Park. Alberta Naturalist 19:141-142.

Delcourt, H.R. and P.A. Delcourt. 1984. Ice age haven for hardwoods. Natural History 93 (9): 22-28.

Depper, M. 1989. First report of a yellow-bellied marmot (*Marmota flaviventris*) in the Calgary area. Pica 9:19-21.

Dice, L.R. 1943. The biotic provinces of North America. University of Michigan Press, Ann Arbor. 78 pp.

Dice, L.R. 1952. Natural communities. University of Michigan Press, Ann Arbor. 547 pp.

Edmonds, E.J. 1986. Woodland caribou: their status and distribution. Alberta Naturalist 16:73-78.

Fuller, T.K. and L.B. Keith. 1980. Physical characteristics of woodland caribou in northeastern Alberta. Canadian Field-Naturalist 94:331-333.

Gainer, B. 1985. Free roaming bison in northern Alberta. Alberta Naturalist 15:86-87.

Gleason, H.A. 1926. The individualistic concept of the plant association. Torrey Botanical Club Bulletin 53:7-26.

Gleason, H.A. 1939. The individualistic concept of the plant association. American Midland Naturalist 21:92-110.

Gunson, J.R. 1983. Status and management of wolves in Alberta. Pp. 25-29, in Wolves in Canada and Alaska. (L.N. Carbyn, ed.) Canadian Wildlife Service, Report Series No. 45.

Hagmeier, E.M. 1966. A numerical analysis of the distributional patterns of North American mammals. II. Re-evaluation of the provinces. Systematic Zoology 15:279-299.

Hagmeier, E.M. and C.D. Stults. 1964. A numerical analysis of the distributional patterns of North American mammals. Systematic Zoology 13: 125-155.

Hall, E.R. 1981. The mammals of North America. John Wiley and Sons, New York, 2nd Edition. 1181 pp.

Harington, C.R. 1978. Quaternary vertebrate faunas of Canada and Alaska and their suggested chronological sequence. Syllogeus 15:1-105.

Haynes, W.S. 1951. A preliminary survey of the rodents and lagomorphs in central and southern Alberta. M.Sc. Thesis, University of Alberta. 88 pp.

Hennings, D. and R.S. Hoffmann. 1977. A review of the taxonomy of the *Sorex vagrans* species complex from western North America. Museum of Natural History, University of Kansas, Occasional Papers, 68:1-35.

Hoffmann, R.S. and D.L. Pattie. 1968. A guide to Montana mammals: identification, habitat, distribution, and abundance. University of Montana, Missoula. 133 pp.

Hoffmann, R.S. and C. Jones. 1970. Influence of late-glacial and post-glacial events on the distribution of Recent mammals of the northern Great Plains. Pp. 355-394 *in:* Pleistocene and Recent environments of the central Great Plains. (W. Dort, Jr. and J.K. Jones, Jr. eds.). University Press Kansas. 433 pp.

Holroyd, G.L. and K.J. Van Tighem. 1983. Ecological (biophysical) land classifications of Banff and Jasper National Parks. Vol. III. The wildlife inventory. Environment Canada, Canadian Wildlife Service, Edmonton. 690 pp.

Hultén, E. 1937. Outline of the history of the arctic and boreal biota during the Quaternary period. Bokförlags Aktiebolaget, Thule, Greenland. 168 pp.

Jones, J.K., Jr., D.M. Armstrong, R.S. Hoffmann, and C. Jones. 1983. Mammals of the northern Great Plains. University of Nebraska Press, Lincoln. 379 pp.

Jones, J.K., Jr., D.C. Carter, H.H. Genoways, R.S. Hoffmann, D.W. Rice, and C. Jones. 1986. Revised checklist of North American mammals north of Mexico, 1986. The Museum, Texas Tech University, Occasional Papers, 107:1-22.

Junge, J.A. and R.S. Hoffmann. 1981. An annotated key to the long-tailed shrews (Genus *Sorex*) of the United States and Canada, with notes on Middle American *Sorex*.. The Museum of Natural History, The University of Kansas, Lawrence, Occasional Paper 94:1-48.

Junge, J.A., R.S. Hoffmann, and R.W. Debry. 1983. Relationships within Holarctic *Sorex arcticus - Sorex tundrensis* species complex. Acta Theriologia 28:339-350.

Kelsall, J.P. and E.S. Telfer. 1973. Biogeography of moose with particular reference to western North America. Naturaliste Canadien 101:117-130.

Kurtén, B. and E. Anderson. 1980. Pleistocene mammals of North America. Columbia University Press. 442 pp.

Macpherson, A.H. 1965. The origin of diversity in mammals of the Canadian arctic tundra. Systematic Zoology 14:153-173.

Mitchell, G.J. 1971. Measurements, weights, and carcass yields of pronghorn in Alberta. Journal of Wildlife Management 35:76-85.

Moore, J.E. 1952a. Notes on three additions to the fauna of Alberta. Canadian Field-Naturalist 66:142-143.

Moore, J.E. 1952b. The gray fox in Alberta. Journal of Mammalogy 33:253.

Nielsen, P.L. 1973. The mammals of Waterton Lakes National Park, Alberta. Environment Canada, Canadian Wildlife Service, Edmonton. 176 pp.

Nielsen, P.L. 1975. The past and present status of the plains and boreal grizzly bear in Alberta. Canadian Wildlife Service, Edmonton. 61 pp.

Pall, O. 1986. Cougar in Alberta. Pp. 209-212, *in* Alberta Wildlife Trophies. Alberta Fish and Game Association, Edmonton.

Preble, E.A. 1908. A biological investigation of the Athabaska-Mackenzie region. United States Biological Survey, North American Fauna 27. 274 pp.

Reynolds, H.W. and A.W.L. Hawley. 1987. Introduction. Pp. 10-12, *in* Bison ecology in relation to agricultural development in the Slave River lowland, N. W. T. (H.W. Reynolds and A.W.L. Hawley, eds.). Canadian Wildlife Service, Occasional Paper 63.

Ross, I. and M. Jalkotzy. 1989. The Sheep River cougar project, Phase II. Final Report. Arc Associated Resource Consultants Ltd., Calgary. 56 pp.

Russell, R.H., J.W. Nolan, N.A. Woody, and G. Anderson. 1979. A study of the Grizzly Bear (*Ursus arctos* L.) in Jasper National Park,

1975-1978, Final Report. Unpublished Canadian Wildlife Service report.

Saunders, M.B. 1990. Fourth red bat found in Alberta. Blue Jay 48:57-58.

Shelford, V.E. 1963. The ecology of North America. University of Illinois Press, Urbana. 610 pp.

Smith, H.C. 1979. Mammals of the Edmonton area. Provincial Museum of Alberta, Natural History Occasional Paper No. 2. 34 pp.

Smith, H.C. 1986. Mammals of southeast Alberta. Provincial Museum of Alberta, Natural History Occasional Paper No. 7. 52 pp.

Smith, H.C. and E.J. Edmonds. 1985. The brown lemming, *Lemmus sibiricus*, in Alberta. Canadian Field-Naturalist 99:99-100.

Soper, J.D. 1942. Mammals of Wood Buffalo Park, northern Alberta and District of Mackenzie. Journal of Mammalogy 23:119-145.

Soper, J.D. 1947. Observations on mammals and birds in the Rocky Mountains of Alberta. Canadian Field-Naturalist 61:143-173.

Soper, J.D. 1964. The mammals of Alberta. Queen's Printer, Edmonton. 402 pp.

Strong, W.L. and K.R. Leggat. 1981. Ecoregions of Alberta. Alberta Energy and Natural Resources Technical Report No. T/4. 64pp.

Udvardy, M.D.F. 1969. Dynamic Zoogeography with Special Reference to Land Animals. Van Nostrand Reinhold Company, New York. 445 pp.

van Zyll de Jong, C.G. 1980. Systematic relationships of woodland and prairie forms of the common shrew, *Sorex cinereus cinereus* Kerr, and *S. c. haydeni* Baird, in the Canadian prairie provinces. Journal of Mammalogy 61:66-75.

van Zyll de Jong, C.G. 1983. Handbook of Canadian Mammals. Vol I: Marsupials and Insectivores. National Museum of Natural Sciences, National Museums of Canada, Ottawa. 210 pp.

van Zyll de Jong, C.G. 1985. Handbook of Canadian Mammals. Vol II: Bats. National Museum of Natural Sciences, National Museums of Canada, Ottawa. 212 pp.

van Zyll de Jong, C.G. 1986. A systematic study of recent bison, with particular consideration of the wood bison (*Bison bison athabascae* Rhoads, 1898). National Museum of Natural Sciences, Publications in Natural Sciences No. 6. Ottawa. 69 pp.

Walker, D.N. 1987. Late Pleistocene/Holocene environmental changes in Wyoming: The mammalian record. Pp. 334-392 *in:* Late Quaternary mammalian biogeography and environments of the Great Plains and prairies. (R.W. Graham, H.A. Semken, Jr., and M.A. Graham, eds.). Illinois State Museum Scientific Papers, Vol. XXII, Springfield. 491 pp.

Wallmo, O.C. 1981. Mule deer and black-tailed deer distribution and habitats. Pp. 1-25, *in* Mule and Black-tailed Deer of North America (O.C. Wallmo, ed.). A Wildlife Management Institute Book, University of Nebraska Press, Lincoln.

Whittaker, R.H. 1952. A study of summer foliage insect communities in the Great Smoky Mountains. Ecological Monographs 22: 1-44.

Whittaker, R.H. 1960. Vegetation of the Siskiyou Mountains, Oregon and California. Ecological Monographs 30: 279-338.

Whittaker, R.H. 1967. Gradient analysis of vegetation. Biological Review 42: 207-264.

Wishart, W.D. 1984. Western Canada. Pp. 475-486, *in* White-tailed Deer, Ecology and Management (L.K. Halls, ed.). A Wildlife Management Institute Book, Stackpole Books, Harrisburg.

Wishart, W.D. 1986a. White-tailed deer and mule deer. Pp. 134-143, *in* Alberta Wildlife Trophies. The Alberta Fish and Game Association, Edmonton.

Wishart, W.D. 1986b. The Wainwright deer herd (1966-1984): A comparative study of Whitetails and Mule Deer. Unpublished report, Alberta Energy and Natural Resources, Fish and Wildlife Division.

Selected References to the Mammals of Western Canada

Banfield, A.W.F. 1974. The mammals of Canada. University of Toronto Press, Toronto. 438 pp.

Cowan, I.McT. and C.J. Guiguet. 1965. The mammals of British Columbia. British Columbia Provincial Museum, Handbook No. 11. 3rd edition (revised). 414 pp.

Hall, E.R. 1981. The mammals of North America. John Wiley and Sons, New York. 2nd edition, 2 volumes. 1181 pp.

Hoffmann, R.S. and D.L. Pattie. 1968. A guide to Montana mammals: identification, habitat, distribution and abundance. University of Montana Printing Services, Missoula. 133 pp.

Jones, J.K., Jr., D.M. Armstrong, and J.R. Choate. 1985. Guide to the mammals of the Plains states. University of Nebraska Press, Lincoln. 371 pp.

Jones, J.K., Jr., D.M. Armstrong, R.S. Hoffmann, and C. Jones. 1983. Mammals of the northern Great Plains. University of Nebraska Press, Lincoln. 379 pp.

Larrison, E.J. and D.R. Johnson. 1981. Mammals of Idaho. A Northwest Naturalist Book, The University Press of Idaho, Moscow. 166 pp.

Rand, A.L. 1948. Mammals of the eastern Rockies and western plains of Canada. National Museum of Canada, Bulletin No. 108. 237 pp.

Youngman, P.L. 1975. Mammals of the Yukon Territory. National Museum of Natural Sciences, Publications in Zoology No. 10. 192 pp.

Index

Index of Common and Scientific Names

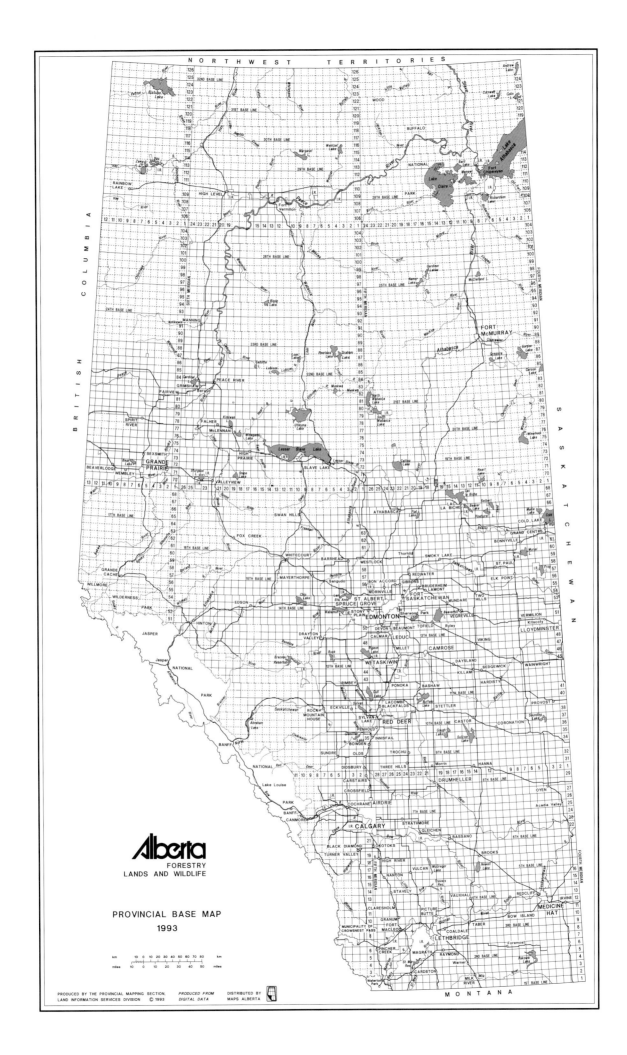

Alberta
FORESTRY
LANDS AND WILDLIFE

PROVINCIAL BASE MAP

1993

PRODUCED BY THE PROVINCIAL MAPPING SECTION,
LAND INFORMATION SERVICES DIVISION © 1993

PRODUCED FROM
DIGITAL DATA

DISTRIBUTED BY
MAPS ALBERTA